VOLUME 569 MAY 2000

THE ANNALS

of The American Academy *of* Political
and Social Science

ALAN W. HESTON, *Editor*
NEIL A. WEINER, *Assistant Editor*

THE AFRICAN AMERICAN MALE IN AMERICAN LIFE AND THOUGHT

Special Editor of this Volume

JACOB U. GORDON
University of Kansas
Lawrence

Ⓢ Sage Publications, Inc. *THOUSAND OAKS LONDON NEW DELHI*

The American Academy of Political and Social Science

3937 Chestnut Street   Philadelphia, Pennsylvania 19104

Origin and Purpose. The Academy was organized December 14, 1889, to promote the progress of political and social science, especially through publications and meetings. The Academy does not take sides in controverted questions, but seeks to gather and present reliable information to assist the public in forming an intelligent and accurate judgment.

Meetings. The Academy occasionally holds a meeting in the spring extending over two days.

Publications. THE ANNALS of the American Academy of Political and Social Science is the bi-monthly publication of The Academy. Each issue contains articles on some prominent social or political problem, written at the invitation of the editors. Also, monographs are published from time to time, numbers of which are distributed to pertinent professional organizations. These volumes constitute important reference works on the topics with which they deal, and they are extensively cited by authorities throughout the United States and abroad. The papers presented at the meetings of The Academy are included in THE ANNALS.

Membership. Each member of The Academy receives THE ANNALS and may attend the meetings of The Academy. Membership is open only to individuals. Annual dues: $61.00 for the regular paperbound edition (clothbound, $90.00). Add $12.00 per year for membership outside the U.S.A. Members may also purchase single issues of THE ANNALS for $14.00 each (clothbound, $19.00). Add $2.00 for shipping and handling on all prepaid orders.

Subscriptions. THE ANNALS of the American Academy of Political and Social Science (ISSN 0002-7162) is published six times annually—in January, March, May, July, September, and November. Institutions may subscribe to THE ANNALS at the annual rate: $327.00 (clothbound, $372.00). Add $12.00 per year for subscriptions outside the U.S.A. Institutional rates for single issues: $59.00 each (clothbound, $66.00).

Periodicals postage paid at Thousand Oaks, California, and at additional mailing offices.

Single issues of THE ANNALS may be obtained by individuals who are not members of The Academy for $20.00 each (clothbound, $31.00). Add $2.00 for shipping and handling on all prepaid orders. Single issues of THE ANNALS have proven to be excellent supplementary texts for classroom use. Direct inquiries regarding adoptions to THE ANNALS c/o Sage Publications (address below).

All correspondence concerning membership in The Academy, dues renewals, inquiries about membership status, and/or purchase of single issues of THE ANNALS should be sent to THE ANNALS c/o Sage Publications, Inc., 2455 Teller Road, Thousand Oaks, CA 91320. Telephone: (805) 499-0721; FAX/Order line: (805) 499-0871. *Please note that orders under $30 must be prepaid.* Sage affiliates in London and India will assist institutional subscribers abroad with regard to orders, claims, and inquiries for both subscriptions and single issues.

Printed on recycled, acid-free paper

THE ANNALS

© 2000 by The American Academy of Political and Social Science

Editorial Office: 3937 Chestnut Street, Philadelphia, PA 19104.

For information about membership* (individuals only) and subscriptions (institutions), address:

SAGE PUBLICATIONS, INC.
2455 Teller Road
Thousand Oaks, CA 91320

Sage Production Staff: MARIA NOTARANGELO, LISA CUEVAS, DORIS HUS, and ROSE TYLAK

From India and South Asia, write to:	*From Europe, the Middle East, and Africa, write to:*
SAGE PUBLICATIONS INDIA Pvt. Ltd	SAGE PUBLICATIONS LTD
P.O. Box 4215	6 Bonhill Street
New Delhi 110 048	London EC2A 4PU
INDIA	UNITED KINGDOM

*Please note that members of The Academy receive THE ANNALS with their membership.
International Standard Serial Number ISSN 0002-7162
International Standard Book Number ISBN 0-7619-2257-1 (Vol. 569, 2000 paper)
International Standard Book Number ISBN 0-7619-2256-3 (Vol. 569, 2000 cloth)
Manufactured in the United States of America. First printing, May 2000.

The articles appearing in the ANNALS are abstracted or indexed in *Academic Abstracts, Academic Search, America: History and Life, Asia Pacific Database, Book Review Index, CAB Abstracts Database, Central Asia: Abstracts & Index, Communication Abstracts, Corporate ResourceNET, Criminal Justice Abstracts, Current Citations Express, Current Contents: Social & Behavioral Sciences, e-JEL, EconLit, Expanded Academic Index, Guide to Social Science & Religion in Periodical Literature, Health Business FullTEXT, HealthSTAR FullTEXT, Historical Abstracts, International Bibliography of the Social Sciences, International Political Science Abstracts, ISI Basic Social Sciences Index, Journal of Economic Literature on CD, LEXIS-NEXIS, MasterFILE FullTEXT, Middle East: Abstracts & Index, North Africa: Abstracts & Index, PAIS International, Periodical Abstracts, Political Science Abstracts, Sage Public Administration Abstracts, Social Science Source, Social Sciences Citation Index, Social Sciences Index Full Text, Social Services Abstracts, Social Work Abstracts, Sociological Abstracts, Southeast Asia: Abstracts & Index, Standard Periodical Directory (SPD), TOPICsearch, Wilson OmniFile V,* and *Wilson Social Sciences Index/Abstracts,* and are available on microfilm from University Microfilms, Ann Arbor, Michigan.

Information about membership rates, institutional subscriptions, and back issue prices may be found on the facing page.

Advertising. Current rates and specifications may be obtained by writing to THE ANNALS Advertising and Promotion Manager at the Thousand Oaks office (address above).

Claims. Claims for undelivered copies must be made no later than six months following month of publication. The publisher will supply missing copies when losses have been sustained in transit and when the reserve stock will permit.

Change of Address. Six weeks advance notice must be given when notifying of change of address to ensure proper identification. Please specify name of journal. **POSTMASTER:** Send address changes to: THE ANNALS of the American Academy of Political and Social Science, c/o Sage Publications, Inc., 2455 Teller Road, Thousand Oaks, CA 91320.

THE ANNALS

of The American Academy *of* Political
and Social Science

ALAN W. HESTON, *Editor*
NEIL A. WEINER, *Assistant Editor*

--- **FORTHCOMING** ---

DIMENSIONS OF GLOBALIZATION
Special Editors: Louis Ferleger and Jay R. Mandle
Volume 570   July 2000

FEMINIST VIEWS OF THE SOCIAL SCIENCES
Special Editor: Christine L. Williams
Volume 571   September 2000

PRESIDENTIAL CAMPAIGNS: SINS OF OMISSION
Special Editors: Kathleen Hall Jamieson and Matthew Miller
Volume 572   November 2000

See page 2 for information on Academy membership and
purchase of single volumes of **The Annals.**

CONTENTS

BOOK DEPARTMENT CONTENTS

PREFACE

A recent publication on the African American male has documented nearly a thousand annotated bibliographical references covering a wide range of subjects: education, health, arts and entertainment, civil rights, crime and violence, family, leadership, literature, media, religion, sports, economic development, and so on (Gordon 1999). The book also includes an impressive list of doctoral dissertations and other published works on the African American male. It reflects the current understanding of the treatment of the African American male in the American academy. No longer can scholars and practitioners ignore this considerably large body of literature. This volume of *The Annals* of the American Academy of Political and Social Science is another step in the right direction. This direction appears to be at least twofold: (1) African American male studies as a legitimate field of academic inquiry and (2) viewing the African American male experience within the context of American life and history. Thus the original essays included in this volume have been designed to examine specific aspects of the African American male in American life.

According to the United States Census Bureau population estimate for August 1999, the total African American population is nearly 35.0 million, or 12.8 percent of the U.S. population. Of this number, 16.6 million are males, representing about 6 percent of the U.S. population. This figure does not include several million foreign-born African American males.

In preparing this volume, we were guided by a simple academic principle, namely, to present a balanced perspective of the African American male. The images of the African American male portrayed through the American media have been distorted, to say the least. Jewelle Taylor Gibbs once noted how African American males have been labelled by the media as dropouts, delinquents, dope addicts, street-smart dudes, and welfare pimps (Gibbs 1988, 22). Some of the men refer to themselves as "home boys," "bloods," and "soul brothers." These labels hold powerful clues to the ways in which black males are perceived and valued in American society. The neglected part of the story is that black males in America are also products of their rich African heritage. They are sons of African kings and queens who have made enormous and valuable contributions to Western civilization, particularly to American life and thought. Capitalism, as scholar Eric Williams puts it, could not have thrived without the sweat and tears of the slaves who were predominantly black men (Williams 1944). African American men not only are pioneers in sports but have proven themselves in practically all walks of life, including the sciences, medicine, law, engineering, and the American armed forces. Obviously, this volume cannot cover all areas of the contributions made by the black male. Thus some neglected areas have been selected for this volume.

SOCIOLOGY

Among several neglected questions addressed in this volume are, Who are the black males? How do we define this population? What are their demographic characteristics? What impact does the black male have on American life and thought?

To examine these and related questions, a group of nationally recognized scholars and practitioners has been assembled. They represent several disciplines and areas of expertise in American studies. I am indebted to all of the contributors for meeting the challenge of academic excellence in African American studies. I am grateful to my colleague in the National African-American Male Collaboration, Inc., Dr. Lynn Curtis, for encouraging the publication of this volume. Finally, I dedicate this volume to the Village Foundation for its leadership, courage, and commitment to improve the quality of life of African American men and their families.

JACOB U. GORDON

References

Gibbs, Jewelle Taylor. 1988. *Young, Black and Male in America: An Endangered Species*. New York: Auburn House.

Gordon, Jacob. 1999. *The African-American Male: An Annotated Bibliography*. Westport, CT: Greenwood Press.

Williams, Eric. 1944. *Capitalism and Slavery*. Chapel Hill: University of North Carolina Press.

ANNALS, *AAPSS*, **569**, May 2000

The Role of African American Males in Politics and Government

By TRACY D. SNIPE

ABSTRACT: This article examines the contributions of African American males to government and politics during the latter half of the twentieth century. More specifically, it chronicles the careers of Kweisi Mfume, Colin Powell, J. C. Watts, Jr., Ralph Bunche, Adam Clayton Powell, Jr., Andrew Young, Jr., and Edward Brooke. The purpose of this critical analysis is threefold: (1) to present a historical overview of prominent African American males in the executive, judicial, and legislative branches of government as well as state and local government; (2) to discuss crucial variables that determined the selection of individuals to be examined in this case study, upon which the author's typology is based, and to reflect critically upon the unique contributions of the seven aforementioned individuals to national and international affairs; and (3) to explore some future implications for black males in the totality of the current American political spectrum. This study takes on considerable magnitude given the fact that it delineates the closing of the twentieth century and the entrance into the new millennium.

Tracy D. Snipe is an assistant professor in the Department of Political Science at Wright State University. He is the author of Arts and Politics in Senegal: 1960-1996 *and several other recent publications on African American politics and film.*

We've come this far by faith. . . . Can't turn around. We've come this far by faith.

—African American spiritual

One ever feels his twoness,—an American, a Negro; two souls, two thoughts, two unreconciled strivings; two warring ideals in one dark body, whose dogged strength alone keeps it from being torn asunder.

—W.E.B. Du Bois

And so this saga continues. These two quotations capture the essence of black religiosity and the African American presence throughout the American body politic in the perpetual quest of black people to make the American dream and creed more applicable to their lives. As a nation, we struggle with this "racial divide," which shows no sign of abating at the dawn of the twenty-first century. This article examines the contributions of African American males to governance in relation to the concept of twoness. A soldier, a conquering son of kings, a quarterback, a diplomat, a lawyer, a minister, and an activist all have left an indelible imprint on American politics despite the prophetic issue of the color line. This is not to suggest that Colin Powell, Kweisi Mfume, J. C. Watts, Jr., Ralph Bunche, Edward Brooke, Adam Clayton Powell, Jr., and Andrew Young, Jr., were not the benefactors of years of struggle waged by other leaders. Each one of them qualifies for the accolade "all-American." The purpose of this study is threefold. First, I present a historical overview of black males in governance.[1] Second, I discuss variables that determined the selection for this case study (which is complemented by a typology), emphasizing the unique contributions of the aforementioned men. Finally, I explore some future possibilities for black males in the context of the American sociopolitical spectrum with the advent of the second millennium and the election year of 2000.

FROM THE EARLY PIONEERS
TO THE CONTEMPORARY ERA

One of the towering early pioneers was Frederick Douglass, whose life was epitomized by struggle and progress. Formerly in servitude, Douglass literally fought his master Covey to obtain what he believed to be his God-given right—freedom. In a speech titled "Oration Delivered in Corinthian Hall, Rochester, July 5, 1852," the charismatic abolitionist decried religious institutions in the United States of America as well as the government for celebrating Independence Day while black people remained enslaved (Hord and Lee 1995). He also advocated equal rights for women. One of the most high-profile African American political or governmental appointees, during his long and distinguished career Douglass served as an adviser to President Lincoln, head of the Freedmen's Bureau, and minister resident and consul general to the Republic of Haiti (Douglass 1962).

There were conservative, liberal, and radical strains to Douglass's political thought that are reflective of the praxis of black politics to this day. His critical rhetoric set the mode for numerous influential black leaders and organizations to follow.

Douglass, however, did pose some contradictions. By the time of his death in 1895, his discourse had become socially conservative and was "characterized by a hostility to the working class and labor unions, a fear of radicalism, and a powerful loyalty to the Republican Party and support of its probusiness policies" (Eisenstadt 1996, 646). Booker T. Washington was catapulted into national prominence after delivering "The Atlanta Exposition Address" in 1895, advocating accomodationism. One century later, in 1995, Louis Farrakhan, leader of the Nation of Islam, and co-organizer Ben Chavis spearheaded the Million Man March in Washington, D.C. This show of unity amounted to a moral reawakening for black men in America, in part mirroring an essentially mainstream conservative critique.

Blacks have been elected at the local, state, and federal levels of government since the second half of the nineteenth century. In 1854, John Langston became the first recorded black elected official, holding the title of clerk of Brownhelm Township, Lorain County, Ohio (Hill 1999, 202). During the short-lived era of Radical Reconstruction, the first major wave of black political participation, African American males were elected to state legislatures and the U.S. Congress. South Carolina sent a record eight black legislators to Congress, including the notable Robert Smalls (Franklin and Moss 1994, 210, 242). Following the impeachment of H. C. Warmoth in Louisiana, P.B.S. Pinchback, who had been popularly elected as lieutenant governor, became the first African

American governor. He served from 9 December 1872 until 13 January 1873 (Vincent 1999, 61). In 1869, John Roy Lynch was elected the Mississippi Speaker of the House and in 1872 was elected to the U.S. House of Representatives. Mississippi also sent two blacks to the United States Senate, Hiram R. Revels and Blanche Kelso Bruce. Revels replaced the ex-Confederate president Jefferson Davis in 1872, and Bruce was elected to serve a full term in 1874 (Franklin and Moss 1994, 239-45). Robert Jenkins (1999) posits that "except for Frederick Douglass, perhaps no black American's name during the last quarter of the nineteenth century was more widely known that than of Blanche K. Bruce" (32). By the time that the U.S. Supreme Court declared that "separate but equal" was the law of the land in *Plessy* v. *Ferguson* (1896), white retrenchment and black disfranchisement were virtually complete as a result of poll taxes, literacy clauses, and gerrymandering. State constitutions were rewritten to nullify the black vote in the South. As a last resort, lynchings and politically inspired violence curtailed black political participation (Franklin and Moss 1994, 259-63). With the advent in 1915 of D. W. Griffith's *Birth of a Nation*, hailed as the genesis of American cinema, black politicians of the Reconstruction Era became the subject of ridicule.

From this period onward, black political progress was slow but significant. In 1928, Oscar DePriest (D-Ill.), formerly an alderman in Chicago, became the first black to be elected to the House of Representatives since Reconstruction. Blacks made unprecedented gains in government service with the formation of President Roosevelt's Black Cabinet[2] during the New Deal, but discriminatory practices stemmed the tide of progress. In protest of such measures, A. Philip Randolph, president of the Brotherhood of Sleeping Car Porters, organized a proposed march on Washington for 1 July 1941. At the eleventh hour, President Roosevelt signed an executive order that banned discriminatory hiring practices in the defense industries and federal government (Franklin and Moss 1994, 436-37). African Americans were also challenging discrimination in the field of education. Argued by Thurgood Marshall on behalf of the National Association for the Advancement of Colored People (NAACP), the *Brown* v. *Board of Education* case (1954) led to the reversal of the separate but equal doctrine and to the desegregation of public schools. Marshall later became the first black justice on the U.S. Supreme Court and was succeeded, ironically, by the ultraconservative Clarence Thomas. Other notable appointments to the judiciary include William Henry Hastie, the first black American to be appointed a federal appellate judge, and the late Judge A. Leon Higginbotham, who was also a former U.S. civil rights commissioner.

Blacks have been elected to the federal, state, and local branches of government in increasing numbers since the passage of the Voting Rights Act of 1965; this constitutes the second major wave of black political participation. Black mayors have reaped major political victories, although they generally inherit city governments beset by shrinking tax bases and enormous institutional problems. In 1967, Carl Stokes became the first African American to be elected mayor of a major city, after effectively employing "a massive grass roots mobilization of the black vote" in Cleveland (Nelson 1982, 176). Utilizing a similar strategy, Kenneth Gibson was elected mayor of Newark, New Jersey, in 1970, and Coleman Young was elected mayor of Detroit in 1973. Black mayors reached the apex of their influence during the 1980s, when virtually all of the major American cities were led by African American mayors: David Dinkins (New York), Tom Bradley (Los Angeles), Harold Washington (Chicago), Wilson Goode (Philadelphia), Norman Rice (Seattle), Maynard Jackson (Atlanta), and Marion Barry (Washington, D.C.). Willie Brown was the first African American elected mayor of San Francisco in 1995. According to Preston, Henderson, and Puryear (1982), "Black mayors, like black congressmen, speak as local and as national representatives of black people in America" (viii). In 1989, L. Douglass Wilder became the first African American to be elected a governor in the United States. At the presidential level, the Reverend Jesse Jackson organized several highly effective voter registration drives in his bid for the presidency as a Democrat in 1984 and 1988.

In 1965, Robert Weaver, secretary of the newly created Department of Housing and Urban Development, became the first black American to hold an actual cabinet ranking (Henry 1999, 34). From the Carter administration to the Clinton administration, the nomination of African Americans to such appointments has fluctuated. During the Carter administration, Andrew Young was appointed the U.S. ambassador to the United Nations. During the Reagan presidency, Samuel R. Pierce, Jr., was appointed secretary of housing and urban development, and General Colin Powell, national security adviser. A member of the Bush transition team, Powell was later appointed to the Joint Chiefs of Staff, while Louis W. Sullivan was named secretary of the Department of Health and Human Services. Though President Clinton hastily withdrew the appointment of Lani Guinier for U.S. attorney general, the Clinton presidency, in comparison to preceding administrations, has been a watershed for African American appointees at the cabinet level. Vernon Jordan was the chairman of President Clinton's transitional team. A former chairman of the Democratic National Committee, Ron Brown, served as the secretary of the Department of Commerce until his death in a plane crash in 1996. Clifton Wharton served as deputy secretary of state for one year, while Mike Epsey served as the secretary of the Department of Agriculture until allegations of financial improprieties (of which he was exonerated) led to his resignation. In 1998, David Satchell was appointed U.S. surgeon general. Eric Holder currently serves as deputy U.S. attorney general. Will other appointments be forthcoming in 2000?

ON THE TYPOLOGY

A broad array of factors were considered in the selection of African American males for this particular case study. These individuals range from some of the most long-standing influential politicians and policymakers in America to some of the relatively new movers and shakers. Contrary to public opinion, there has never been one monolithic black political tradition. Be they Democrats, Republicans, or independents, the individuals selected for this case study embody the liberal, conservative, and radical components of black politics. African Americans have also established and served in third parties such as Lenora Fulani's now "defunct New Alliance Party, which promoted minority rights and redistribution of wealth" (Leavitt 1999).[3] At present, this analysis is not theory driven.[4] Herein I provide succinct political biographies for Ralph Bunche, Andrew Young, Jr., Adam Clayton Powell, Jr., Kweisi Mfume, Edward Brooke, J. C. Watts, Jr., and Colin Powell. These men come from different regions of the nation and diverse socioeconomic backgrounds. Attesting to the influence of the black church in particular on American politics, two of the individuals selected for this study have been ministers, Adam Clayton Powell, Jr., and Andrew Young, Jr., albeit Young began as a member of the Congregational Church. Second, I examine their domestic and international influence during the latter half of the twentieth century, as blacks began then to take on significant leadership roles. Finally, I situate each of these men with respect to the issue of twoness. Some 30 years after the Kerner Commission's initial proclamation in 1968, race is still the red herring of American politics and society. Yet too often anyone who brings divisive issues into discussions of race and politics in America is accused of race baiting and promoting victim status. "I love America more than any other country in the world, and exactly for this reason, I insist on the right to criticize her perpetually," proclaimed the preeminent essayist James Baldwin (1984, 9). He could have been writing on behalf of most of the individuals highlighted in the present analysis. How can their Americanness and blackness (that is, Negritude) be applied to their political fortunes or misfortunes? Given the past and current lexicon of politics, if a black candidate chooses to emphasize or deemphasize the race card, how does this affect his political aspirations? What is the price of this ticket?

INTERNATIONAL DIMENSIONS
OF RALPH BUNCHE
AND ANDREW YOUNG, JR.

The educational and diplomatic career of scholar and world statesman Ralph Johnson Bunche was punctuated by numerous firsts, like the careers of all of the other men in this study. Born in Detroit in 1904, Bunche spent his formative years in Los Angeles. He studied political science and philosophy at the University of California (now the University of California at Los Angeles). After graduating as class valedictorian, Bunche subsequently enrolled in the doctoral program in political science at Harvard and became the first African American in the nation to earn a Ph.D. in this discipline. In 1953, Bunche would become the first black president of the American Political Science Association. Immediately after earning an M.A. in political science from Harvard, Bunche was invited to teach at Howard University, where he developed the school's first political science department. As a young scholar, Bunche wrote about the "race problem," African development, and colonialism. After completing research in Africa on a Julius Rosenwald Fellowship, Bunche wrote an award-winning dissertation, "French Colonial Administration in Togoland and Dahomey." Bunche later wrote the monograph *A World View of Race*. Eventually, he completed postdoctoral research in anthropology at Northwestern University and more extensive research throughout Africa. In 1936, during the most radicalized stage of his career, Bunche cofounded the National Negro Congress, an organization that he disavowed after it became pro-Communist. Several years later, Bunche became one of the senior associates for Gunnar Myrdal's momentous book, *An American Dilemma: The Negro Problem and Modern Democracy*. In conjunction with this publication, Bunche wrote the treatise *The Political Status of the Negro in the Age of FDR*, which was published posthumously in 1973 (Rivlin 1990, xxii).

Ralph Bunche came to have an enormous influence on the formation of American foreign policy during his career as an international states- man. Within a year of his appoint- ment at the Office of the Coordinator of Information Service (OCI) in 1941, Bunche led the Africa Section of the Office of Strategic Service (OSS), the name of the newly reformed OCI. By the time of his retirement in 1971, Bunche was the under-secretary- general for special political affairs in charge of deploying U.N. peacekeep- ing forces. In any news story today related to the ongoing Israeli- Palestinian peace talks, typically there will be no reference made to Ralph Bunche or his groundbreaking role in the initial Palestinian nego- tiations. In 1948, after the assassina- tion of the Israeli Count Folke Berna- dotte, Bunche was named the acting mediator for these talks. In 1950, he became the first African American to be awarded the Nobel Peace Prize; it was awarded in recognition of his role in "successfully negotiating an armistice agreement between Egypt and Israel" (Rivlin 1990, xxiii). Bunche was one of the principal architects of the Trusteeship Divi- sion of the United Nations, which employs peacekeeping forces, an idea that he first espoused. Such forces are deployed throughout the world at present. Bunche also organized U.N. peacekeeping operations in Congo and Cyprus.

At the height of his career as a dip- lomat, Bunche came under increas- ing criticism for not offering a visible critique of the U.S. government for its double standard on human rights, promoting them abroad but denying them at home for millions of African Americans. Other famous black Americans such as Malcolm X sought redress for American racism and eco- nomic exploitation from the United Nations. In 1965, Bunche marched at the front of the line with civil rights leader Martin Luther King, Jr., in Selma. Given his stature at the United Nations, Bunche avoided hos- tile criticism of the American government.

Charles Henry posits that "Bunche avoided marginality by attempting to synthesize the duality or dichotomy set forth by Du Bois" (Henry 1999, 5). Though he gradu- ated as valedictorian at Jefferson High School, Bunche was not inducted into the Los Angeles chap- ter of the honor society because he was black (Henry 1999). To counter this affront, undoubtedly, Bunche had to draw on the lessons that his grandmother Nana, who could pass for white, emphasized about race pride. There were additional instances of discrimination. The cir- cumspect ways in which prejudice and white privilege operated pre- vented Ralph Bunche from teaching at any of the elite schools in the nation despite his credentials. In this respect, he was no different from many of the other brilliant African American intellectuals of this period. During the early phase of his govern- ment career, Bunche refused an offer to work for the U.S. State Depart- ment because of the racially entrenched atmosphere that was pervasive in Washington during the

1950s. Two years after winning the Nobel Prize, Bunche's American patriotism came under attack during the era of McCarthyism because of his past close association with the National Negro Congress. Bunche was exonerated but not before publicly disavowing Paul Robeson, the American singer and civil rights activist, who, like Du Bois, came under attack by the House Un-American Activities Committee. For a period during his career, Bunche was promoted as the "model Negro," which later alienated him from a more militant generation of black Americans. In a glowing tribute to his mentor, the distinguished psychologist Kenneth Clark writes that Bunche was "the model of a human being who by his total personality demonstrated that disciplined human intelligence and courage were most effective instruments in the struggle for social justice" (Clark 1990, 212).

In 1977, Andrew Young became the highest-ranking black American at the United Nations when he was appointed U.S. ambassador to the United Nations by President Jimmy Carter, whom he vigorously endorsed for the presidency. Young has worn many hats during his lifetime: minister, civil rights activist, Georgia legislator, mayor of Atlanta, and cochair of the Olympic Games held in Atlanta in 1996. Born into a middle-class black family in New Orleans in 1932, Young briefly studied at Dillard University in New Orleans but later transferred to Howard University, where he received a B.A. in biology. Spurning familial pressures to venture into the dentistry profession in his father's footsteps, Young chose to pursue a career in the ministry after his revelation on top of Kings Mountain at a Christian retreat for youths (Young 1996). Inspired by the leadership of the charismatic Reverend Dr. Martin Luther King, Jr., Young joined the Baptist-oriented Southern Christian Leadership Conference. The civil rights movement had gained momentum throughout the South. Young would become one of King's major lieutenants in an organization that minimized the influence of black women within its ranks despite the visibility of Rosa Parks, Ella Baker, and Fannie Lou Hamer (Young 1996). Eventually Young channeled his energies into an active political career, and in 1972 he became the first black American in Georgia to be elected to the U.S. Congress since the period of Reconstruction.

In terms of diplomatic protocol, Ralph Bunche and Andrew Young make for an arresting study in contrasts. Both men were involved with the civil rights movement and were preoccupied with African development, but the comparisons end here. Whereas the former gained a reputation as a "troubleshooter," Young was portrayed as a "troublemaker" unaccustomed to the "niceties of diplomacy." Lee Clement (1978) infers that the anti-Young sentiment was spread throughout the ranks of the Carter administration from almost the first day of his appointment as U.N. ambassador because he endorsed the Cuban presence in Angola, which the State Department refuted swiftly. Whereas the Palestinian negotiations led to Bunche's greatest diplomatic achievement, Young's decision to meet behind closed doors with leaders of the Palestinian Liberation Organization ultimately triggered his political downfall and resignation. Young championed human rights during his brief tenure and was a vocal critic of the brutal Ugandan dictator Idi Amin. Among the topics of the addresses he gave at the United Nations were South Africa's racial policies; independence for Mozambique and Rhodesia; illegal Israeli measures in the occupied Arab territories; the Sadat-Begin meeting; East-West détente; and the admission to the United Nations of the Socialist Republic of Vietnam and Djibouti (Clement 1978). Even in his capacity as the American ambassador to the United Nations, the concept of twoness came into play. Young had to defend his identification with blacks in southern Africa but not to the exclusion of the whites there, who, from his vantage point, had a complex about race and harbored deep-seated prejudices. Rhodesia's Ian Smith tacitly approved of Young's willingness to shirk the oftentimes staid diplomatic protocol (Clement 1978).

Young's involvement in the civil rights movement addressed the "American dilemma." Young and his cohorts protested to ensure that America would become "one nation under God, with liberty and justice for all." From the streets of Montgomery to the U.N. General Assembly to the pulpit, Young has persevered by virtue of his deeply held religious faith. At his recent installation as president of the National Council of Churches, which has a membership of 50 million, Young proclaimed, "I can't think of a better ship to move into the 21st century on than this old ship of Zion" (Affleck 1999).

ADAM CLAYTON POWELL, JR., AND KWEISI MFUME: THE POLITICS OF PROTEST

"Keep the faith, baby" was what protesters yelled to the beleaguered Harlem congressman who is perhaps the most powerful and intriguing individual of this study. "Rabble-rouser," "irritant," "magnetic," and "militant" are some of the words that have been used do describe this indomitable man of the "silk" cloth, Adam Clayton Powell, Jr., who was a rebel with a crusade. In addition to his political prowess, Powell introduced many symbolic changes that augmented his stature in the Harlem community, which became for him a microcosm of black America. Whereas Bunche relinquished an appointment in the State Department in an understated protest against the practice of racism in Washington, Powell the astute politician thumbed his nose at the establishment, exploiting this defiance for partisan gain. He forced the desegregation of a barbershop patronized by congressmen as well as the integration of the White House press corps.

Although he was born in New Haven in 1908, Powell was a son of Harlem. Under the watchful eyes of his doting parents, Mattie Powell and Adam Clayton Powell, Sr., pastor of the nationally renowned Abyssinian Baptist Church, Adam was groomed to succeed his father. Some of the famed individuals who have spoken at Abyssinian include Mary McCleod Bethune, Marcus Garvey, Haile Selassie, and President Franklin Roosevelt. After the resignation of his father, Powell was installed as the new minister (but, against his father's wishes, he later married nightclub dancer Isabelle Washington). The industrious, socially conscious Powell used the church as a base of support as he rallied the Harlem community around issues of continuing racial injustice. Powell became recognized as a legitimate political power after forcing Con Edison and Harlem Hospital to redress racial segregation and discrimination in the workplace (Haygood 1993, 34-36, 77). He led the highly effective "Don't Buy Where You Can't Work" campaign. These early victories propelled Powell into the crux of politics. "You can't fight city hall" was not a creed that Powell adhered to in his nascent rise in city politics. He fought Tammany Hall and won, becoming the first African American to be elected to the New York City Council in 1941. He ran as an independent. Utilizing the black church as a broad base of institutional support, Powell was elected to the U.S. House of Representatives in 1943 by the newly created district in Harlem. In later years, he went on to chair the House Education and Labor Committee, where the Powell Amendment was attached to numerous bills. In a private letter, President Johnson praised Powell for the "successful reporting to the Congress of 49 pieces of bedrock legislation" (Hamilton 1991, 24). Powell has been one of the single most influential blacks in politics and government throughout the course of American history. How Powell amassed this degree of influence and lost it is legendary.

Powell earned the title "Mr. Civil Rights" but was often at odds with the NAACP and Dr. King, whom he dubbed Martin "Loser" King (Cutler 1972, 3). Powell later expeditiously co-opted the Stokely Carmichael–led chant of "black power" but redefined it to suit his political purposes, much to the chagrin of some of the younger militants in the movement. Powell was also unafraid to chart his own path on international issues. Against the wishes of President Eisenhower and the State Department, he attended the Bandung Conference held in Indonesia in 1955. Powell made international headlines there when he announced that racism in America was passé, much to the dismay of stunned participants at this conference of nonaligned Asian and African nations. The announcement had been orchestrated to score political points at home; when Powell returned to Congress, he was given a standing ovation by his colleagues— but was roundly condemned in other circles. Powell advocated President Johnson's War on Poverty but opposed the Vietnam war.

Powell was the embodiment of the two warring souls, as is thoroughly documented in Charles Hamilton's seminal study, *Adam Clayton Powell, Jr.: The Political Biography of an American Dilemma* (1991). He could pass for white and initially did not disclose his true racial identity while he was enrolled at Colgate University, where he majored in biblical literature. The eventual discovery of Powell's dark secret led to profound embarrassment. Admonished by his father, Powell never repeated this mistake again; however, he remained entangled in the web of racial politics. He made an enemy of President Truman for life when he publicly described Mrs. Truman as the "last lady" because she did not condemn the Daughters of the American Revolution (DAR) for refusing to permit his second wife, Hazel Scott, to sing at Constitution Hall in 1945. Unlike her counterpart Eleanor Roosevelt, who resigned from this organization when Marian Anderson was refused the same privilege in 1939, Mrs. Truman chose to attend a tea sponsored by the DAR over Powell's objection. Powell never received a personal invitation to the White House after this incident. President Truman deferred perks to Powell's rival, Chicago congressman Willie Dawson (Hamilton 1991, 165). Over time, Powell's stature in Congress grew exponentially. Nonetheless, unlike Senator Strom Thurmond, who filibustered a key civil rights bill, Powell could not flaunt his power (or womanizing) without raising the ire of his peers. In 1966, Powell was stripped of his chairmanship and temporarily of his congressional seat in light of the mounting evidence of his abuse of power, ranging from nepotism to the illegal use of funds for the purchase of trinkets. His claim of a double standard in Congress was to no avail. Though Powell took his case to the U.S. Supreme Court and won, his political career was all but finished. Powell had also lost a defamation-of-

character suit to a resident of Harlem, Esther James, whom he described on television as a "bag woman," or "someone who carried money from gamblers to the police as payoff to permit the continuance of illegal activities in the community" (Hamilton 1991, 36). In 1970, Charles Rangel defeated Powell by 150 votes, ending a political dynasty.

Kweisi Mfume, the current president of the NAACP, continues in the tradition of protest, minus the grandstanding and theatrics of Powell. Born into a working-class black family in West Baltimore in 1948, Mfume's life underwent a radical transformation after he experienced a spiritual epiphany while shooting dice on Hankin's Corner (Mfume with Stodghill 1996). The untimely death of his mother had temporarily caused young Frizzel Gray to go astray. His decision to employ the name "Kweisi Mfume," which his aunt had bestowed upon him following her trip to Africa years before, was symbolic of the new path in life that he had chosen in his early twenties (Snipe 1999, 197). Kweisi Mfume (translated as "conquering son of kings") studied at the Community College of Baltimore but transferred to Morgan State University, where he received a bachelor's degree in urban planning. He completed a master's degree in liberal arts, emphasizing international relations, at Johns Hopkins University. Like Powell, Mfume began his political career in city politics. He served on the Baltimore City Council for seven years and in 1979 was elected to the U.S. House of Representatives, representing Maryland's Seventh

District for five successive terms. While in Congress, Mfume served on the Committees for Finance, Banking, and Urban Affairs and presided over the largest Congressional Black Caucus to date. Dating back to his days of student activism, Mfume had pushed for sanctions against South Africa. The cumulative effect of the divestment movement was the dismantling of apartheid. Mfume has since befriended former president Nelson Mandela, whom he regards as a great leader and a father figure (Mfume 1998). Most of Mfume's work in foreign affairs centered on a vocal critique of an American foreign policy that allowed for the repatriation of Haitian refugees seeking asylum in the United States.

Mfume has been one of the most visible leaders of the NAACP since Walter White. Thus far during his tenure, Mfume has steadfastly addressed this continuing twoness in American society. He was arrested along with fellow supporters for leading a demonstration on the Supreme Court grounds. At issue was the Supreme Court's dismal record of hiring minority clerks (Mauro 1998). He has challenged the Detroit Tigers to create a more diversified workplace by improving its minority-hiring practices. Mfume and the NAACP have also taken the major networks to task for virtually excluding black shows from prime-time television. Mfume gives the issue of twoness a more inclusive frame of reference. In an interview, he declared that "racism, sexism, and anti-Semitism" are as aberrant as "gay bashing," "immigrant bashing," and "union bashing":

Hate radio, hate speech, hate crimes, and hate groups are attempting to further divide the American public as never before. And legislators cannot hide from that and say, "Well, that's outside my legislative jurisdiction." Members of the clergy cannot hide from that and say God will simply take care of this. (Mfume 1998)

EDWARD BROOKE, J. C. WATTS, JR., AND THE GOP

What pronouncements or solutions have black Republican legislators posed to some of these prevailing issues, and how have they shaped the national platform? The present-day electoral status of African Americans in the Grand Old Party (GOP), better known as the Republican Party, is at a critical juncture. While I disagree with John Cutler's (1972) contention that "the most exciting step forward for American blacks since Lincoln freed the slaves was the election by popular vote of Edward William Brooke III of Massachusetts to the United States Senate," it was, nonetheless, a historic achievement (1). Ironically, while Senator Brooke was being sworn in, Representative Powell was being censured by the House. Brooke has often been described as the antithesis of Powell (41). In 1966, Brooke became the first African American to be elected to the Senate since Reconstruction. Blacks had realigned with the Democrats with the advent of President Roosevelt's New Deal in the wake of a national economic boom following World War II. Since this date, only two other black Republicans have been elected to Congress, Gary Franks of Connecticut and J. C. Watts, Jr., of

Oklahoma. That all three men were elected from districts or a state with a white-majority population is noteworthy.

Born in Washington, D.C., in 1919, Edward Brooke attended Howard University, where he earned a bachelor of science degree and was a member of the Reserve Officer Training Corps. He was called into combat during World War II. A decorated war hero, when he returned to the United States, he enrolled at the Boston University Law School as a result of his legal experiences defending black GI's overseas in court-martial cases. Brooke had a successful law practice but was persuaded to enter politics by former colleagues from law school, business associates, and friends. Moreover, he was motivated by the personal desire to effect positive change in Roxbury's growing black community, though even in his early political defeats Brooke easily demonstrated his widespread political appeal. In 1960, Brooke was elected state attorney general on the Republican ticket, which was a stepping stone to his bid for the United States Senate (Hayden and Hayden 1999, 162). He was elected to two terms in the Senate, where he crafted a reputation as a moderate. Brooke served on the Banking, Housing, and Urban Affairs Committees and the President's Commission on Civil Disorders, where he fought to safeguard the open house clause in the 1968 Civil Rights Act. With respect to foreign affairs, within six months in office Senator Brooke toured Japan, Taiwan, Hong Kong, South Vietnam, Cambodia, and Thailand (Cutler

1972, 221). After this fact-finding tour, Brooke publicly stated his support for the Vietnam war. This position boosted his standing among the rank and file of his party but alienated Brooke from leaders of the civil rights movement as well as many of his constituents.

In 1968, Brooke went on a tour of 12 African nations. He saw Africa as a crucial region of the world in terms of the ongoing ideological struggle, despite problems associated with underdevelopment and illiteracy. When Brooke returned to Congress, "he proposed a policy that would isolate all white regimes of Southern Africa which subjugate black majorities" (Cutler 1972, 284). While Brooke was lecturing to a group of students in Kenya, echoes of the issue of twoness resurfaced. Students wanted to know whether, as a black Republican, his election was merely an example of political acquiescence, to which Brooke responded, "Nobody in Massachusetts decided they just wanted to put a Negro in the Senate. . . . It isn't a question of race. It's a question of power politics frankly" (Cutler 1972, 283). Brooke played down the issue of race, as does Cutler, who posits that "Brooke [was] a Republican who happen[ed] to be black, just as Jack Kennedy was a Democrat who happened to be Catholic" (4). It implies that, like Bunche, Brooke had transcended race, which did not matter. Would those individuals who voted for Brooke have allowed their children to be bused to achieve integration? Recall the volatile struggle in Boston over the issue during this period.

Brooke, who reentered the law practice after his electoral defeat in 1978, may address some of these key points in his upcoming biography.

Elected to Congress almost two decades later, conservative Republican J. C. Watts has rapidly emerged as one of the leading spokespersons for the GOP. Watts is the current House Republican Conference chairman, the fourth-ranking post in his party. He was a featured speaker at the 1996 Republican National Convention as a freshmen congressman, delivered the official GOP response to President Clinton's State of the Union address in 1997, and was appointed to George W. Bush's presidential exploratory committee.

Born in Efufala, Oklahoma, in 1957, Watts was the fifth of six children. Watts's family owned land but was relatively impoverished. A Democrat, his father inculcated in his children a solid work ethic and other values to which Watts would later attribute his future political reorientation. An athlete turned politician in the mode of former Democratic presidential candidate Bill Bradley, Watts was a star quarterback for the nationally renowned University of Oklahoma Sooners and played professionally in Canada (Kuharsky and Largeant 1995). He majored in journalism, which eventually spawned his interest in politics. In 1989, Watts switched his political party due to his increasing disaffection from the Democrats. When he was elected to the Oklahoma Corporate Commission in 1990, Watts became the first black American to hold a statewide office in Oklahoma, and in 1994 Watts

became the first African American Republican to be voted into Congress from below the Mason-Dixon line since Reconstruction (Ringle 1997). With only five years of experience behind him, Watts, as should be expected, has played a more prominent role in domestic policies as opposed to foreign affairs. More moderate on some issues, along with John Lewis (D-Ga.), Watts helped to defeat the Republican-sponsored Riggs Amendment, which sought to curtail affirmative action amendments in higher education. He supported a recent bipartisan congressional agreement that provides $1.3 billion to hire additional teachers and retrain others as necessary. As of November 1999, other future items for Congress to debate during Watts's tenure as House Republican included "environmental laws in mining," "debt relief for poor nations," and "barring U.S. funds to international family planning groups that support abortion overseas" (Leavitt 1999).

The media often make reference to Watts's race in their descriptions of him. Watts has been termed "the black Republican," which offends him, yet he clearly benefits from this portrayal. Watts has declared,

I didn't win because of my skin color. . . . I won because I had a strong message that resonated across the racial and ideological spectrums. I won because the vision I represent is universal. That vision entails hard work, equality of opportunity, church-oriented families, and family-orientated communities rooted in American society and black American culture. (Ringle 1997)

Watts has shunned membership in the Congressional Black Caucus, insisting that he has no obligation to cave into that "group identity thing." Some members of the caucus have stated that this decision is politically motivated. Representatives Bennie Thompson (D-Miss.) and Earl Hillard (D-Ala.) have been vocal critics (Booker 1999). Watts refers to Jesse Jackson and Marion Barry as "race-hustling pimps" who "talk a lot about slavery . . . but they're perfectly happy to have just moved us to another plantation" with a dependence on the government (Ringle 1997). But to what extent is the GOP merely "hustling" Watts to increase its appeal to black voters?

COLIN POWELL: AND THE
GENERAL STANDS ALONE

The only military leader included in this case study, Powell stands alone on the American political frontier. Four-star general Colin Powell was the first African American to hold the position of chairman of the Joint Chiefs of Staff. Powell considered a run for the presidency in 1996 but bowed out because he did not have the passion for politics.

The son of Jamaican immigrants, Colin Powell was born in Harlem in 1937 but grew up in a racially diverse working-class neighborhood in the Bronx. He attended City College, where he excelled as a student in the Reserve Officer Training Corps program. His career in the military progressed despite the era of Jim Crowism, a fact that the soldier does not dwell on in his autobiography, *My American Journey* (Powell with

Persico 1995). Powell saw action in the Vietnam war and commanded American troops in Panama. The "mastermind of Desert Storm," the Persian Gulf war brought Powell directly into the homes of millions of Americans via television in this carefully monitored conflict. Once again, Powell was thrust into the national headlines when President Clinton instituted the "don't ask, don't tell" policy in reference to gays in the military. Like most of the other top military brass, Powell objected to this policy. He has more liberal views on other controversial issues such as affirmative action.

That Colin Powell titled his book *My American Journey*, not *My Journey as a Black American*, is revealing but not surprising given his unwavering patriotism. His advancement in the military is indicative of the fact that African Americans have progressed in the armed services and military academies. (Major Charles Young was once the highest-ranking black officer in the U.S. Army, and Henry Flipper was the first black American to graduate from West Point.) Yet, according to a recent study, African Americans and Hispanics still believe that "racially offensive behavior" persists in the military in much higher numbers than do their white peers (Stone 1999). Past surveys also indicated that white Americans would have voted for Colin Powell as president, at least in theory. However, Earl Ofari Hutchinson (1994) points out many of the contradictions on the part of Powell, his political adversaries, and the mass media as well as the American electorate (147-51).

Suffice it to say, even in 1996, General Powell could not follow the precedent set by General Eisenhower, who was elected president. In 1995, Powell retired from public life, having twice been a recipient of the Medal of Freedom. He lectures across the United States and leads America's Promise (The Alliance for Youth), which he hopes will be a catalyst for change.

"YET THERE ARE
GLIMMERS OF HOPE"

As the census and election year of 2000 gathers momentum, the expression "yet there are glimmers of hope" put forth by Johnson and McCluskey (1997) points to the future horizons for black males in governance. In the future, black leaders in politics and government will be like the charismatic Jesse Jackson, Jr. (D-Ill.), and William E. Kennard, chairman of the Federal Communications Commission. On the other hand, there is a more ominous side that entails the alarming number of African American males incarcerated in the nation's penal system and the highly publicized few who have fallen victim to police brutality or racial profiling, a topic that President Clinton has addressed. Is building more prisons the answer? The prison industry is one of the fastest-growing ones in America today. Legislators and government leaders need to be at the forefront in addressing these dilemmas in spite of the political risks. Moreover, when and how black males communicate with each other or choose to remain alienated and embittered can be life

sustaining or lead to chaos and destruction. For the most part, the mainstream media foster an essentially three-dimensional image of black males as criminals, entertainers, or sports heroes to be worshipped—at least until they are charged with a heinous offense. In reality, the individual personas of black males are as diverse as the prism of black politics. They run the gamut from Barry Rand (chief executive officer of Avis) to Benjamin Carson, M.D. (director of pediatric neurosurgery at Johns Hopkins Hospital) to the late astronaut Ronald McNair. How young African American males see the concept of twoness (if they discern it at all) and the difference it makes to them and society at large is of paramount importance. There are far too many young people who cannot appreciate the significance of a King much less care about Harriet Tubman (*Black Is* 1995). This dislocation is reinforced by the inability of one generation to pass the baton of knowledge and history to the next. Referred to in some circles as "Generation X" or "Generation Next," the youths of today are less politicized. But to place all young people in this category would be to err. Who could forget the electrifying speech delivered by Alleynde Baptiste at the Million Man March? Socially conscious rap and hip-hop music, created primarily by urban black youths, often points out the inherent contradictions of being black in America today. This case study on governance suggests that until we live in a truly color-blind society, there will be opportunities for advancement but obstacles far into the twenty-first century. Prophecies and dreams aside, we must realize that "man has created artificial boundaries for race, religion and culture. If we can get past that we can realize that there is much in life which connects us"[5] (in Morris 1999).

Notes

1. This critical study does not negate the considerable achievements of African American females in government and politics. Among the most heroic and distinguished are Mary McLeod Bethune, founder of Bethune-Cookman College and director of Negro Affairs of the National Youth Administration during the New Deal; the late Representative Barbara Jordan (D-Tex.); Shirley Chisolm (D-N.Y.), who in 1972 became the first black person to be in serious contention for the American presidency; the late Patricia Harris, former secretary of housing and urban development; Constance Motley, the first African American woman to be elected to the New York State Senate and appointed as a federal judge; Dr. Joycelyn Elders, the former U.S. surgeon general; and Carol Mosley-Braun (D-Ill.), the first black woman to be elected to the United States Senate.

2. These African American advisers helped President Roosevelt to coordinate programs pertaining primarily to blacks. This cabinet was precedent setting. Some sources cite it as a defining moment for blacks in government service, while others indicate that it was largely a symbolic gesture.

3. Lenora Fulani is now slated to cochair Buchanan's campaign to be the presidential nominee for the Reform Party. As this unlikely pairing demonstrates, "politics can make for strange bedfellows" (Leavitt 1999).

4. This topic lends itself to future theoretical discourse. In terms of national prominence, black males have been most consistently visible and influential in the legislative arena, which is why the vast majority of the individuals selected for the case study have been congressmen. Black mayors could have been selected, but the extent of their influence is primarily local and national as opposed to national and international. In the future, this case study may be expanded to include a mayor and an African American in the judiciary.

5. This quotation is attributed to the late Jeraldyn Blunden, who has been described as a "cultural warrior." She founded the Contemporary Dance Company of Dayton.

References

Affleck, John. 1999. Young Takes Reins of Church Council. *Dayton Daily News*, 12 Nov.

Baldwin, James. 1984. *Notes of a Native Son*. Boston: Beacon Press.

Black Is . . . Black Ain't. 1995. Produced by Marlon Riggs. California Newsreel. Videorecording.

Booker, Simeon. 1999. Ticker Tape. *Jet*, 11 Oct., 53.

Clark, Kenneth. 1990. Postscript: Ralph Bunche, the Human Being and the International Statesman. In *Ralph Bunche: The Man and His Times*, ed. Benjamin Rivlin. New York: Holmes & Meir.

Clement, Lee. 1978. Introduction. In *Andrew Young at the United Nations*, ed. Lee Clement. Salisbury, NC: Documentary.

Cutler, John Henry. 1972. *Ed Brooke: Biography of a Senator*. Indianapolis, IN: Bobbs-Merrill.

Douglass, Frederick. 1962. *The Life and Times of Frederick Douglass*. New York: Collier Books.

Eisenstadt, Peter. 1996. Conservatism. In *Encyclopedia of African American Culture and History*, ed. Jack Salzman, David Lionel Smith, and Cornel West. 2:644-51. New York: Simon & Schuster.

Franklin, John Hope and Alfred A. Moss, Jr. 1994. *From Slavery to Freedom: A History of African Americans*. New York: McGraw-Hill.

Hamilton, Charles V. 1991. *Adam Clayton Powell, Jr.: The Political Biography of an American Dilemma*. New York: Atheneum.

Hayden, Robert C. and Karen Hayden. 1999. *African Americans on Martha's Vineyard and Nantucket: A History of People, Places and Events*. Boston: Select.

Haygood, Wil. 1993. *King of the Cats: The Life and Times of Adam Clayton Powell, Jr.* Boston: Houghton Mifflin.

Henry, Charles. 1999. *Ralph Bunche: Model Negro or American Other?* New York: New York University Press.

Hill, Ricky. 1999. Contemporary Black Politics. In *The Legacy of African American Leadership: For the Present and Future*, ed. Bernard E. Powers, Jr., Madlyn Williams Calbert, and Deborah Wright. Washington, DC: Association for the Study of Afro-American Life and History.

Hord, Fred Lee and Johnathan Scott Lee. 1995. *I Am Because We Are: Readings in Black Philosophy*. Amherst: University of Massachusetts Press.

Hutchinson, Earl Ofari. 1994. *The Assassination of the Black Male Image*. New York: Simon & Schuster.

Jenkins, Robert. 1999. Blanche K. Bruce: A Black Mississippi Political Leader. In *The Legacy of African American Leadership*, ed. Bernard E. Powers, Jr., Madlyn Williams Calbert, and Deborah Wright. Washington, DC: Association for the Study of Afro-American Life and History.

Johnson, Charles and John McCluskey, Jr. 1997. Introduction. In *Black Men Speaking*, ed. Charles Johnson and John McCluskey, Jr. Bloomington: Indiana University Press.

Kuharsky, Paul and Steve Largeant. 1995. Former Football Stars Bring Game Plans to Capital. *New York Times*, 28 Jan.

Leavitt, Paul. 1999. Congress, White House Keep Looking for Budget Savings. *USA Today*, 12 Nov.

Mauro, Tony. 1998. Mfume Arrest. *USA Today*, 6 Oct.

Mfume, Kweisi. 1998. Interview by author. Baltimore, MD, 24 Sept.

Mfume, Kweisi with Ron Stodghill II. 1996. *No Free Ride: From the Mean Streets to the Mainstream*. New York: One World.

Morris, Terry. 1999. From Humble Roots, Hard Work Earned Worldwide Acclaim. *Dayton Daily News*, 23 Nov.

Nelson, William E., Jr. 1982. The Evolution of Black Political Power in Cleveland. In *The New Black Politics: The Search for Political Power*, ed. Michael B. Preston, Lenneal J. Henderson, Jr., and Paul L. Puryear. New York: Longman.

Powell, Colin with Joseph E. Persico. 1995. *My American Journey*. New York: Random House.

Preston, Michael B., Lenneal J. Henderson, Jr., and Paul L. Puryear, eds. 1982. Introduction. In *The New Black Politics: The Search for Political Power*. New York: Longman.

Ringle, Ken. 1997. Carrying the GOP Ball; Rep. J. C. Watts Absorbed His Father's Lessons. Work Hard. Play Fair. But Be a Democrat? *Washington Post*, 4 Feb.

Rivlin, Benjamin. 1990. Preface and Introduction. In *Ralph Bunche: The Man and His Times*, ed. Benjamin Rivlin. New York: Holmes & Meir.

Snipe, Tracy. 1999. Kweisi Mfume: "Conquering Son of Kings." In *The Legacy of African American Leadership*, ed. Bernard E. Powers, Jr., Madlyn Williams Calbert, and Deborah Wright. Washington, DC: Association for the Study of Afro-American Life and History.

Stone, Andrea. 1999. Poll: Minority Troops Encounter Racism in Military. *USA Today*, 24 Nov.

Vincent, Charles. 1999. Louisiana's Black Governor: Aspects of His National Significance. In *The Legacy of African American Leadership*, ed. Bernard E. Powers, Jr., Madlyn Williams Calbert, and Deborah Wright. Washington, DC: Association for the Study of Afro-American Life and History.

Young, Andrew. 1996. *An Easy Burden: The Civil Rights Movement and the Transformation of America*. New York: HarperCollins.

African American Males in Foreign Affairs

By JAKE C. MILLER

ABSTRACT: The making and implementation of American foreign policy is a process that involves many actors, including the president, his advisers, legislators, nongovernmental organizations, and private citizens. Absent, for the most part, have been African Americans. During recent decades, however, some progress has been made in including them. A major purpose of this article is to determine the extent to which African American males have been and are involved in the foreign affairs arena, including the military. Likewise, it will seek to determine the impact that foreign policy has had and continues to have on African American males and the extent to which their involvement in the military can be considered a curse or blessing.

Jake C. Miller is a professor of political science emeritus at Bethune-Cookman College, where he taught for 22 years. Prior to that he taught at Fisk University. Among his publications are The Black Presence in American Foreign Affairs *(1979) and* The Plight of Haitian Refugees *(1984). He also has written several articles for professional journals.*

I N order to have a major impact on foreign policy, it is necessary to be in the right place at the right time, and African American males too often have not been near the scene of foreign policy-making. Until the entry of Ralph Bunche in the State Department as an African specialist in 1944 and his later accomplishments as under-secretary-general of the United Nations, African American males could aspire to be only minister either to Haiti or Liberia. Bunche provided the inspiration needed to motivate others of his race to seek careers in foreign affairs.

In regard to African American males, a major void existed in foreign affairs until 1869, when Ebenezer D. Bassett was commissioned U.S. minister to Haiti—a rank lower than that of ambassador. With this appointment, a trend was begun whereby African American males were appointed as ministers to Liberia and Haiti—two black republics—on a regular basis. From 1869 to 1913, 8 African American males served with ministerial rank in Haiti, and from 1871 to 1949 there were 23 who headed the U.S. legation in Liberia. Perhaps the best-known minister was Frederick Douglass, the famed abolitionist who served as minister to Haiti from 1889 to 1891 (Miller 1979, 393).

Another plateau was reached in 1949, when Edward Dudley became the first African American to represent this country abroad with ambassadorial rank. At the time of his elevation to this level, he was serving in Liberia as minister. He was followed by two other African American males

at that post before the trend was changed and assignments in other embassies became available to them. In 1961, Clifton Wharton became the first African American male to head a mission in a nation that was not predominantly black, when he was appointed ambassador to Norway. Likewise, he was the first of his race to obtain the position by advancing through the regular ranks of the Foreign Service. Of the first 20 assignments of African American males, 15 were in Africa, 3 in Europe, and 2 in Asia—Syria and Malta (Miller 1979, 293).

Ambassadorial positions are obtained by political appointment or by advancement through the ranks of the Foreign Service. An African American male seeking to make the Foreign Service a career may find the résumé of Terence A. Todman to be encouraging. He entered the State Department as an international relations officer in 1952 and served in a number of positions before being appointed country director for Kenya, Tanzania, Seychelles, and Uganda. While at that post, he acquired his first ambassadorship in Chad, where he served from 1969 to 1972. Following that assignment, he headed missions in Guinea (1972-74), Costa Rica (1974-77), Spain (1978-83), Denmark (1983-89), and Argentina (1989-93). He also served a brief tour of duty in the State Department as assistant secretary of state for Latin American affairs (1977-78). Other African American males who have served in three or more ambassadorial positions are Irvin Hicks, Ronald D. Palmer, and Edward J. Perkins.

To what extent do ambassadors influence American foreign policy? For an answer, one needs to take into consideration the ambassador, the particular nation to which he is assigned, and the perceived American interests. At times, the advice he transmits to Washington may be crucial to decision making in regard to the assigned nation. In addition to representing the United States in foreign capitals, ambassadors are accredited to international organizations, including the United Nations. Two African American males, with cabinet-level rank, have headed the United States Mission to the United Nations, and during their tenure they were very influential in the foreign policymaking process. They were Andrew Young and Donald McHenry.

According to President Jimmy Carter, he took into consideration Congressman Andrew Young's closeness to Martin Luther King, Jr., and the civil rights movement when he appointed him ambassador to the United Nations. He was perceived as the right person to push the human rights agenda of Carter's administration. Young gladly accepted the appointment, viewing it as a position from which he could help change American foreign policy (Young 1994, 124). Even though the United Nations is closely associated with diplomacy, Young perceived himself as being a politician rather than a typical diplomat. He noted that "a diplomat, in the traditional sense, is instructed by his government to maintain the status quo. A politician is generating activity, hoping to produce change, trying to make things happen in a positive way for his country" (Finger 1988, 262).

Seymour Finger (1988) viewed Young as a politician who employed diplomacy in achieving success (262). He credited him with having utilized a different approach to Africa, perceiving it in African terms rather than from the perspective of the Soviet-American rivalry. According to Finger, by using this approach, Young made the United States more acceptable to "third world" nations (267).

As the permanent U.S. representative to the United Nations, Young served on a rotating basis as president of the Security Council. He expressed pride in his accomplishments in this role, noting that it was during his tenure that the Anglo-American plan for ending the civil war in Rhodesia (Zimbabwe) was begun and the five Western nations' plan for independence in Namibia was initiated. While these were among his noted accomplishments, there also were disappointments. During his tenure as president in August 1977, the U.N. Committee on Palestinian Rights prepared a resolution to submit to the Security Council that Young preferred not being presented at that time. He realized that as the representative of the United States he would have had to veto it. After he met unofficially with the Palestinian representative to discuss the matter, a storm of protest arose, and, in response, he submitted his resignation.

In accepting Young's resignation, President Carter praised him for his "dedication and sensitivity," which he observed had helped to prove "that our country is sympathetic to the deepest social and political aspirations of increasingly awakened human beings throughout the world." Carter observed that Young "earned for us the friendship, trust and respect of many nations which had previously considered the United States to be suspect and unworthy of such a relationship" (*Public Papers* 1979, 1436).

After accepting Young's resignation, Carter named Donald McHenry to succeed him. He was well qualified for the assignment, having served under Young as deputy representative to the U.N. Security Council. In this role, he had already established diplomatic skills, serving as the chief negotiator on the question of Namibia. McHenry served until the end of the Carter administration and was credited with doing a superior job.

In the State Department, the position of assistant secretary is regarded as the highest in a bureau. Several African American males have held that position, including Terence A. Todman, assistant secretary for Latin American affairs; John Rhinehart, assistant secretary for public affairs; Alan Keyes, assistant secretary for international organizations; and George E. Moose, assistant secretary for African affairs.

Perhaps no African American has exerted more influence on the making of U.S. foreign policy than General Colin Powell, who served as adviser to the president for national security during the Reagan administration. In this key position, he was responsible for advising the president in regard to "the integration of domestic, foreign and military policies relating to national security" (Powell with Persico 1995, 332). He sat on a council composed of the secretaries of state and defense, chairman of the Joint Chiefs of Staff, and director of the Central Intelligence Agency. During his tenure as adviser (November 1987 to January 1989), he played a major role in the preparation for three summit conferences: Moscow, 1988; Governor's Island, New York, 1987; and Iceland, 1986. He regards as his major accomplishment the drafting of the Intermediate-range Nuclear Forces (INF) Treaty.

Another major actor in the foreign affairs arena was Ronald H. Brown, secretary of commerce from 1993 to 1996. His chances of becoming secretary of state during the second term of the Clinton administration were considered good, but he was killed in a plane crash prior to the president's reelection. During his tenure as commerce secretary, he was actively involved in negotiations with Congress concerning the North American Free Trade Agreement and the General Agreement on Tariffs and Trade. Brown led several major trade missions abroad, including those to South Africa in 1993 and China in 1994. He was killed in a plane crash during a mission to Bosnia-Herzegovina and Croatia in 1996. James Hackney, a counselor to Brown, observed, "As he grew into the position, Brown defied Clinton in a sense by combining the positions of commerce secretary and secretary of state, ushering in a new era of commercial diplomacy" (Jones 1996, 92).

Depending upon his or her committee assignment, a member of Congress can exert major influence on foreign affairs. Among African American males who have played important roles are Congressman Charles Diggs, who, as chairman of the House Subcommittee on Africa, for several years appeared to be a voice in the wilderness pleading the cause for that continent. Likewise, Congressman Mickey Leland, chairman of the House Select Committee on Hunger, gave his life in the struggle against world hunger. Congressman Ronald Dellum also found himself in a crucial position as chairman of the Armed Services Committee. He was the leading congressional voice in the employment of sanctions against South Africa and the changing of policies in regard to Haiti.

When we consider private individuals who have had a major impact on foreign affairs, Randall Robinson comes to mind. His influence, for the most part, results from his leadership of TransAfrica, which was organized in 1977. He was very instrumental in the campaign to end minority rule in South Africa and the restoring of the elected government to power in Haiti. In order to achieve the latter, he undertook a successful fast, which was followed by discussions with top U.S. governmental officials.

Jesse Jackson, acting as a private citizen, also has been a major actor in foreign affairs. He was credited with obtaining the release of hostages and prisoners in Lebanon, Cuba, and Iraq, and he has been used for certain missions abroad, especially during the Clinton administration.

As a rule, foreign policy is effective to the extent that there is military power to guarantee its enforcement; therefore, good foreign policymakers do not make decisions without taking into consideration the advice of leaders of the military. In a sense, it can be said that military leaders, indeed, are major actors in the making and implementation of foreign affairs. In this arena, Colin Powell, the chairman of the Joint Chiefs of Staff in the Bush administration, exerted major influence. In this role, he was the principal adviser to the secretary of defense and the president on all military issues. He presided over the Just Cause operation in Panama, which resulted in the capture and imprisonment of Manuel Noriega, the country's leader, and the Desert Storm operation in the Persian Gulf. In both cases, he provided critical information that led to the making of major decisions.

While no African American military leader exercised near the influence of General Powell, several of them are noteworthy, including Brigadier General Benjamin O. Davis, Sr., who was the first of his race to achieve the rank of general. One of the major assignments given to him was that of assistant to the inspector general. In that role, he advised the War Department (forerunner of the Defense Department) "on how to handle the racial problems generated by its segregation policies." During his tenure in office, he made many recommendations concerning how to improve race relations in the military and how to provide fairer treatment for blacks, including their participation in combat. In considering race problems in the general society, he felt that the Army was in a very good position to lead the way in improving race relations. He viewed racial discrimination as posing a problem to the United States' war efforts (Fletcher 1989, 122).

During his tenure in the Army, Davis experienced more than his share of racial discrimination, but he endured. As he was inspired by Charles Young, the leading black military man of his day, Davis has been an inspiration to many others in all branches of the armed forces, including his son, Benjamin O. Davis, Jr., who became the first to achieve general rank in the Air Force. Other African American males whose achievements are often applauded include Samuel L. Gravely, Jr., who became the first African American to hold admiral rank in the Navy; Frank E. Petersen, the first of his race to obtain general rank in the Marine Corps; Daniel "Chappie" James, who was the first to receive a four-star general rank in the Air Force; and Roscoe Robinson, Jr., who was the first African American to become a four-star general in the U.S. Army. Civilians who have held high positions in the Defense Department include Clifford Alexander, who served as secretary of the Army in the Carter administration, and Togo West, who held a similar position in the Clinton administration. Edwin Dorn served as assistant secretary for personnel and readiness in the Defense Department.

IMPACT OF FOREIGN AFFAIRS DECISIONS OF AFRICAN AMERICAN MALES

The making of U.S. foreign policy should be of concern to all Americans since they are affected by its implementation. Aside from this general interest, African Americans have a more specific interest in issues that have affected them as a racial group or an economic class. Although historically American foreign policy has had a more negative than positive impact on them, we will begin this analysis with the latter.

African Americans benefited racially from some of the policies this country pursued in response to the influx of African nations to the international community during the decade of the sixties. In the Cold War era, these new nations were of great importance to the United States since it needed their votes to continue to exert maximal influence in the United Nations. The obtaining of friends in Africa, however, depended, in large part, upon race relations here at home. In referring to the principles of racial equality and nondiscrimination, Secretary of State Dean Rusk suggested that "the degree to which we ourselves practice those principles our voice will carry conviction in seeking national goals in the conduct of foreign relations" (U.S. Department of State 1961b). A major problem that confronted the State Department was that of protecting African diplomats from racial discrimination here in the United States. In a sense, the State Department became a lobbyist seeking to convince state and local governments that our foreign policy was being harmed by discrimination against visiting diplomats. As it achieved success in removing obstacles against diplomats, owners of segregated facilities decided that if they allowed foreign blacks to partake of their services, then morally, they should grant African Americans the same privileges.

The State Department perceived not only a need for insulating diplomats from racial discrimination but also a need to resolve the racial problems as they were practiced here against African Americans. It acknowledged that while the immediate problem was assuring foreign visitors that they would "face no affront to their racial dignity," its eventual goal was the complete elimination of "racial discrimination and segregation from American public life" (U.S. Department of State 1961a). In later years, the impact of race relations upon foreign policy goals became a consideration in the adoption of major civil rights legislation, including the Civil Rights Act of 1964 and the Voting Rights Act of 1965.

African American males also have been affected by certain trade and tariff agreements that have had the effect of encouraging indirectly the purchase of goods manufactured abroad. Congresswoman Barbara Collins, chair of the Anti-NAFTA Task Force of the Congressional Black Caucus, and the Reverend Jesse Jackson opposed the North American Free Trade Agreement, citing the adverse effect it would have on minority employment (U.S. Congress 1993, 58-61, 72-77). A closing down of factories here in the United States, which was perceived as resulting from the treaty, would more than likely cause an increase in unemployment, especially among African American males.

Critics have maintained that the United States' participation in foreign military actions has constituted major obstacles to the progress of African Americans. Perhaps the most vocal critic of this nation's policies in regard to Vietnam was Martin Luther King, Jr., who bemoaned the fact that the war efforts were preventing necessary funds and energies from being used to rehabilitate the poor in this country (King 1968, 22-23).

The war in Vietnam was criticized not only for its drain on men and funds but also for the large number of casualties suffered by African Americans, mostly males. Once again, King was very vocal, noting that the United States "was sending their [African Americans'] sons and their brothers and their husbands to fight and to die and in extraordinarily higher proportions relative to the rest of the population" (King 1968, 23).

As was the case with the war in Vietnam, African Americans, in large numbers, opposed the war in the Persian Gulf in 1991. The reasons that were given were the same. The spending of money to pursue warfare was perceived as preventing the expenditure of money to alleviate domestic problems. Second, there was the issue of disproportionality as it related to the number of African Americans involved in the war. The Congressional Black Caucus was virtually unanimous in its opposition to involvement in the Persian Gulf (Puddington 1991, 28-29). The issue of disproportionality will be analyzed in greater depth later in this article.

AFRICAN AMERICAN MALES IN THE MILITARY: BENEFIT OR CURSE?

Serving in the armed forces of the United States is regarded as the highest form of patriotism, considering that often one's life is at risk. Critics, therefore, have raised questions concerning the wisdom of African American males' enlisting in the military, contending that they are required to spend too much time fighting racism rather than foreign enemies. Those who disagree with this view acknowledge that there are vestiges of discrimination remaining in the military, but discrimination is less there than in the larger American society. While there is truth in this observation, historically the military was a bastion of segregation.

It was not until after the close of World War II that steps were taken to eliminate racial discrimination in the military. On 26 July 1948, President Harry Truman issued Executive Order 9981, which directed the armed services to provide "equality of treatment and opportunity for all personnel without regard to race, color, religion, or national origin." He also appointed a presidential committee to study the situation and recommend ways to ensure equality of treatment and opportunity in the military. In the meantime, the Air Force and Navy began taking steps to integrate on their own.

The Army resisted, maintaining that it provided equal opportunities and facilities and that blacks usually benefited from segregation since they would not have to compete against "more qualified" whites for positions (Dalfiume 1969, 179-80). According to Secretary of the Army Royall, "Voluntary segregation was the normal condition in civilian life and since a large portion of the Army's volunteers came from the South ... integration would seriously disrupt the Army and impede its mission of national defense" (Dalfiume 1969, 181).

In spite of the Army's objection, the Defense Department eliminated official racial segregation in the armed forces, but that did not mean that integration was a reality. In the years that followed, there were numerous complaints concerning racial discrimination. The National Association for the Advancement of Colored People conducted an investigation in Germany in 1971 and concluded that there were urgent problems that needed to be addressed. It made recommendations concerning the Armed Forces Qualification Test, promotion, administration of military justice, off-base housing, and several other areas (MacGregor and Nalty 1977).

Often it has been stated that the military is neither white nor black but, instead, one unified force. There are African Americans who disagree with this statement, contending that culturally their values are submerged in a predominantly white society. In recent years, they have demanded "an official recognition of their distinctive life-style and culture." Jack Foner (1974) perceived these protests as "simply reflecting changes in the larger black community and its consciousness" (207). The military was challenged to provide literature that reflects the African American experience, as well as make available products, supplies, music, and food associated with African Americans. A modified Afro haircut became acceptable in many situations.

Some black leaders decried the efforts to meet these cultural demands, suggesting that the armed forces should be integrated with one set of standards. Typical of those were General Benjamin Davis, Jr., who had encountered various forms of segregation during his military career. He declined to have his portrait displayed at West Point as a source of pride for black cadets, recalling that he had gone "through the separate unit segregated phase into a phase which the black serviceman was simply another serviceman who was treated and employed without regard to his race." In noting that some blacks are now interested in emphasizing their race and seeking special treatment because of it, Davis expressed the view that all servicemen should be treated alike in every respect and that no official notice should be given to their race (Davis 1992, 419).

In response to critics who insist that, because of racial discrimination, African Americans encounter serious obstacles in the military, some maintain that although racial discrimination continues to exist in the armed forces, it does not compare with what one would face in the broader society. General Colin Powell noted that "the military had given African-Americans more equal opportunity than any other institution in American society" (Powell with Persico 1995, 501). This view was shared by many others, including Roger Wilkins (1989), who concluded that "the military does a better job of making, enlarging, and sustaining opportunities for minorities than do most other segments of society" (164). Earlier, Richard Stillman (1968) suggested that the military not only provides "a materially better place for Negroes," but it is the "colored man's haven from worldly oppression." He perceived the military as offering three types of rewards: "for the Negro, an institutional haven; for the military, troops to fill its ranks and for the American white, a salve for his conscience" (123). Like Powell and Wilkins, he, too, considered it an irony that the least democratic organization—the armed forces—had introduced equality more rapidly than other institutions. He attributed this to its organizational structure, which was equally effective years earlier in maintaining segregation (124-25).

When we move beyond the argument that racial discrimination should be a deterrent to African American males' enlisting in the armed forces, the point of debate shifts to the disproportionate number of black males in the military with the possibility of a higher percentage of casualties. As indicated earlier, some critics question whether young African Americans are sacrificing too much for a country that, because of economic discrimination, has forced them into the military in the first place. Several suggestions have been made relative to providing incentives to make enlistment more attractive to middle-class whites in order to bring about a greater racial balance. Some whites, who fear that the armed services may become "too black," also support such reform. Ironically, this was one of the arguments made against integration at the time it was proposed by President Truman in 1948 (Dalfiume 1969, 197).

An aggressive campaign to encourage enlistment of whites in order to increase their percentage in the military was perceived by Wilkins (1989) as having a negative effect upon young economically deprived African American males. He viewed it as shifting the question from "whether it is fair for many of them to have no economic option but military service to whether it is fair that some of them lose the valuable economic option of military service so that we can entice more middle-class youngsters into the military" (162).

Returning to the issue of proportionality and the risk that it poses for African American males, the question may be asked, Are young men not aware of the risk involved when they enlist in the military? According to Robert Fullinwider (1989), one joining the military "must weigh the benefits he will gain against the drawbacks of service." The most important drawback is the risk of being killed or injured in war. He suggested that in peacetime, a recruit may not view the overall risk as being very high, unless war is clearly imminent. Fullinwider concluded that the recruit "will find military service an attractive option if the combination of its economic and non-economic returns compensates fully not only for the unpleasantnesses of service, but also for the risks" (105).

Consistent with the latter, a black youth who cannot easily find a job may be attracted to the military. Once there, he may consider what he has to gain as worth the risk; therefore he reenlists. Because of the higher reenlistment ratio of blacks to whites, the likelihood of becoming a noncommissioned officer in charge of others is great. Moskos and Butler (1996) have noted that "what makes the Army's enlisted ranks unique is that blacks are more likely to be superiors and whites subordinates" (47). In this regard, Moskos and Butler perceived the military as perhaps outranking civilian institutions regarding blacks' having whites under their command. Moskos and Butler viewed this as having a very "tangible and positive" impact on the black community when these men return as veterans (47). They also envisioned many benefits that a person having served in the military would have over nonveterans, including better opportunities for employment, education, and the purchase of homes.

Employment opportunities may be viewed as both a curse and a blessing. On the negative side, some servicemen may find that they have spent years in the military only to face unemployment as civilians because their skills cannot be transferred. On the positive side, some businesses and governmental agencies give high priority to the employment of veterans. In addition to this advantage, Moskos and Butler (1996) noted that many young men improve their chances of employment merely because of general skills that they usually cultivate while in service, including the ability to work with others cooperatively, accept authority, and cope successfully with the "bureaucratic complexity of large organizations" (104). Moskos and Butler also suggested that enduring the rigid life of the military without giving up may itself be a valuable recommendation for a veteran seeking employment.

In general, based on the statistics relative to both initial enlistment and reenlistment, African Americans apparently consider the military to be a blessing more than a curse. Critics, however, maintain that their choice of the military was not much of an option since the civilian economy is not willing or able to accommodate them. Colin Powell observed that as long as this imbalance exists, blacks will continue to flock to the military. He issued this challenge: "Let the rest of American society open its doors to African Americans and give them the opportunities they now enjoy in the armed forces" (Powell with Persico 1995, 501). Then and only then, Powell concluded, is their flow into the military likely to be stemmed. The curse lies more in the inequities in American society, generally, than in the military.

ASSESSMENT

In this study, we have sought answers to the following questions: (1) What is the role of African American males in American foreign affairs, including the armed forces? (2) How have foreign affairs policies affected African American males? (3) Are the American armed forces a curse or benefit to African American males?

A major assumption is that the greater the number of African Americans holding strategic foreign affairs positions, the more likely the policies will result in reflecting their interest. It will be difficult to test this assumption since so few African Americans have held positions crucial to the process. An exception to the rule was Ambassador Andrew Young, who, in his cabinet-level post at the U.S. Mission to the United Nations, was able to give visibility to African issues and human rights, both of which were of concern to the African American community. Perhaps it can be better argued that when blacks occupy major positions in foreign affairs, their presence may not promote the interests of the African American community as much as serve as a deterrent to the adoption of policies that the community would consider detrimental. It should be kept in mind that an African American, even though very sensitive to issues of a racial interest, must help to formulate policies for the entire nation. These policies sometimes will not be as beneficial to his race as to the rest of the nation; therefore, he is left with no choice but to note his objection and then to proceed to endorse the policy. An effective foreign policy, as perceived here, is one that will be good for the nation at large and at the same time not have an adverse effect on a particular racial group.

It appears that, at times, too much is expected of African Americans in foreign affairs positions. Because these officials must adhere to the policies of the State Department, they are too often labeled "stooges" or "Uncle Toms." Likewise, those in the military are at times referred to as "fighters in the white man's war." This type of rejection may convince many young men not to pursue careers in the Foreign Service or military.

It also has been suggested that the involvement of African American males in foreign affairs depends upon the extent to which they perceive themselves as being affected by foreign policy decisions. Policies that have a major negative impact upon them may lead to a response in the form of a protest. Illustrative of such issues were the U.S. policies in regard to the racist regime of South Africa and tolerance of military rule in Haiti. A logical outgrowth of the slow but successful change of policies through protest can result in more African Americans' being placed in positions of influence, in the hope that this will ensure more positive policies in the future. Likewise, the perceived exerting of influence in foreign affairs may encourage ambitious young men to seek careers in the Foreign Service since they would view international affairs as being relevant to them. Assuming the foregoing, the African American community more than likely would support with greater enthusiasm a disproportionate percentage of members of its community participating in military engagements in defense of policies that it approves. The African American men involved in such conflicts probably would be viewed as heroes making sacrifices for worthy causes; therefore, their being in the military would most likely not be perceived as a curse.

References

Dalfiume, Richard M. 1969. *Desegregation of the Armed Forces*. Columbia: University of Missouri Press.

Davis, Benjamin O., Jr. 1992. *Benjamin O. Davis, Jr.: American*. New York: Plume Book.

Finger, Seymour. 1988. *American Ambassadors at the United Nations*. New York: Holmes & Meier.

Fletcher, Marvin E. 1989. *America's First Black General*. Lawrence: University Press of Kansas.

Foner, Jack. 1974. *Blacks and the Military in American History*. New York: Praeger.

Fullinwider, Robert K. 1989. Choice, Justice and Representation. In *Who Defends America?* ed. Edwin Dorn. Washington, DC: Joint Center for Political Studies.

Jones, Joyce. 1996. The Best Commerce Secretary Ever. *Black Enterprise* 26(11):90-98.

King, Martin Luther, Jr. 1968. *The Trumpet of Conscience*. New York: Harper & Row.

MacGregor, Morris J. and Bernard C. Nalty, eds. 1977. *Blacks in the United States Armed Forces*. Wilmington, DE: Scholarly Resources.

Miller, Jake C. 1979. *The Black Presence in American Foreign Affairs*. Washington, DC: University Press of America.

Moskos, Charles C. and John S. Butler. 1996. *All That We Can Be*. New York: Basic Books.

Powell, Colin L. with Joseph E. Persico. 1995. *My American Journey.* New York: Random House.

Public Papers of the Presidents: Jimmy Carter. 1979. Washington, DC: Government Printing Office.

Puddington, Arch. 1991. Black Leaders vs. Desert Storm. *Commentary,* 5(May):28-34.

Stillman, Richard J., II. 1968. *Integration of the Negro in the U.S. Armed Forces.* New York: Praeger.

U.S. Congress. House of Representatives. Committee on Government Operations, Employment, Housing and Aviation Subcommittee. 1993. *NAFTA: A Negative Impact on Blue Collar, Minority and Female Employment?* 103rd Cong., 1st sess., 10 Nov.

U.S. Department of State. 1961a. Press release 267, 27 Apr.

———. 1961b. Press release 359, 1 June.

Wilkins, Roger. 1989. Right Issues, Wrong Questions. In *Who Defends America?* ed. Edward Dorn. Washington, DC: Joint Center for Political Studies.

Young, Andrew. 1994. *Way out of No Way.* Nashville, TN: Thomas Nelson.

ANNALS, *AAPSS*, **569**, May 2000

Black Males in the Civil Rights Movement

By JACOB U. GORDON

ABSTRACT: The civil rights movement has had a tremendous impact on American life and history. Its public policy impact includes the landmark Supreme Court decision of 1954, the comprehensive Civil Rights Act of 1964, and the Voting Rights Act of 1965, to name a few. Although much has been written about the civil rights movement, there is a paucity of comparative in-depth analyses of the leadership role of African American men. This article seeks to fill this gap in the literature. It focuses on five nationally and internationally recognized African American male civil rights leaders of the twentieth century: W.E.B. Du Bois, A. Philip Randolph, Martin Luther King, Jr., Malcolm X, and Kwame Toure (formerly Stokely Carmichael). Notwithstanding the vast differences in their backgrounds, leadership styles, tactics, philosophies, and strategies, they had a common goal and shared vision for America, the land of the free. Their legacies are immortal.

Jacob U. Gordon is professor of African and African American studies and research fellow at the University of Kansas. He is also the executive director of the Center for Multicultural Leadership in the Schiefelbusch Institute for Life Span Studies. Dr. Gordon is the author of 12 books, including The African American Male: An Annotated Bibliography *(1999),* The African American Male: His Present Status and Future *(1994), and* A Search for Equal Justice by African-American Lawyers: A History of the National Bar Association *(1999). He is the recipient of several honors and awards for academic and public service.*

Oppressed people must assume responsibility . . . to free themselves.
—A. Philip Randolph ([1942] 1970)

The civil rights movement in America produced, among other things, many black national leaders. They all practically agreed on a common cause of freedom, justice, and equality for blacks. To be sure, they were men who believed in the American dream, the American revolutionary philosophy, and America's promise of life, liberty, and the pursuit of happiness. They often differed, however, in approach and style.

The purpose of this article is twofold: (1) to document the impact of African American males in the civil rights movement and (2) to examine the extent to which the civil rights movement has affected American life and thought. Obviously, it is not possible to include all the black men of national stature who made significant contributions to the civil rights movement. I decided at the outset that in order to achieve a better perspective of the role of black men in the civil rights movement and its impact on American life, persons still alive would not be treated. In addition, space limitations, historical period covered, and the current state of research in African American studies have helped shape the choices. Obvious omissions include men like Marcus Garvey, James Weldon Johnson, Adam Clayton Powell, Jr., Charles Houston, Medgar Evers, Roy Wilkins, and Thurgood Marshall.

On the other hand, attempts have been made to include men whose principal base was their organizational affiliations, representing different ideologies and personalities: nationalists and integrationists, radical and nonviolent. Thus this article analyzes five nationally recognized male civil rights leaders representing five organizations: W.E.B. Du Bois, National Association for the Advancement of Colored People (NAACP); Martin Luther King, Jr., Southern Christian Leadership Conference (SCLC); Malcolm X, Nation of Islam; A. Philip Randolph, Brotherhood of Sleeping Car Porters; Kwame Toure (formerly Stokely Carmichael), Student Nonviolent Coordinating Committee (SNCC). These leaders sought in diverse ways to advance African Americans and overcome the racial barriers and oppression that pervaded American society. The period selected for this examination is the twentieth century.

W.E.B. DU BOIS
AND THE NAACP

One of the most prominent and influential black leaders of the twentieth century, William Edward Burghardt Du Bois, was a free black born on 23 February 1868, in Great Barrington, Massachusetts, the year of President Andrew Johnson's impeachment (White 1985, 48). Educated at Fisk University, a predominantly black private university (A.B., 1888), the University of Berlin, and Harvard University (A.B., 1890; Ph.D., 1896), Du Bois went on to become an articulate intellectual and distinguished scholar. His first book, *Suppression of the African Slave Trade to the United States,*

1638-1870 (1969), was a pioneering book that, until recently, was considered the definitive study of the slave trade in the United States. It was based on his 1896 doctoral dissertation. In addition to his writing, Du Bois held teaching positions at Wilberforce University, the University of Pennsylvania, and Atlanta University.

Du Bois is best remembered as the leader of those early-twentieth-century black intellectuals who challenged the accommodationist leadership of Booker T. Washington. Washington, of course, stressed the concept of industrial and vocational education for blacks, conciliation with the white South, and submission and silence as to black civil and political rights. Writing in *The Souls of Black Folk* (1903), Du Bois asserted that the Washington program practically accepted the alleged inferiority of black people. The function of education, according to Du Bois, was to train individuals for social leadership. Blacks would continue to be led by whites until an African American intelligentsia (what Du Bois called the "talented tenth") was allowed to emerge. By straitjacketing blacks with vocational education, as opposed to traditional liberal arts education, such an emergence would never occur. "Mr. Washington's programme," Du Bois commented, "ignores the Negro's right to vote, his right to attend universities to secure a liberal arts education and his right to share equally in the American dream" (Huggins 1986, 392-404).

In 1905, Du Bois founded the Niagara Movement and, five years later, became one of the prominent leaders of the NAACP. Throughout this time, he continued to hammer away at Washington's leadership of American blacks. Du Bois advocated and genuinely believed in what modern sociologists called "cultural pluralism." Rejecting the concept of the melting pot, he realized that complete amalgamation of the races in America probably would never occur. He insisted, however, that blacks wanted to be both black and American, maintaining their racial identity and integrity while associating with and participating in American culture to the fullest extent. As early as 1897, Du Bois had written that "one feels [the Negro's] two-ness—an American, a Negro, two souls, two thoughts, two unreconciled strivings, two warring ideals in one dark body. He simply wishes to make it possible for a man to be both a Negro and an American without being cursed and spit upon" (Du Bois 1903, 3).

A major influence over all twentieth-century black protest, Du Bois worked within the NAACP until after World War II, serving as editor of the organization's monthly magazine, *The Crisis*, from 1910 to 1934. As the director of publications and research and editor of *The Crisis*, Du Bois made significant contributions to the growth and influence of the NAACP. For example, in 1919, the NAACP published *Thirty Years of Lynching in the United States, 1889-1918*, which estimated that 3224 blacks had been lynched during this period.

He was also devoted to the cause of pan-Africanism and, as a result of his persistent attacks upon colonial rule in Africa, is often referred to as the "Godfather of African Independence." During his later life, Du Bois became increasingly discouraged by the lack of genuine racial progress in the United States. As a result, he emigrated to Ghana at the age of 93. A close friend of Ghanaian leader Kwame Nkrumah, Du Bois became a citizen of Ghana two months before his death in 1963.

Aside from Du Bois, the first group of NAACP officials, including the organization's first president, Moorfield Storey, were whites. Bringing most of the black intellectuals from the Niagara Movement into the new group with him, Du Bois was assured an important role in the NAACP.

Notwithstanding contemporary accusations of conservatism and Uncle Tomism leveled by many young black militants, the NAACP was in the vanguard of the black struggle for civil rights and equality in America. Founded in 1909 in response to the prevailing pattern of American segregation, disfranchisement, and racial violence, the NAACP from the outset has been an interracial organization (Hughes 1962).

By maintaining a strong lobby in Washington, the NAACP has successfully campaigned for laws designed to protect and, when necessary, extend the rights of African Americans. Equally significant have been the NAACP's legal battles in the courts against unjust laws and inadequate enforcement of constitutionally guaranteed rights. The organization's most notable success came as a result of its steady and skillful assault on public school segregation, an assault that culminated in 1954 when the Supreme Court of the United States, in *Brown* v. *Board of Education*, declared that racially segregated schools are "inherently unequal" (Martin 1998). Legal victories such as these set the stage for the subsequent civil rights revolution during the 1960s.

Since Du Bois's era, the NAACP has continued its historic tradition and strategies for social equity in a civil society. Currently headed by a former congressman, Kweisi Mfume, as the executive director, and Julian Bond as the chairman of the board of directors, the NAACP appears to be at a crossroads. It promises to broaden its base, to be more inclusive, and to move toward economic opportunities for all Americans, especially the underrepresented populations. The future of the NAACP remains to be seen as the color of America's future will change dramatically (Chideya 1999, 5).

ASA PHILIP RANDOLPH AND THE WORKING CLASS

A. Philip Randolph came to prominence during and after World War I as editor of the radical Socialist magazine *The Messenger*. He established himself as a race leader by his successful effort to organize and secure recognition of the Brotherhood of Sleeping Car Porters during the 1920s and 1930s. In 1936, he became the first president of the National Negro Congress, an "organization of organizations," created on the initiative of a group of black intellectuals.

A civil rights leader, Randolph was born in Crescent City, Florida, on 15 April 1889. He completed his high school courses at the Cookman Institute in Jacksonville before moving to the North. He attended the College of the City of New York, taking courses in economics and political science.

In 1917, Randolph and Chandler Owen launched the publication of *The Messenger*. Randolph was arrested in June 1918 by the Department of Justice for his militant stand against World War I. He was released after a few days.

Also in 1917, he organized a union of elevator operators in New York City. He also participated in many organizational campaigns among garment-trade workers and motion-picture operators. In August 1925, Randolph was elected president and general organizer of the Brotherhood of Sleeping Car Porters. He changed the name of his publication from *The Messenger* to *The Official Organ of the Brotherhood of Sleeping-Car Porters*. Randolph was the vice president of the American Federation of Labor and Congress of Industrial Organizations (AFL-CIO) in 1957 and a member of Mayor La Guardia's Commission on Race in 1935.

Concerned about discrimination in the expanding defense industries, Randolph proposed and organized a mass march of 10,000 blacks to the nation's capital in 1941 to petition for equal opportunities in employment. As a result of the pressure from the preparation for the march, President Franklin D. Roosevelt in June 1941 promulgated his executive order establishing the Fair Employment Practices Committee. Randolph called off the march but tried to keep the movement intact.

As Randolph ([1942] 1970) noted, "This aggressively all-black movement excluded white participation" (392). Criticized by a number of his contemporaries, Randolph and his followers defended the color barrier on the ground that white participation inevitably led to Communist infiltration. This policy was certainly also rooted in a genuine belief in the necessity for blacks to direct their own fight for freedom—as Frederick Douglass had declared nearly a century before. Yet the movement's ideology not unexpectedly revealed the common ethnic paradox, and Randolph made it clear that it was in no way anti-white, nor did he close the doors on cooperation with white and interracial groups. However, as to the composition of the movement itself, Randolph's policy was that it be all-black and pro-black but not anti-white or anti-Semitic or anti-labor or anti-Catholic.

The most significant step toward the unionization of African Americans was the organization of the Brotherhood of Sleeping Car Porters and Maids by Randolph in 1925 (Brazeal 1946, 15-30). When the brotherhood made an effort to secure from the Pullman Company better working conditions and higher wages, the employer would have nothing to do with the brotherhood. It attacked the brotherhood as a dangerous radical organization and condemned Randolph as a professional agitator. Considerable opposition to the brotherhood arose from both white and black groups, but its endorsement by the AFL, the NAACP, and the National Urban League bolstered its fight considerably. Partial recognition came in 1926 and 1929 in wage agreements; full recognition of the brotherhood as the bargaining agency for the porters and maids employed by the Pullman Company came only in 1937, when more than 8000 employees benefited by a wage increase that totaled $1,152,000 (Harris 1977, 150-200).

Thus Randolph's demand for a new deal was accomplished. It was only a year later, in 1938, that Congress passed the Fair Labor Standards Act, better known as the wages and hours bill. It was another step in the direction of the emancipation of the working class in America. The stand of the CIO in favor of abolishing racial discrimination and the liberal programs of the Political Action Committee gave new hope to many blacks and whites of goodwill. They were no longer suspicious of labor organizations per se and were inclined to join and even provide leadership for strikes with much enthusiasm. A feeling of security and belonging arose among black workers that was one of the most significant developments in their struggle for greater integration into American life. In testimony of the courageous efforts of A. Philip Randolph, an institute named after him was created in 1968 in New York City. He died on 7 May 1979.

MARTIN LUTHER KING
AND THE SCLC

Without any doubt, the one name most clearly associated with the civil rights movement during the mid-twentieth century was that of Martin Luther King, Jr. Apostle of nonviolence and dedicated humanitarian, King attracted broader support from both the American black and white communities than any previous black leader, including Booker T. Washington. His violent and premature death on 4 April 1968 in Memphis, Tennessee, represented one of the most tragic and ominous developments in the history of the United States.

Born Michael Luther King, Jr., on 15 January 1929, in Atlanta, Georgia (Bennett 1968, 15), King's given name was changed to Martin while still a child. His mother, the late Alberta Williams King, was the daughter of the Reverend Alfred D. Williams, who founded the Ebenezer Baptist Church in Atlanta during the late nineteenth century (Lincoln 1984). King's father, Michael Luther King, Sr. (whose given name was also later changed to Martin), succeeded Williams as pastor at Ebenezer in 1932. Under his leadership, Ebenezer became one of the most prominent black churches in the United States.

King was a precocious youth. He graduated from high school and matriculated at Morehouse College, a predominantly black institution, before he was 16. Following in his father's footsteps, he decided to devote his life to the ministry, being ordained at Ebenezer in 1947. A year later, he graduated from Morehouse College, where he was mentored by Benjamin Mays (Carter 1998, 250), and entered Crozer Theological Seminary in Chester, Pennsylvania.

Following a distinguished academic career at Crozer, King enrolled in a Ph.D. program at Boston University's School of Theology, receiving his doctorate in 1955 (Lewis 1970). During his sojourn in Boston, King met and married Coretta Scott, a native of Alabama and an alumnus of Antioch College (King 1993).

While King was completing his doctoral dissertation in 1954, he was offered and accepted the pastorate of the Dexter Avenue Baptist Church in Montgomery, Alabama. Quickly gaining local recognition in Montgomery's black community, he was called upon to lead the now-famous Montgomery Bus Boycott of 1955-56. It is important to note here that the Montgomery Bus Boycott is of special significance to the student of American studies in at least two respects. In the first place, the boycott provided a pattern of resistance that other blacks in other Southern cities soon followed. In this respect, historian Louis E. Lomax has written that the refusal of Rosa Parks to give up her seat to a white man, and the subsequent bus boycott, represent the "birth of the Negro Revolt" (Lomax 1962). Second, the Montgomery boycott provided the setting for the emergence of a new black leader, Martin Luther King, Jr. King was relatively unknown before he more or less led the bus boycott.

Representing 75 percent of Montgomery's bus-riding population, the city's blacks continued the boycott (notwithstanding tremendous white indignation and terrorist retaliation) until a federal court injunction prohibiting racial segregation on buses went into effect a year later. It was King who united the blacks of Montgomery, utilizing, for the first time, Gandhi's principle of passive resistance. This act was a great victory for King. The result of King's first success was the desegregation of public transportation. As a result of this successful beginning and of his own charismatic personality, King was catapulted into the national limelight. The civil rights revolution, it appeared, had found its leader.

In 1957, a group of black ministers led by Dr. King laid the groundwork for a new civil rights organization, the Southern Christian Leadership Conference. Calling for "total integration" and "full citizenship rights," the SCLC under the leadership of King dedicated itself to the nonviolent elimination of Jim Crow practices throughout the South. Although not always successful in its efforts, the SCLC's participation in the Birmingham demonstrations of 1963 and the Selma march of 1965 did much to secure the passage of the Civil Rights Acts of 1964 and 1965, respectively. These acts have had far-reaching impact on American life. The Civil Rights Act of 1964 was undoubtedly the most comprehensive and significant piece of civil rights legislation ever passed by Congress. Despite an extended Southern filibuster, supporters of the legislation had sufficient strength to muster the necessary votes for passage on 2 July 1964 (Franklin 1994, 502). The legislation prohibited racial discrimination in public accommodations and in programs receiving federal assistance. In addition, discrimination by employers and unions was prohibited; the Equal Employment Opportunity Commission was established; and the enforcement apparatus of voting laws and of school and public facilities desegregation orders was significantly strengthened.

Dr. King's participation in the March on Washington during August 1963 cemented his position as the most dynamic, charismatic, and meaningful black civil rights leader of his day. It was on this occasion that he delivered his passionate "I Have a Dream" oration, evoking the prospect of a day in the future when white children and black children would walk hand in hand "on the red hills of Georgia" and when black children as well as white would "one day live in a nation where they [would] not be judged by the color of their skin, but by the content of their character" (Fairclough 1987, 48). Millions of Americans, black and white, were deeply moved by King's "dream," and for a moment—fleeting as it might have been—the "dream" seemed a distinct possibility.

Recognition of King's sincerity, zeal, and leadership in the civil rights struggle came when he was named *Time* magazine's "Man of the Year" for 1963 and, later, when he was awarded the 1964 Nobel Peace Prize, perhaps his greatest triumph. In 1967, King announced his opposition to American policy in Southeast Asia, characterizing the Vietnam conflict as a "tragic adventure." Protesting that money spent for bombs should be spent instead to improve domestic conditions among the poor and oppressed, King declared that the United States was playing "havoc with the destiny of the entire world."

Shortly thereafter, he began to formulate plans for a Poor People's March on Washington to demonstrate in a dramatic manner the needs of the ignored masses of downtrodden Americans. But on 4 April 1968, while in Memphis, King was shot down by an assassin's bullet outside of his motel room. The fact that the confessed killer, James Earl Ray, was a white man caused a shock wave of terror and incredible racial violence throughout the United States. For many black and white friends, King's death symbolized the death of his dream. "The extent to which this dream became a nightmare," according to historian Edgar Toppin (1973), "is an index of the degree to which the racism King optimistically hoped to erase permeates America" (29).

Regrettably, King did not live long enough to pursue his effort to internationalize the civil rights movement and thereby affect American foreign policy, especially on the Vietnam war. His limited effort, however, apparently helped to change the minds of most Americans about American intrusion in Vietnam. In the end, history sided with King; the war was one that most Americans rejected. David Garrow, one of his major biographers, reminds readers of King's unyielding opposition to war and his unwavering commitment to economic and social justice (Garrow 1986, 35). More recently, the late civil rights leader and the historic March on Washington were commemorated with the unveiling of a new stamp by the U.S. Postal Service in Atlanta. The ceremony was part of an event at the Martin Luther

King, Jr., Center for Nonviolent Social Change, Inc., to recognize the thirty-sixth anniversary of Dr. King's historic "I Have a Dream" speech (*Jet* 1999, 4).

MALCOLM X AND THE NATION OF ISLAM

Born Malcolm Little on 19 May 1925, in Omaha, Nebraska (X 1970, vii), Malcolm X emerged as one of the most eloquent, fiery, and controversial leaders of the Black Muslim movement in the 1950s and 1960s. Saddled with a string of unfortunate childhood experiences, including the tragic death of his father and his mother's mental instability, the young Malcolm left school after the eighth grade, traveled to New York, and subsequently drifted into a life of crime. Following a number of petty offenses, Malcolm turned to pimping, drug trafficking, and, finally, burglary, for which he was sentenced to a 10-year prison term in 1946.

During his six years of incarceration (he was pardoned in 1952), Malcolm became acquainted with and subsequently devoted to the teachings and writings of Elijah Muhammad, the leader of the Nation of Islam, frequently referred to as the "Black Muslims." Following his release from prison, he became active in the Muslim movement, ultimately becoming Elijah Muhammad's confidant and right-hand man. As such, he vigorously defended the Muslim assumption that worldly evil was the direct result of the existence of the "devil" white race. "The greatest crime the white man ever committed," he was fond of saying, "was to teach black people to hate themselves." As a result of this belief, Malcolm X advocated a militant and uncompromising stand against white racism as well as an "eye for an eye" philosophy of vengeance, retaliation, and the defense of black people by any means necessary (X 1970).

His verbal attacks against the "white devils" often assumed extreme proportions. When John F. Kennedy was assassinated in 1963, for example, Malcolm characterized the tragedy as being a vivid illustration of "chickens coming home to roost." Elijah Muhammad, who had become increasingly resentful of Malcolm's growing personal popularity, used this statement as a pretext to suspend him from the Muslim movement.

Undaunted, Malcolm quickly formed his own black protest movement, the Organization of Afro-American Unity (OAAU). This organization was still in an embryonic stage of development when, in early 1965, Malcolm X was assassinated in New York City. Described by many as a "vendetta murder" perpetrated by his former Muslim associates (a trio of Muslims were subsequently convicted and sentenced to life imprisonment for the crime), Malcolm's premature death provided the black masses and a sizable number of young militant black leaders with a significant martyr image for years to come.

Shortly before his death, Malcolm X had concluded that not all whites were necessarily "devils." Asserting that the OAAU was not an anti-white organization, he maintained that "if the white man doesn't want us to be anti-him, let him stop oppressing and exploiting and degrading us" (Carson 1991; Breitman 1965, 185). This philosophy, coupled with his insistence that blacks should politically and economically control those areas where they constitute a majority of the population, would subsequently form an important aspect of the black power movement during the late 1960s.

As a people, the Nation of Islam provides an alternative institution from which blacks articulate their search for freedom and equal opportunity. One of its most articulate leaders was Malcolm X.

The Nation of Islam was founded in 1930 by W. Fard Muhammad as a breakaway faction of the Moorish Science Temple; after 1933, the faction was led by Elijah Muhammad. It slowly built up its strength among the lower black masses, especially prison inmates. The Muslim program, while espousing equal opportunity and equal justice, contrasts radically with the integrationist ideology that dominated the civil rights movement. Elijah Muhammad states clearly his desire for "complete separation in a state or territory of our own" and for prohibition of "intermarriage or race mixing." He moved to set up Muslim schools and established Muslim businesses such as dry cleaning shops, grocery stores, and restaurants as a first step toward developing black self-sufficiency. These actions in the economic sector carry on Marcus Garvey's ideas and foreshadow the black capitalist ideology of the late 1960s. *Muhammad Speaks*, the Muslim

weekly newspaper, published accounts of the activities and struggles of black people throughout the world in addition to those of the Muslims themselves (Essien-Udom 1962, 89).

In enunciating the Muslim program in 1960 at the Harlem Unity Rally, Malcolm X declared, among other things, his separatist philosophy:

We want some land where we can create unity, harmony, and brotherhood . . . and live together in peace. Since America now sees that this false show of integration and intermarriage will not work, she should take immediate steps to set aside a few of these states for us, and put us there to ourselves. (*Muhammad Speaks*, 8 Mar. 1960)

Clearly, Malcolm X symbolized the nationalist revival of the 1960s as the brilliant, articulate, and charismatic spokesman for the Nation of Islam and then as a revolutionary nationalist. Leading the short-lived OAAU, Malcolm X kept separatism before the American public as an alternative to racial integration and nonviolence.

In March 1964, Malcolm left the Nation of Islam because of differences with Elijah Muhammad and issued a Declaration of Independence. Shortly afterward, he formed the OAAU, apparently inspired by the Organization of African Unity and his pilgrimage to Mecca and Africa. Since his assassination in February 1965, Malcolm's status has grown, and his autobiography has a commanding place in the nationalist literature of the sixties.

It was not until another three decades that the Nation of Islam had a significant impact on American life. The occasion was the Million Man March on Monday, 16 October 1995, in Washington, D.C. The leader of the Nation of Islam then and of the Million Man March was Minister Louis Farrakhan.

The principal organizers of the march, Farrakhan and former NAACP president Benjamin Chavis, said that the march was a response to "an increasingly conservative and hostile climate growing up in America toward the aspirations of black people and people of color for justice" (Farrakhan 1996). They hoped to combat negative stereotypes and destructive federal legislation affecting blacks, especially black males, by mobilizing "one million disciplined, committed, and dedicated black men" for the march on Washington (*Million Man March* 1995). To the organizers, the march was a "Day of Atonement and Reconciliation," a call to power for black men, intended to celebrate their ability to stop black-on-black violence, spousal abuse, and illegal drug traffic (Sadler 1996, xi).

The impact of the march was felt throughout America, especially in the black community. Following the march, local groups organized black male marches in their local communities. Farrakhan had gained a national reputation and was admired by millions of young blacks. Commemorating the first anniversary of the march, on 16 October 1996, thousands of African Americans gathered in New York, this time for a rally billed as "World Day of Atonement." Again Farrakhan was the featured speaker. If this trend continues, the Million Man March will not have been in vain, and Malcolm X would have appreciated it, as did his widow.

KWAME TOURE: SNCC
OR BLACK POWER?

Kwame Toure was born as Stokely Carmichael in Port of Spain, Trinidad, in 1941. He came to the United States when he was 11 years old. His early experience in Harlem formed his viewpoints, which were further strengthened in the Bronx High School of Science. In 1964, Toure graduated from Howard University and joined SNCC. His first political act was to organize the Lourdes County Freedom Organization, an independent political group. He joined the James Meredith Freedom March in Mississippi and by shouting "black power" to the sharecroppers drove a wedge into the civil rights movement. He became the most dynamic black spokesman on record, delivering speeches for black aspirations around the world. He later moved to Guinea, Africa, where he changed his name to Kwame Toure. He died of cancer in 1999.

On 1 February 1960, four black students from the black Agricultural and Technical College in Greensboro, North Carolina, entered a downtown Woolworth store, made several purchases, and then sat down at the lunch counter and ordered coffee. As David Richmond recalled, they were refused service because they were black, but they continued to sit at the counter until the store closed. This was the beginning of the sit-in movement, which spread rapidly throughout the South and numerous places in the North (Zinn 1964, 16). In the spring and summer of 1960, young Americans, black and white, participated in similar peaceful forms of protest against segregation and discrimination. They sat in white libraries, swimming pools, churches, and restaurants, waded at white beaches, and slept in the lobbies of white hotels. Some of them were arrested for trespassing, disorderly conduct, and disobeying police officers. Notwithstanding the inevitable heckling, harassment, beatings, and arrests that ensued, the students patiently and nonviolently stood their ground.

The sit-in movement came as the stage was already set for the beginning of the most profound, revolutionary changes in the status of black Americans that had occurred since emancipation. These activities led to the formation of a national organization, the Student Nonviolent Coordinating Committee, on 15 April 1960. It was an interracial direct-action civil rights organization.

One of the leaders of SNCC and its articulate spokesperson was Kwame Toure, formally known by his American name of Stokely Carmichael. Following his election as chairman of SNCC in 1966, the organization became increasingly militant and dedicated to black liberation and black nationalism as opposed to mere integration. Toure himself resigned his office in 1967 to join forces with the emerging Black Panther Party. After the assassination of Martin Luther King, Jr., in 1968, H. Rap Brown, who succeeded Toure as head of SNCC, changed the name of the organization to the Student National Coordinating Committee. The name change, however, was merely a token gesture since SNCC had already lost much of its momentum and membership as the result of defections to the black power and Black Panther movements. The mysterious disappearance of Brown in 1970 limited the activities of SNCC.

The slogan "black power" was popularized by Toure. Beginning in the summer of 1966, when the "black power" slogan first gained national prominence, SNCC spokesperson Carmichael espoused his brand of racial solidarity and black revolution (Wright 1967). SNCC, reflecting a growing disillusionment with the inadequate progress of the civil rights movement in the South and the mounting rebelliousness of the ghettos, shifted its focus from civil rights protest and voter registration in the South to radicalizing youths in the ghettos and on college campuses. Typical of the new militancy of black students to which Toure addressed himself was the confrontation that took place at Northwestern University in Evanston, Illinois, in the spring of 1968. He noted,

Everybody in this country is for "Freedom Now" but not everybody is for Black Power because we have got to get rid of some of the people who have white power.... We have to move to control the economics and politics of our community. (Hamilton and Carmichael 1996, 102)

Toure's speech incited the black students at Northwestern University to take action: "If our demands are impossible, then peace between us is impossible" was the theme that led to policy changes that swept through American white universities in the late sixties and the seventies. The black students, joined by many white students, demanded changes such as the inclusion in university curricula of black history; the hiring of black faculty, including a visiting chair in black studies; and other changes in admissions policy, scholarships, financial aid, housing, and facilities.

As the leader of the youthful, radical wing of the civil rights movement, SNCC was a crucible for most of the social movements associated with the 1960s. Recent scholarship and American culture, however, have been far more focused on the charismatic leadership and mediagenic activities of Martin Luther King, Jr., and his SCLC. Nonetheless, in recent years, there has been a growing recognition of the necessity to document and analyze the SNCC experience and trace its many legacies. A number of scholars, most notably Clayborne Carson (1982) and Emily Stoper (1989), have begun this process.

Since SNCC's destiny was in a way a reenactment of the abolitionist movement, the first reconstruction, and numerous antebellum slave revolts, it should be noted that SNCC's history confirms once again the inexplicable way in which human beings (and their cultures) everywhere reenact their tragedies. Perhaps in the final analysis, the many human imperfections of SNCC and its elites simply authenticate the sincerity of the whole. At least Carson (1982) seems to suggest as much.

In this article, attempts have been made to document the thoughts, works, and leadership of five African American men in the civil rights movement: Du Bois, Randolph, King, Malcolm X, and Toure. Although these men had different backgrounds and leadership styles, they held a common vision for America. And although their organizations, strategies, and tactics were often different, they always kept their eyes on the prize—respect for human dignity. In so doing, their contributions to American quality of life in the twentieth century will remain an enduring legacy for the future.

References

Bennett, Lerone, Jr. 1968. *What Manner of Man: A Biography of Martin Luther King, Jr.* Chicago: Johnson.

Brazeal, Brailsford Recse. 1946. *The Brotherhood of Sleeping Car Porters.* New York: Harper & Brothers.

Breitman, George. 1965. *Malcolm X Speaks: Selected Speeches and Statements.* New York: Grove Weidenfeld.

Carson, Clayborne. 1982. *In Struggle: SNCC and the Black Awakening of the 1960s.* Cambridge, MA: Harvard University Press.

———. 1991. *Malcolm X: The FBI File.* New York: Carroll & Graf.

Carter, Lawrence. 1998. *Walking Integrity: Benjamin Elijah Mays, Mentor to Martin Luther King, Jr.* Macon, GA: Mercer University Press.

Chideya, Farai. 1999. *The Color of Our Future.* New York: William Morrow.

Du Bois, W.E.B. 1903. *The Souls of Black Folk.* New York: Bedford Books.

———. 1969. *The Suppression of the African Slave Trade to the United States, 1638-1870.* New York: Schocken Books.

Essien-Udom, Essien Udosen. 1962. *Black Nationalism: A Search for an*

Identity in America. Chicago: University of Chicago Press.

Fairclough, Adam. 1987. *To Redeem the Soul of America: The Southern Christian Leadership Conference and Martin Luther King, Jr.* Athens: University of Georgia Press.

Farrakhan, Louis. 1996. *Let Us Make Man: Select "Men Only" and "Women Only" Speeches.* Atlanta, GA: Uprising Communications.

Franklin, John. 1994. *From Slavery to Freedom*. New York: McGraw-Hill.

Garrow, David J. 1986. *Martin Luther King, Jr., and the Southern Christian Leadership Conference.* New York: William Morrow.

Hamilton, Charles and Stokely Carmichael. 1969. *Black Power: The Politics of Liberation in America*. Harmondsworth: Penguin.

Harris, William Hamilton. 1977. *Keeping the Faith: A. Philip Randolph, Milton P. Webster, and the Brotherhood of Sleeping Car Porters, 1925-37.* Urbana: University of Illinois Press.

Huggins, Nathan. 1986. *Du Bois Writings*. New York: Library Classics of the United States.

Hughes, Langston. 1962. *Fight for Freedom: The Story of the NAACP*. New York: Berkley.

Jet Magazine. 1999. 96(16).

King, Coretta Scott. 1993. *My Life with Martin Luther King, Jr.* New York: Henry Holt.

Lewis, David Levering. 1970. *King: A Critical Biography.* New York: Praeger.

Lincoln, C. Eric. 1984. *Martin Luther King, Jr.: A Profile*. New York: Hill & Wang.

Lomax, Louis. 1962. *The Negro Revolt*. New York: Harper.

Martin, Waldo. 1998. *Brown v. Board of Education*. New York: Bedford, St. Martin's.

Million Man March. 1995. 178 min. CNN. Videocassette.

Randolph, A. Philip. [1942] 1970. *A. Philip Randolph and the March on Washington: "Oppressed People Must Assume the Responsibility . . . to Free Themselves."* In *Black Nationalism in America*, ed. John Bracey, Jr., August Meier, and Elliott Rudwick. New York: Bobbs-Merrill.

Sadler, Kim Martin, ed. 1996. *Atonement: The Million Man March*. Cleveland: Pilgram Press.

Stoper, Emily. 1989. *The Student Nonviolent Coordinating Committee: The Growth of Radicalism in a Civil Rights Organization*. New York: Carlson.

Toppin, Edgar. 1973. *The Black American in United States History*. Boston: Allyn & Bacon.

White, John. 1985. *Black Leadership in America, 1895-1968*. New York: Longman.

Wright, Nathan, Jr. 1967. *Black Power and Urban Unrest*. New York: Hawthorn Books.

X, Malcolm. 1970. *By Any Means Necessary*. New York: Pathfinder.

Zinn, Howard. 1964. *SNCC, the New Abolitionists*. Boston: Beacon Press.

ANNALS, *AAPSS*, **569**, May 2000

A Reform for Troubled Times: Takeovers of Urban Schools

By ROBERT L. GREEN and BRADLEY R. CARL

ABSTRACT: Increasing pressure to improve low-performing schools—particularly those in central cities serving disadvantaged and minority students—has led to a host of reform efforts. This article focuses on a strategy that involves takeovers of troubled schools or entire systems by mayors, state legislatures, or control boards. Following the takeover of the Jersey City, New Jersey, schools in 1989, at least partial control of schools has been taken from elected boards in Chicago, Baltimore, Cleveland, Washington, D.C., and Detroit. Discussed in this article are some of the major issues involved with takeovers, including arguments for and against the practice, the policy questions it raises, and the all-important role race has played in the debate. The authors close with thoughts for evaluating the effectiveness of this increasingly popular, yet unproven, attempt at reforming low-achieving schools.

Robert L. Green is a professor in the David Walker Research Institute in the College of Human Medicine at Michigan State University. He is the author of several publications, including Racial Crisis in American Educations *(1969).*

Bradley R. Carl is a research analyst at the Pelavin Research Center of the American Institute for Research in Washington, D.C., and a doctoral candidate in sociology and urban studies at Michigan State University.

I N response to growing concern over the dismal performance of public school systems in major urban areas, a variety of reform-minded strategies have been proposed, debated, and enacted. One such reform initiative that has been proposed and used with increasing frequency in the 1990s has been the takeover of urban school districts. In a takeover, some or all of the powers held by elected local school boards are removed and transferred by a mayor, an appointed oversight board, or a state legislative body. Large urban school systems, including Chicago; Washington, D.C.; Cleveland, Ohio; and, most recently, Detroit, have been the most frequent targets for takeovers, the authority for which is granted by state legislatures. These school systems, as a rule, have had high concentrations of poor and non-white students, especially African American males, and often have a history of low academic performance, high drop-out rates, financial mismanagement, and other negative performance indicators (Green 1998; Reinhard 1998; Hornbeck and Harmon 1999; Reecer 1989; Guskey 1993; Suarez et al. 1991; Hendrie 1996a).

The politics, issues, and legalities surrounding the takeover of urban school systems have been immense from the start. In cities across the country, proposed or actual takeovers have divided neighborhoods, cities, and state governing bodies along lines of geography and race, and they have sparked intense debate and lawsuits over their legality and their potential to serve as the critically needed catalyst for comprehensive urban school reform. Thus far, no conclusive and defensible evidence has been presented that demonstrates either the success or failure of this reform initiative. Therefore, it is imperative that providing this evidence be a high priority for mayors, academics, and policymakers seeking to improve urban education. Takeovers clearly constitute a dramatic departure from urban school governance as we have known it, but differences of opinion as to their viability must eventually be backed by solid evidence. Takeovers must not cause us to lose sight of the end result that all parties seek, namely, the best possible educational opportunities for youths in our nation's great cities.

This article will outline some of the major components of the takeover issue. It will include a brief history and background of takeovers and an overview of the complex and controversial arguments surrounding them, including the all-important role of race in the takeover issue. The article will close with some thoughts on evaluating the takeover initiative to date.

Jersey City, New Jersey, was the first urban school district to be taken over by an outside authority when it was taken over by the state of New Jersey in 1989 (Hendrie 1996a; Dolan 1992; Tewel 1991; Reecer 1988). This was followed in 1994 by takeover of the troubled East St. Louis district by Illinois (Reinhard 1998; Ziebarth 1998). Since these pioneering ventures, some 21 districts have had control transferred from an elected board to a mayor, a state legislature, or an appointed oversight board, and the opportunity to undertake such action is now possible in 23 states (Reinhard 1998). In addition to the previously mentioned takeovers, there have been many instances in which districts have been threatened with the same fate, including Philadelphia (Hendrie 1998) and Milwaukee (Keller 1998).

Takeovers of urban school systems share at least one characteristic: a perceived need to install new leadership into educationally and financially troubled districts. They have differed significantly in other details, however, including when they occurred, who was tapped to lead the new governance structure, and what became of the former board. In several cases (for example, Jersey City, Paterson, and Newark, New Jersey; and East St. Louis, Illinois), control by local school boards was replaced by state government control. In others (most notably Washington, D.C.), an appointed oversight board was given control, with the elected board relegated to an advisory capacity.

A third and even more celebrated form of takeover has involved mayors. In Cleveland, the 70,000-student Cleveland Public Schools were first taken over by the state of Ohio in 1995, with control then given to Mayor Michael White a year later (Hendrie 1996b). In perhaps the most well-known takeover initiative, Mayor Richard M. Daley was given control of the 430,000-student Chicago Public Schools by the Illinois legislature in 1995. Long-time Daley budget aide Paul Vallas was then appointed chief executive officer of the system. In the most recent episode, Detroit mayor Dennis Archer

was given the authority to appoint six of the seven new board members for the 180,000-student Detroit Public Schools. Michigan governor John Engler named State Superintendent Arthur Ellis as the seventh member. The elected board has been relegated to an advisory role, and residents of Detroit are scheduled to vote after five years on whether this arrangement should continue (Keller 1999).

THE CASE FOR TAKEOVERS

Across the group of urban school systems that have been subject to takeovers by an outside authority, a fairly consistent set of issues and arguments emerges as the rationale for taking such action. At the most basic level, the rationale has been based on two circumstances: first, the prolonged dismal performance of urban districts in accordance with both academic indicators (such as standardized test performance, suspensions, expulsions, special educational placement, drop-out rates, graduation rates, and teacher absenteeism) and leadership and management issues (including financial mismanagement and bureaucratic waste); and second, the apparent inability and/or unwillingness of the existing school governance system to respond to this increasingly desperate situation. Simply put, sufficient support has built in many cities and state legislatures for the notion that the situation has become so grim that an unproven, but drastic change in course is necessary. The current system is seen as broken, and the existing governance structure shows little or no ability to take the needed steps to arrest its decline. Cleveland mayor Michael White expressed this sentiment when he declared, "We have a broken system [and] we have to have enough guts, I think, to try some new strategies even though we may not know whether or not they'll completely work" (in Hendrie 1996b, 1). Chicago mayor Richard Daley echoed this when he stated, "All over the country, public education is in crisis" and "we have to take dramatic steps to change it" (Council of the Great City Schools 1995, 2). Perhaps the simplest and most eloquent comment on the proposed takeover of Detroit's schools was made by a well-known black-owned weekly newspaper in Detroit. The newspaper declared, "We cannot go on this way" ("School Reformists" 1999, 4A).

Efficiency and accountability

When the pro-takeover argument is broken down into more detail, several key points are frequently made. One major component of this thinking centers on the notions of efficiency and accountability in budgeting and other aspects of the school decision-making process. Rather than having a 7-, 9-, or even 11-member board of education and its appointed superintendent, the notion of having one person or a control board of smaller size holds great appeal to takeover proponents. The logic here is that one person will be able to make decisions far more quickly than will a large board and that this person can then be held accountable for the success or failure of the decisions.

The politics of urban school governance

A second, closely related justification for urban school takeovers relates to the goal of depoliticizing urban school governance. The argument here, essentially, is that the process of electing multimember school boards (which then choose superintendents and then rehire or fire them) has become hopelessly politicized. The view is that increasingly smaller percentages of citizens are voting in school board elections, and special interest groups (such as teachers' unions) are able to wield considerable influence over the election and policymaking processes. In its recent editorial on the proposed takeover of the Detroit Public Schools, the *Michigan Chronicle* argued, "Educating our kids takes a backseat when the number one agenda of a politically elected board is staying in power, making a good impression at public meetings, controlling contracts, dispensing favors, and building a base to launch future political campaigns . . . as [an elected body]; it is driven and run by politics" ("Endorses Reform" 1999, 1A).

Denial of responsibility

A final piece of the pro-takeover argument relates to a perceived denial of responsibility for problems in minority-dominated, urban school systems. Those who advocate takeovers have frequently argued that major cities and their school systems have made excuses for too long while denying the existence and scope of the problems they face. Quoting again from the *Michigan Chronicle,* which endorsed the takeover of the Detroit Public Schools, "True reform happens only when the Detroit community rises up and takes responsibility for educating our children the way Black folks did years ago. Real healing can happen only when we admit there's a problem" ("School Reformists" 1999, 1A). This illustrates one of the most powerful planks of the pro-takeover platform: opposing a takeover is tantamount to endorsing a broken status quo and denying there is a problem that demands a serious (and perhaps radical) change of course.

THE CASE AGAINST TAKEOVERS

Just as a common set of arguments has tended to characterize the case that is made in favor of the takeover of troubled urban school systems, a competing justification against this practice has also developed. One of the major planks of the anti-takeover campaign involves the race-based notion that takeovers are little more than an attempt by white-dominated political bodies and leaders (who abandoned central cities and watched their decay with little concern) to deny minorities self-governance. Aside from issues involving race, however, other objections to the use of takeovers have arisen as well, several of which are discussed below.

*Identifying criteria
to justify takeovers*

An initial problem with the pro-takeover strategy concerns the criteria upon which these controversial

actions are taken. Generally, the primary justification has been a history of poor performance on standardized tests, but the use of this benchmark has at least two potential problems. The first is a lack of specificity about just how poor test scores must be, and for how long, to warrant talk of a takeover. It is generally true that urban districts score lower than state averages on most standardized tests, but how low is unsatisfactory, given the constraints and challenges under which urban schools operate—and what of a district that shows continued improvement, even if it remains below state averages?

A second objection concerns standardized testing itself, which has long been subject to charges of bias against some students, particularly those who are poor and nonwhite. There has been continued concern, furthermore, that tests have become a far too narrow and simplistic means of assessing school and student performance that ignores much more complex processes of learning and assessment (Ziebarth 1998; Tirozzi 1998; Olson 1998). Notwithstanding a general consensus that a need for evaluating the progress of students and schools exists, therefore, there is far from unanimous agreement that standardized tests are the most appropriate means for making such determinations.

*The conditions for
ending takeovers*

Closely related to the criteria for launching takeovers is the matter of how these initiatives should be ended. Under all of the takeover attempts to date, the expressed hope has been that these are temporary, emergency situations brought about by desperately low performance and that control should and will eventually return to a local level. In addition to the previously discussed problems of how to determine when a situation is sufficiently desperate to warrant a takeover, however, how does the state determine when to relinquish control—and how does it prevent the district from "backsliding" once local control is returned (Ziebarth 1998)? Finally, and perhaps most importantly, what should happen if a state takeover fails to produce the desired result—what then?

Doubts about depoliticizing school governance

An additional problem that takeover opponents have with this new and increasingly popular reform strategy is significant doubt over the claim that takeovers have depoliticized school governance. However true it may be that school board elections and the board's selection of a superintendent are highly political processes subject to significant influence by special interest groups, some observers of the takeover process have wondered whether it is any less political to put a mayor, a control board appointed by the mayor or governor, or a state legislature in charge. As Stanford University education professor Michael Kirst noted, "If the aldermen replace school boards, I'm not sure we come out ahead" (in Lewis 1998, 1). Rather than a true depoliticizing of school governance, most takeovers to date might more accurately be characterized as the replacement of one kind of politics with another, with unclear progress toward the true goal of improved performance of urban schools and their students. As Hunter (1997) observed, in order to accomplish objectives in major cities, it is important to gain the mayor's support. "The best way to gain this support is to do something for the mayor ... [to] help keep the mayor in office. When public education becomes part of this political process, educational policy decisions become commodities bought, sold, bartered, and bestowed like patronage positions and building permits" (219). School board members appointed by the mayor are likely to support the mayor's reelection or face nonappointment. How can this situation be less political than having locally elected school boards?

Are governance problems unique to education?

Similarly, it might well be wondered whether the alleged excessive politicization of urban school districts is unique enough to warrant their takeover by other governmental agencies. If it is true, for example, that low voter turnout leads to domination of school board races by special interests, should the governor or control board appoint the mayors of major cities as well if the same conditions exist in a mayoral race? At what point would the threshold for low voter turnout be established? School takeover proponents might argue here that the importance of school systems and their especially dismal performance makes them a different species from city government. But should cities be subject to takeovers, too, if they are thought (by outsiders) to be poorly run and failing in their most basic and important duties (such as providing safe streets and trash collection)? This becomes somewhat of a slippery-slope argument against school takeovers that perhaps extrapolates the situation a bit, but it is not without some precedent. The city of East St. Louis, for instance, was partly taken over by the state of Illinois in the late 1980s because of financial mismanagement and corruption. As takeovers of urban school systems become increasingly popular as a way to reform the schools, several larger questions are worth considering: How far does this authority extend—only to school systems or to entire cities? At whose discretion are the judgments made—a governor's, a state legislature's? What criteria are used to make these decisions—by whose judgment and along which indicators is a school system or perhaps a city deemed to be failing?

A daunting task for mayors?

A further objection to a common form of the takeover strategy arises from questions of whether mayors charged with reforming troubled urban school systems are up to the enormous task set before them. If it is assumed that a mayor is in a better position to make necessary changes than a multimember school board and superintendent, what of the day-to-day demands of the mayor's own job? As Washington, D.C., mayor Anthony Williams recently noted, "I am not lobbying to take over the schools because . . . I don't think I have any credibility because we have

got to run the government well first and foremost" (in ElBoghdady 1999). San Francisco mayor Willie L. Brown stated clearly at the National Association of Black School Educators conference in November of 1998 that he had no interest in taking over the San Francisco Unified School District, envisioning the mayor's role in urban communities as supporting the local superintendent. Mayors should concentrate on their own job of making cities good, efficient, and hospitable places in which to live, Brown maintained, and those qualities will greatly assist efforts to improve urban schools. Some would argue that having an efficient and hospitable city is impossible with a low-performing school system. The point here, however, is to draw attention to the enormous responsibility of just being a mayor, much less taking on the additional role of school superintendent. Clearly, the cities in which takeovers have been proposed or undertaken have significant problems—with crime, attracting business, poorly functioning city services, and a host of other issues—that occupy the attention of mayors and make it at least somewhat questionable as to whether they have the time and resources needed to tackle the monumental task of overhauling and running a large and troubled school system.

Delegating authority to others

Perhaps acknowledging that they are, indeed, too busy running their cities to take on troubled school systems, mayors such as Chicago's Richard Daley have delegated school oversight powers to leaders of their own choosing—but this strategy has also raised questions. In general, the trend has been to install as chief (or chief executive officer, as in the case of Chicago) an outsider who is either not from the city or someone with little or no experience as an educator or school administrator, or both. These appointees may know little about the culture and problems of school systems, and they may be unfamiliar with the dynamics between school administrators and teachers. Another variation of this strategy has been the use of retired armed forces personnel (in Washington, D.C., and Seattle, among other locations) as the head of an urban district (ElBoghdady 1999). Proponents of these moves insist that someone from outside the system who takes a no-nonsense and businesslike approach to school oversight and who has no accumulated local loyalties is precisely what is needed to "shake things up"—and there is probably a good deal of truth here. Critics have made the case, however, that it is naive to presume that running a school system, with thousands of often impoverished children, is the equivalent of running a business or an army battalion. They decry the lack of involvement by those most involved in and knowledgeable about schools and their problems—teachers and principals.

*Leadership change
    without social change?*

A final component of the doubt regarding the takeover phenomenon centers on the root causes of urban school decay and whether school governing bodies can effectively address them. It would be difficult to deny, on one hand, that some major urban districts have been hampered by inefficient spending practices, resistance to change, a lack of leadership, and other factors that a takeover may well be able to correct. Critics have long noted, however, that the true roots of the urban school crisis lie much deeper—in poverty, family dysfunction, urban abandonment, institutionalized racism, and the "curse of low expectations" (Green 1999). While a takeover may be appropriate for and successful in dealing with issues of petty corruption and incompetent administration, is it sound reasoning to presume that these are the most serious problems facing urban schools? It is surely a road to nowhere to claim that urban schools can do nothing to overcome social and economic woes, as we have seen precisely the contrary in places like East Harlem and from dynamic school reformers such as Marva Collins and James Comer. At the same time, however, critics have wondered what long-term effect a simple change in leadership—without accompanying social change—will have on urban school performance. What basis is there for believing that a mayor or any other politician or board has answers that have eluded educational professionals? If the answer to urban school woes is to place more power for hiring and firing teachers, setting budgets, and so on in the hands of one person, why not make the superintendent or the school board president this person?

THE ROLE OF RACE IN
URBAN SCHOOL TAKEOVERS

If little else is clear about the controversial practice of urban school takeovers by mayors and other political actors, the all-important role of race in this issue has been seen time and time again. Districts that have been targeted for takeovers generally have had majority, if not almost exclusively, nonwhite student populations, have been located in minority-dominated cities, and have been overseen by nonwhite superintendents and boards of education. A survey by *Education Week* of the 21 districts that had been taken over in some form by early 1998 showed that 18 had predominantly black enrollments, and most had student populations that were at least 80 percent minority. In addition, 6 of the 8 districts where takeovers had been proposed at the time of this survey had predominantly black enrollments, and 3 of these 6 were at least 93 percent nonwhite (Reinhard 1998, 2).

Racial mismatch

Racial considerations immediately arise when contrasting the makeup of the aforementioned urban school systems with many of the people proposing and sponsoring legislation seeking takeovers. Since much educational policy is made at the state level, the impetus for takeovers has often come from leaders (including governors and state legislators) who are almost exclusively white. At all phases of the history of takeovers—from early efforts in Jersey City and East St. Louis to more recent efforts in Chicago, Cleveland, and Detroit—white governors and white-dominated state legislatures have been the driving force behind these initiatives. While it is certainly true that takeover initiatives have been supported and sometimes welcomed by minority leaders and parents (a point discussed later in this article), these reform attempts have generally arisen at a legislative level from the work of white politicians who sometimes resisted providing educational funding for these same districts. What of the notion of local control, and is it fair for white suburban legislators whose constituents abandoned central cities to then blame minority-run cities for problems that may not be of their own making?

Historical considerations

The issue of race has been a staple in urban school takeovers not only due to the immediate and obvious racial mismatch between many of those pushing a takeover and the makeup of the districts being taken over but also because of larger, historical considerations. A long history of institutional racism—from the legally segregated schools that characterized public education until 1954 to the underfunded and de facto segregated schools of today—has clearly been a part of our educational history and strongly influences much of the debate over the takeover issue. This history of school segregation, North and South, was accompanied by limited funding to black students, poor facilities, and a belief (accompanied by low expectations) that black and Hispanic students could not learn. In addition to the admittedly grim situations in many urban districts, many observers see something else motivating takeover attempts: a continued belief in the inability of black and other minority school boards, superintendents, and principals to govern their own schools. As the Reverend Michael DeBose, a black former school board candidate in Cleveland who opposed the mayoral takeover of the Cleveland Public Schools in 1996, argued, "When you've got Black people in charge and a majority-Black district, people think they don't know what they're doing. . . . It's really insulting" (in Reinhard 1998, 1). This quote captures the sentiment of many black and other minority leaders, who see takeovers as an attempt by white citizens and legislators (who have abandoned central cities in droves and retreated to suburban white enclaves) to deny urban minorities the right of self-governance.

Questions about race and constitutionality

In addition to the larger history of institutional racism that is so deeply interwoven into the takeover issue, there have also been questions about race and the constitutionality of urban school takeovers. In several locations where takeovers have been attempted, lawsuits have been filed alleging that these initiatives violate the federal Voting Rights Act of 1965, which was intended to prohibit actions that inhibit the voting rights of racial and ethnic minorities (Reinhard 1998). Although a takeover has yet to be overturned on this basis, it does raise compelling questions not just about the Voting Rights Act but also about the notion of local control,

which has been a cornerstone of educational policy in this country. It is not surprising that attempts to circumvent this tradition, especially in urban areas where it was so long in coming to blacks and Hispanics, have aroused significant opposition.

Takeovers and the race card

Notwithstanding the often-compelling case made by those who have objected on racial grounds to takeovers of largely minority-populated and minority-run urban school systems by white legislative bodies, however, the issue of race in urban school takeovers is by no means simple or one-sided. Although many of the governors and state legislators who have pushed most aggressively for takeovers of urban and minority-dominated school systems are white, these initiatives have enjoyed support from minority leaders as well. Among the leaders who have sought to wrest control of urban schools from elected school boards are well-known, high-ranking black political figures, including Cleveland mayor Michael White, Maryland delegate Howard Rawlings (who helped write a 1997 law giving the state significant control over the Baltimore Public Schools), and Detroit mayor Dennis Archer. These leaders have broken ranks with and drawn the wrath of civil rights organizations such as the National Association for the Advancement of Colored People and traditional allies such as teachers' unions for their pro-takeover stances. Nevertheless, they have been willing to ruffle the feathers of takeover opponents due to their commitment to transforming the leadership and governance structure of the schools in their cities.

In the frequent instances in which the matter of race has entered the public debate over urban school takeovers, some takeover proponents have even sought to turn the tables by using the race card themselves. In responding to allegations that the takeover of the East St. Louis schools by the state of Illinois was racist, Richard J. Mark, the chair of the state-appointed panel that oversaw the district's financial operations, declared, "It's an easy alibi to make it a race issue. If we continue to let so many of our kids fail to learn to read and write, that's what would be racist" (in Reinhard 1998, 2). Michigan governor Engler made a similarly compelling point when he responded to a question about his motives for proposing state takeovers of minority-dominated districts by asking, "You tell me which is more racist: my proposing to do something about the situation in Detroit, or my sitting back and doing nothing?" (in Cantor 1998). These comments reflect a critical question that lies at the heart of the takeover issue, namely, which is more racist: white politicians' pushing a takeover of a minority-dominated district or their failure to seek such a takeover when the system in question is producing such continually dismal outcomes?

ASSESSING THE IMPACT OF
URBAN SCHOOL TAKEOVERS

Assessing the results of urban school takeovers is a complex, controversial, and as yet inconclusive

matter. It underscores the need for mayors, academicians, and policymakers to undertake clear and defensible evaluations of this increasingly popular educational reform initiative.

Have schools improved?
Conflicting evidence
and opinions

By the most important and undoubtedly the most scrutinized criterion—that of student performance as measured by indicators such as standardized tests—the verdict on urban school takeovers is somewhat mixed. On one hand, there is at least some evidence that improvement in student performance has resulted: some 8 percent more students in Chicago, for example, tested above national norms in both reading and math three years into the takeover of that district by Mayor Richard Daley (McWhirter and Kennedy 1999). In Baltimore, where the state of Maryland assumed much of the power in running the city's schools, similar (if modest) gains in performance were made (ElBoghdady 1999).

On the other hand, takeover initiatives other than in Chicago and perhaps Baltimore produced inconclusive results or have shown no improvement. As Daniel Cassidy, the former educational policy aide to the mayor of Jersey City, New Jersey, stated, "There was no change in test scores, dropout rates, or violence. . . . All it did was replace one local bureaucracy with a larger, more remote bureaucracy in the state capital. There was no attempt at systemic change" (in Cantor 1998, 2). It may also be the case that the threat of takeovers is failing to have the intended effect of stimulating urban school improvement. In Maryland, for example, none of the schools placed on a warning list for possible takeover has shown measurable improvement, and the state has yet to make good on its threat to take them over (Argetsinger 1999).

Tempering the apparently positive results shown in places such as Chicago are at least two additional considerations. First, even districts that showed improvement remain far below state and national averages on these indicators, dashing any hopes that there would be quick and measurable changes in student achievement and overall institutional effectiveness. Second, it is not clear that gains in performance can be attributed directly to takeovers themselves. Some analysts have argued that improvements may be due at least as much to increases in funding, teachers' teaching to standardized tests, or other factors as they are to takeovers. Establishing cause and effect when looking at complex variables such as student performance remains exceedingly difficult, and as yet it has not been conclusively shown that the takeover of urban school systems has resulted in improved performance.

With respect to other criteria, there is at least some early evidence that takeover initiatives may be stimulating positive developments in nonacademic areas of school performance and operations. In Chicago, for example, one evaluation (Council of the Great City Schools 1996) gave chief executive officer Vallas high marks for balancing the district's budget and eliminating wasteful practices and spending. Chicago schools also took significant steps toward making themselves smaller and more responsive to parents. They undertook significant renovation of school buildings, cut truancy rates, and tightened security (McWhirter and Kennedy 1999). Even Harvard education professor Gary Orfield, a noted skeptic on the issue of takeovers, has conceded that outside intervention has had at least some positive effects in rooting out corruption and mismanagement, obviously critical steps in the reform process (Hornbeck and Harmon 1999).

In the absence of conclusive and large-scale longitudinal data on the effects of urban school takeovers, it may be that an evaluation of these initiatives for urban school reform should include far less tangible yet critically important qualities, namely, hope and optimism. For years, there has been precious little of either in urban school systems. Despite the fact that takeovers have stirred up a great deal of controversy, they may be cultivating reason for hope and optimism that was sorely lacking. Stanford University professor Kirst notes that "even the harshest critics [of the takeover in Chicago] believe the move established hope" (in Lewis 1998, 1). Ultimately, however, the verdict on the success or failure of takeovers will need to be based upon a foundation of comprehensive evaluation and evidence, which sets forth a clear challenge and mandate to mayors, politicians, and researchers pursuing urban school reform. To be precise, mayors must collect baseline data when they take over school systems, and they must implement an evaluation four or five years after the takeover to determine if their school systems have improved.

Indicators of change after school takeovers include standardized test scores, attendance rates, drop-out and graduation rates, placement rates in special education, classroom discipline, SAT and ACT scores, high expectations for student performance, physical health and accountability, student retention rates, class size, teacher attributes, commitment to improved customer service, and parent involvement.

CONCLUSION

Negative outcomes associated with school systems in our nation's major cities have led to a number of different reform strategies. Among the most controversial and increasingly popular strategies has been takeovers. In some two dozen locations around the country, most of which are in major urban areas, the control over school districts has been involuntarily transferred from elected local school boards to mayors, state legislatures, or appointed control boards, and the threat of this same fate has been held over the heads of many school boards. Issues of race have become deeply intertwined with many of the arguments made both for and against takeovers, producing widespread debate and disagreement. To date, comprehensive and defensible data on the success of takeover initiatives have proven elusive, and filling this gap in

the knowledge base is a priority of the highest order for mayors and others seeking to revitalize their cities through the all-important goal of having successful school systems.

As noted, mayors who assume the responsibility of running school systems must also be responsible for measuring whether these systems improve. Objective, outside research teams should be used to evaluate improvement, measuring criteria against the baseline data collected when the mayors took over the school systems. Political rhetoric will not suffice five years after the takeover. If sensible and measurable data are not collected, the debate around this aspect of school reform becomes meaningless.

Finally, great care should be taken in discussing the role of race in urban school takeovers. The long history of institutional racism in public education makes the race card tempting for both advocates and opponents of takeovers to play, but this must not obscure the true goal of improved educational opportunities for youths in troubled urban schools. Institutional racism is present, but we cannot conclude that it is the only force that has an impact on school achievement.

References

Argetsinger, Amy. 1999. Despite Takeover Threat, Little Gain at MD Schools. *Washington Post*, 24 Jan.

Cantor, George. 1998. Chicago Takes Over School Debate. *Detroit News*, 8 Feb. Available at http://www.detnews.com/1998/outlook/9802/11/020800009.

Council of the Great City Schools. 1995. Mayor Takes over Chicago Schools. *Urban Educator*. Available at http://www.cgcs.org/newslett/educator/1995/aug/a2.

———. 1996. Chicago Schools Report Progress Since Mayor's Takeover. *Urban Educator*. Available at http://www.cgcs.org/newslett/educator/1996/apr/a4.htm.

Dolan, Margaret. 1992. *State Takeover of a Local District in New Jersey: A Case Study*. New Brunswick, NJ: Consortium for Policy Research in Education; Denver, CO: Education Commission of the States.

ElBoghdady, Dina. 1999. D.C. School Chief's Vision, Bold Moves Pay Off. *Detroit News*, 21 Mar. Available at http://www.detnews.com/1999/specials/schools/washington/washington.htm.

Endorses Reform. 1999. *Michigan Chronicle*, 16-23 March, 1A.

Green, Robert L. 1998. *Ownership, Responsibility and Accountability for Student Achievement*. Dillon, CO: Alpine Guild.

———. 1999. Expectations: Research Implications on a Major Dimension of Effective School—Implications for Increasing Student Achievement and Making High Expectations Work: What Effective Teachers Do; What the Research Says. Paper presented at the San Francisco Unified School District Staff Development Workshop.

Guskey, Thomas R. 1993. Policy Issues and Options When States Take Over Local School Districts. *International Journal of Educational Reform* 2(1):68-71.

Hendrie, Caroline. 1996a. Ill Will Comes with Territory in Takeovers. *Education Week on the Web*. Available at http://www.edweek.org.

———. 1996b. Plan Gives Mayor Control over Cleveland Schools. *Education Week on the Web*. Available at http://www.edweek.org.

———. 1998. PA Lawmakers Pass a Takeover Bill for Phila. *Education Week on the Web*. Available at http://www.edweek.org.

Hornbeck, Mark and Brian Harmon. 1999. Reform Can Work in Big City Schools. *Detroit News*, 22 Mar. Available at http://www.detnews.com/1999/specials/schools/lead/lead.htm.

Hunter, Richard C. 1997. The Mayor Versus the School Superintendent: Political Incursions into Metropolitan School Politics. *Education and Urban Society* 29(2):217-32.

Keller, Bess. 1998. Wis. Lawmakers Reject Milwaukee Takeover Plan. *Education Week on the Web*. Available at http://www.edweek.org.

———. 1999. Mich. Lawmakers Approve Takeover Bill for Detroit. *Education Week on the Web*. Available at http://www.edweek.org.

Lewis, Anne C. 1998. District Takeovers Strand School Boards. *America Tomorrow*. Available at http://www.kidware.com/ati-acl80328c.htm.

McWhirter, Cameron and Sheryl Kennedy. 1999. Windy City Shines as School Reform Success. *Detroit News*, 21 Mar. Available at http://www.detnews.com/1999/specials/schools/chicago/chicago.htm.

Olson, Lynn. 1998. Study Warns Against Reliance on Testing Data. *Education Week on the Web*. Available at http://www.edweek.org/ew/1998/28chic.h17.

Reecer, Marcia. 1988. Yes, Boards Are Under Fire, but Reports of Your Death Are Greatly Exaggerated. *American School Board Journal* 176(3):31-34.

———. 1989. Jersey City Stands Firm Against Charges of "Academic Bankruptcy." *American School Board Journal* 175(11):21-23.

Reinhard, Beth. 1998. Racial Issues Cloud State Takeovers. *Education*

Week on the Web. Available at http://www.edweek.org.

School Reformists Must Be Ready to Go the Distance. 1999. *Michigan Chronicle*, 24-30 Mar., A4.

Suarez, Tanya M. et al. 1991. *The Use of Sanctions with Low-Performing School Districts*. ERIC no. ED373411. Chapel Hill, NC: North Carolina Educational Policy Research Center.

Tewel, Kenneth J. 1991. Do State Takeovers Hasten Reform—or Impede Progress? *Executive Educator* 13(3):14-17.

Tirozzi, Gerald N. 1998. It's About Teaching and Learning—Not Testing. *Education Week on the Web*. Available at http://www.edweek.org/ew/1998/43tirozz.h17.

Ziebarth, Todd. 1998. *State Takeovers and Reconstitutions*. Policy Brief: Accountability. Denver, CO: Educational Commission of the States.

African American Males in Dance, Music, Theater, and Film

By I. PETER UKPOKODU

ABSTRACT: The history of African American males in the entertainment industry begins with the African background and extends through the transatlantic slave trade and to the various aspects of the black presence in the Americas. African American males have contributed enormously to the American cultural wealth in dance, music, theater, and film. Minstrelsy, the cakewalk, the Charleston, the lindy hop, the twist, the break dance, rap, jazz, blues, spirituals, soul—these and many others have enriched the American cultural experience at various stages of American history. African American male performers, directors, producers, musicians, playwrights, dancers, choreographers, and filmmakers, working individually or as a group, have made an indelible mark both on the American stage and in the American collective memory. These entertainers, especially those who began their profession at a time of social inequality, prejudice, and the ever present threat of physical violence, laid the foundation for African Americans of a later age to realize their potential and be called stars of Hollywood and Broadway. Their accomplishments have made it possible to look positively toward the future.

Peter Ukpokodu is chairperson of the Department of African and African American Studies and courtesy faculty of theater and film at the University of Kansas. He is past president of the Mid-America Alliance for African Studies. The author of Socio-Political Theatre in Nigeria, *his numerous articles have appeared in* TDR, Theatre Research International, Theatre Annual, Harvard Journal of African American Public Policy, African American Encyclopedia, *and* Literary Griot, *among others. He is a Phi Beta Delta scholar, a playwright, and an award-winning poet.*

THE story of African American males in the entertainment industry is one of the fabled stone rejected by the builders but which eventually turns out to be one of the cornerstones of the house. From the initial total denial to limited access, from their secluded Southern plantation cradle to universal exposure in star-studded Hollywood and Broadway, from the state of forced obscurity to overt, public recognition by awards of Oscars, Tonys, Emmys, and Grammys, African American males have contributed immensely to develop, sustain, and enhance the American entertainment enterprise in the areas of dance, theater, film, and music. As a child of two worlds—Africa and America—the African American male has been influenced by the vitality of the American and African cultures and experiences in creating a unique entertainment history.

DANCE

The beginnings of African American dance are as rough and old as the practice in human merchandise that brought most African American ancestors to the United States. In their long sea voyage to the Americas, African slaves were forced to dance to improvised songs and music as a form of health therapy—possibly one of the precursors of contemporary dancercise or aerobics. On arrival in the United States, the African slaves entertained their masters with dances on the plantations and in the cities. Especially on Sundays, when they were off work, the slaves entertained themselves by dancing, and during the long summer evenings, it was the common practice of slave owners to order their slaves to dance to amuse them. African slave dancers who displayed a more creative spirit than others were sent by their masters to visit other plantations to perform before the owners either as a friendly gesture from their masters to the hosts or simply as a form of a money-making enterprise in an arrangement between the various wealthy plantation slave owners. During the Christmas holidays, slaves were allowed to perform the "Christmas dance"—a lot of fiddling, drumming, and dancing—on the plantations to entertain themselves and their masters. The custom of slave Christmases continued for a long time even after the emancipation; Booker T. Washington witnessed such a performance in Alabama in 1881. These dances were derived from the different aspects of the original dance traditions that existed in the African continent—social, religious, celebratory, ritualistic, funerary, and nuptial—as the African slave, plucked from the original African source of these performances, best remembered them, and as best as he could perform them with the instruments he brought and could improvise in a world that was at that time alien and hostile to him.

Minstrelsy

In African history, minstrels referred to as "griots" have always played key roles as custodians of oral traditions, as counselors to royalty, as genealogists, and as performers. However, the minstrel tradition on which the African American male would have his first significant entertainment impact was unrelated to the dignified griot tradition. Blackface minstrelsy, as it came to be known, was conceived from the Jim Crow dance, which was performed by a deformed, old African American called Jim Crow. A white American stage performer, Thomas D. Rice, was so fascinated by the financial and artistic possibilities of the Jim Crow dance he saw that he developed a comic dance routine that imitated the dance, song, performance style, mannerisms, and physical disability of Jim Crow. So interested was Rice in replicating the dance exactly that he painted his white face black (hence the term "blackface"), costumed himself in Crow's poor clothes, and added "Jim Crow" to his stage name. The chorus of the slightly modified version of "Jump Jim Crow" is now in the annals of dance history:

Wheel about, turn about,
Do jus' so.
An' ebery time I turn about,
I jump Jim Crow. (Emery 1988, 181)

The name "Jim Crow," while receiving thunderous applause theatrically, would later describe the ugliness of racial segregation and discrimination in American life and history.

The first famous African American male to perform in blackface minstrels was "Master Juba" (William Henry Lane). Regarded as the greatest dancer in the world by his contemporaries, Lane created a healthy and appreciative rapport with Irish and African American audiences and dancers. This Irish connection would later manifest itself in cross-cultural dance assimilations by which the Irish jig and clog dancing became part of the African American dance routine that saw the birth of tap dancing.

African American males such as Sam Lucas, Billy Kersands, and James Bland formed and managed their own minstrel companies after the Civil War. The cakewalk dance was soon introduced as a routine in African American minstrel performances. The cakewalk, as did the Charleston, the lindy hop, the jitterbug, the twist, and the break and rap dances much later, took the country by storm. The cakewalk made dancing in African American minstrelsy more diversified than in white minstrelsy.

Vaudeville

African American minstrelsy was mostly absorbed into vaudeville toward the end of the nineteenth century, when early African American musicals were also developing. Both developments luxuriated in dancing and singing. *A Trip to Coontown* and *Clorindy: The Origin of the Cakewalk* exemplified the emphasis on music and dance of the new period. *In Dahomey*, *In Abyssinia*, and *Bandanna Land* all had successful, spectacular dancing by the team of Williams and Walker. Williams and Walker made the cakewalk dance fashionable, opening up cakewalk contests to big names and making it an international favorite. Due to their flawless dances and music, they, with Will Marion Cook, Bob

Cole, and Billy Johnson, pioneered the opening of Broadway to African American performers. In the dazzling constellation of American vaudeville, African American performers like Eddie Rector, Bill "Bojangles" Robinson, John Bubbles (and his team of Buck and Bubbles), Bill Bailey, and "Slow Kid" Thompson were among the brightest. Their tap dancing left an indelible mark on the history of American vaudeville.

Modern dance

Hemsley Winfield is one of the significant African American male pioneers of modern dance. His New Negro Art Theatre Dance Group aimed at creating dances that were socially significant enough to express the "New Negro" philosophy that had been propounded by the Harlem Renaissance. But the single show that captured the excitement of this period was *Shuffle Along*, with music and lyrics provided by Noble Sissle and Eubie Blake. The show set a Broadway standard and launched the careers of two singer-dancers, Florence Mills and Josephine Baker. Both were to mesmerize the world and be idolized in the capitals of contemporary Western civilization.

The Charleston became the dance mania of the 1920s and the harbinger of the Jazz Age. The Savoy Ballroom and the Cotton Club of Harlem promoted jitterbug and the lindy hop. Individual performances that were the forerunner of disco dance fever were also initiated there. Leon James, Pepsi Bethel, and Al Minns refined the air steps of ballroom

dancing at the Savoy. One of the greatest African American choreographers of this era was Buddy Bradley, who coached performers of different ethnicities such as Lucille Ball, Mae West, and Alicia Markova. He drew international respect by choreographing stage shows in England, Italy, France, and Spain. Asadata Dafora (John Warner Dafora Horton) of the Shologa Oloba (later rechristened the African Dance Troupe) emerged in 1934 with *Kykunkor*, an African dance-drama that mesmerized audiences.

Contemporary dance

The post–civil rights era witnessed the participation of African American males in pan-African cultural events. One of these was the Second World Black and African Festival of Arts and Culture (FESTAC '77) in Lagos, Nigeria, in 1977. By the 1980s, African Americans could boast of many prominent choreographers and dancers. Talley Beatty choreographed major ballet works such as *The Blacks* (1961), *Fly, Blackbird* (1962), and *House of Flowers* (1968) and many other dramatic and musical works for Broadway and off-Broadway. Donald McKayle choreographed *The Tempest* (1962), *As You Like It* (1963), and *Sophisticated Ladies* (1981). Gus Solomons, Jr., a former dean of the Dance School at the California Institute of the Arts, emerged as a dancer, choreographer, and dance critic. Arthur Mitchell and Karel Shook, his white ballet teacher, founded the Dance Theatre of Harlem in 1969. Mitchell's most spectacular productions are the *Firebird* and *Gisselle*, but the Dance Theatre of Harlem has a repertoire that ranges from the ballet russe to modernist pieces, dance drama, and contemporary fusion.

But it is Alvin Ailey, the dancer, choreographer, and entrepreneur extraordinaire, who became the epitome of African American quality in contemporary dance. Founder of the Alvin Ailey American Dance Center, Ailey produced and choreographed shows too numerous to list here. His company has attracted students from various ethnic groups and has drawn national and international recognition. Before his death in 1991, Ailey's influence had been felt in most American dance companies, especially the Dayton Contemporary Dance Company, which celebrated its twentieth anniversary in the 1988-89 season, the Philadelphia Dance Company (Philadanco), the Cleo Parker Robinson Dance Ensemble, the Nanette Bearden Contemporary Dance Theater, and the DanceMobile.

Two major developments have occurred in the contemporary scene. The first is the networking and cooperation between African American dance companies that were initiated by Philadanco. The other is the decision by the American Dance Festival to make the contributions of African Americans to dance known to the public.

African American dances have become a significant ingredient in contemporary American dances with such groups as the Garth Fagan's Bucket Dance Company and the Bill T. Jones/Arnie Zane Company. New dance forms that keep emerging—break dance, moonwalk, and rap dance—ensure the continuing contributions of African American males to the American dance medium.

MUSIC

Musical legacy is perhaps the most significant African American contribution to the development of American culture and of the entertainment industry. Starting off from its African cultural roots, each period of the black experience in the Americas, whether one of joy or sorrow, has manifested itself richly in music. African Americans inherited a musical rhythm from Africa and have passed it on in different forms and techniques to the American musical tradition.

Spirituals

Spirituals emerged as the earliest major musical contribution of African Americans. As an expression of Christian religious sentiments during slavery, this unique musical phenomenon, which was often accompanied by a ring shout (a ceremonial, ecstatic collective dance), reshaped "bits of pre-existing songs into new ones" (Stewart 1998, 22). A spiritual always used Ebonics (African American English) as spoken in the Southern United States. Spirituals gave to America such classics as "Nobody Knows the Trouble I See," "Swing Low, Sweet Chariot," and "Go Tell It on the Mountain." Two forms of spirituals, the map and the alert, were specially created to help slaves achieve freedom. Map spirituals such as "Follow the Drinking Gourd" (figurative language for the Big Dipper constellation) and "Sheep, Sheep, Don't You Know the Road?" gave directions to escaped slaves. Alert spirituals such as "I'm Packin' Up" and "Good News, the Chariots Comin'," alerted slaves to secret meetings and escape possibilities. The Fisk Jubilee Singers, under George L. White, toured the United States and helped to popularize spirituals in 1871.

Blues

Ragtime (rag piano music or "jig piano")—that style of music in which the right hand played syncopated melodies on the keyboard while the left hand stomped and patted repeatedly on the bass—was the first African American musical tradition to appeal to international audiences, especially after it was popularized by Scott Joplin. It was the blues, however, that became a more meaningful musical invention by which African American males conveyed their misery and rootlessness. By singing about his misery, sorrow, and the vicissitudes of life, the blues singer achieved an emotional purgation that made life bearable again to both the singer and the listener. The first blues composition was published by William Christopher Handy in 1912. His publication of *St. Louis Blues* made blues an international commodity. Over the years, three styles of the blues have emerged: country; city, or classic; and contemporary, or urban, blues. B. B. King is easily one of the best-known contemporary blues musicians.

Jazz

Ragtime, in conjunction with blues, brass-band music, syncopated dance music, and a repertory of slave songs, "seeded the first manifestation of America's most important twentieth-century development: jazz" (Stewart 1998, 103). New Orleans, Louisiana, is usually associated with the birth of jazz, and, as it happens, the most prominent figure of the classic jazz era, Louis Armstrong, grew up there. Other cities such as New York, Chicago, and Kansas City became jazz centers also.

Jazz has remained very creative, reinventing itself over time in different styles, including swing, bebop, cool jazz, West Coast jazz, third stream, hard bop, free jazz, and jazz rock (or fusion), to become the quintessential, most recognizable American cultural and musical trademark in the world. The prominence and vitality of jazz have been sustained by a galaxy of African American musical talents: Duke Ellington, Lionel Hampton, William "Count" Basie, Cabell "Cab" Calloway, Dizzy Gillespie, Charlie Parker, Miles Davis, Douglas Ewart, Alvin Batiste, and Donald Brown. Dance theater has also been built around jazz music. An example of dance theater is Donald Byrd's *JazzTrain*, which is touring Kansas and Missouri in 1999-2000.

Popular music

African American males have over the years developed various styles of music that have had popular appeal. These styles range from rhythm and blues (R&B) to soul music, pop solos, and rap.

In its earliest appearance, rhythm and blues (rhythm 'n' blues)—popular music by African Americans targeted at the African American market—had its roots in the boogie-woogie blues, gospel, and swing. As a musical genre, it featured an ensemble comprising a rhythm unit, a vocal unit, and a supplementary unit. R&B lyrics have been described as "earthy and realistic," with the singers typically writing "their own songs, both music and lyrics" (Southern 1997, 514). Street language and lifestyles of urban blacks form the thematic background of R&B lyrics. R&B has boasted such luminaries as Louis Jordan, often referred to as the father of rhythm and blues; Ray Charles; Stevie Wonder (Steveland Judkins Morris); William "Smokey" Robinson; and groups such as the Crows, the Temptations, the Flamingos, the Orioles, the Ravens, the Cadillacs, the Four Tops, and the Imperials. A dominant form of R&B was the doo-wop, which used grittier, more ghetto-sounding material in both rhythm and vocals. The dominant theme of R&B is human relationships, especially love. R&B has also been referred to as "Motown sound."

Soul music emerged as a new, expanded form of R&B. Combining some of the characteristics of R&B, doo-wop, and gospel, soul thematically focused on political and social issues: human injustice, black militancy, racial pride, and social protests. Its music was as harsh, intense, and explosive as the social issues it sang about. Its form corresponded with its content; fittingly, soul music was prominent in the 1960s and early 1970s. Solo male artists of that period such as Ray Charles, James Brown, and Marvin Gaye made unique contributions to the American musical scene by making music serve, to a degree not experienced before, as a "vehicle for the expression of the political and social turbulence that characterized black America" of that period. The songs were "outspoken and unapologetic" (Stewart 1998, 222). James Brown's "Say It loud, I'm Black and Proud" so captured the imagination of young African Americans of that era that the song became their rallying cry.

Solo African American musicians who do not readily fit into categories other than the general one of pop but whose individual contributions to the music scene have been stellar include Jimi Hendrix, Prince (Rogers Nelson), and Michael Jackson. Like Chubby Checker (Ernest Evans), who immortalized himself in the musical consciousness of the world with "The Twist," Jimi Hendrix made an impact as a virtuoso guitarist and songwriter. His powerful avant-garde rendering of the American national anthem at Woodstock confirmed him as a superstar. "His influence on . . . vernacular guitarists, particularly rock guitarists, to this day remains enormous" (Stewart 1998, 248). Hendrix's unprecedented stage antics may have influenced Prince (The Artist Formerly Known as Prince), a consummate musical experimentalist and astute businessman who dumbfounded the world by adopting an unpronounceable glyph as his name.

He plays all his recording instruments except the horn.

Described as "the greatest entertainer of all time" (Southern 1997, 597), Michael Jackson has had command performances for the U.S. president and Queen Elizabeth of England, received numerous awards, developed the moon walk dance step, and stayed on top of the musical charts for lengthy periods. His humanitarian spirit is marked by his coauthoring with Lionel Richie the song "We Are the World," whose joint rendition by numerous musicians raised millions of dollars to combat the Ethiopian famine. He brought dance innovations to music video with his video *Thriller* in the 1980s and with *Dangerous* in the 1990s. He is an astute business magnate and always a crowd puller.

Rap has been described as the musical manifestation of the hip-hop culture, just as break dance expresses hip-hop dance and graffiti expresses hip-hop visual arts (Stewart 1998, 252; Roach 1992, 204). Rap is an unconventional musical style that combines spoken poetry or spoken narrative with song (or chants) and a disc-jockey's synthesizer technology. Its origin is generally credited to Afrika Bambaataa, a former gang member, who felt that youths could challenge themselves to nonviolent rap battles instead of violent knife ones. The service that rap has done for the nation is not only the discovery of a financially profitable and spiritually uplifting way of life for African American youths, but the pointing out to the world the brutally harsh reality of the inner-city slums

in America where African Americans seem condemned to live. Among the most successful rap musicians are M. C. Hammer, Run-D.M.C., Public Enemy, Ice-T, Ice Cube, Fresh Prince, L L Cool J (Ladies Love Cool James), Dr. Dre, Snoop Doggy Dogg, Big Daddy Kane, Kool Moe Dee, Puff Daddy, and Coolio.

THEATER

The opening in New York City of the African Grove, a tea-garden theater belonging to Mr. Brown, with a performance in 1821 by the African Company, led by James Hewlett, was a giant step in the African American male theatrical presence in the United States. *King Shotaway* was the first African American play to be produced at the African Grove. Shakespearean plays were also produced there. Ira Aldridge, regarded as the first truly great African American actor, performed at the African Grove before he went to Europe, where he was acclaimed as one of the world's greatest Shakespearean tragedians and was awarded royal honors. But the African Grove was short-lived; racial intolerance by white audiences caused it to shut its doors permanently by 1830.

Early dramatists

Although for over 50 years, following the closure of the African Grove, African American actors did not have any access to theaters where they could perform regularly, African American playwriting did not wait that long to emerge, thanks in part to

William Wells Brown. Brown was an antislavery activist who wrote plays about slavery. Because his plays could not be produced for lack of an African American theater building, they were read at public gatherings. His play *The Escape, or A Leap to Freedom* (1858) is the first published play in America by an African American author. But the situation was different in Europe. There, an African American playwright and actor, Victor Sejour, who had emigrated from New Orleans to Paris, produced his first play, *Diegarias* (1844), at the Theatre Français. Sejour was a prolific playwright; about 21 of his plays were produced by French theaters. In 1903, Joseph S. Cotter, Sr., published his play *Caleb, the Degenerate*. It was not until 1916, when Angelina Grimké wrote *Rachel* for the Drama Committee of the National Association for the Advancement of Colored People (NAACP) that a play written by an African American was produced by African Americans with African American performers. The performance was produced at the Neighborhood Theatre in New York.

Early theater companies

In 1906 in Chicago, some African American actors whose interest in vaudeville and musicals had waned formed the Pekin Players. Their group obtained the support of the management of the Pekin Theater to present serious drama. Their success attracted other African American actors.

In 1912, Lester Walton, an African American theater critic, formed the Lafayette Theater Stock Players in Harlem. Talented African American actors such as Charles Gilpin and E. S. Wright performed with that company. Walton's idea was aimed at making the African American presence in Harlem felt. Many popular plays were successfully produced by the company. The changing taste of the audience from serious drama to musicals, however, brought the end of the Layfayette Theater Stock company as serious dramatists made their exit. It would reappear as the New Lafayette Theater in 1967, with Ed Bullins as playwright-in-residence and Robert Macbeth as director. The Lafayette Theater Stock company influenced the formation of the Lincoln Theatre Troupe at the Lincoln Theatre in New York, where in 1915 Scott Joplin presented a folk opera about real African American life, *Treemonisha*. The production failed because the Harlem audience was not yet ready to look critically at their painful recent past. The Lincoln Theatre quickly went back to presenting vaudeville and musical comedies.

In an effort to integrate the theater, two white social workers, Russell and Rowena Jelliffe, founded the Karamu Theatre in Cleveland, Ohio, in 1916. The Karamu Theatre made a profound impact on the development of African American artistic talents.

The date of 5 April 1917 is a remarkable one in the development of serious drama in African American theater history. That day, for the first time, Broadway witnessed the presentation of white playwright Ridgeley Torrence's three one-act plays "written for the Negro theatre"—*The Rider of Dreams, Granny Maumee*, and *Simon the Cyrenian*—at the Madison Square Garden Theatre. They were performed by the all-African-American Hapgood Players. The high critical acclaim the production won was the beginning of American interest in African American life as artistically interpreted by African Americans themselves. Other white theater practitioners like Eugene O'Neill, Paul Green, David Belasco, and Jim Tully followed in the 1920s the example set by Torrence; they gave Charles Gilpin, Paul Robeson, Freddie Washington, Abbie Mitchell, and many other African American actors the necessary positive exposure they needed to be successful.

Harlem Renaissance theater

All these activities helped usher in and maintain the Harlem Renaissance of the 1920s. The "New Negro" philosophy stimulated a lot of artistic creativity. Noble Sissle, Eubie Blake, Garland Anderson, and Willis Richardson were involved in memorable productions. W.E.B. Du Bois formed the Krigwa Players. The Harlem Experimental Theatre, the Negro Art Theatre, the Dunbar Garden Players, and the Harlem Community Players all flourished. Langston Hughes wrote the *Mulatto* and *Mother and Child*.

The Great Depression

The Great Depression of the 1930s hit the African American community the hardest. The African American theater that had been so buoyant, energetic, and refreshing was halted.

Many African American theater practitioners were unemployed. The Federal Theater Project, which was the theater wing of President Roosevelt's Works Progress Administration, helped to alleviate the crushing unemployment. When Congress brought the Federal Theater Project to an end in 1939, African American theater was strong enough to develop its own path. Langston Hughes's *Mulatto* had played continuously from October 1935 to December 1937; the Harlem Suitcase Theater, the Negro People's Theatre, and the New Negro Theatre had been formed between 1937 and 1939. Also formed was the Rose McClendon Players, featuring Canada Lee, Ossie Davis, Dooley Wilson, and Maxwell Glanville, while the Rose McClendon Workshop Theatre had officially opened in 1930.

Postdepression theater

In 1940, the Negro Playwrights Company was founded to reflect the historical reality of African American life. Abram Hill and Frederick O'Neal formed the American Negro Theatre, which produced many successful plays, including *Anna Lucasta* and *The Natural Man*. Theodore Ward, of the Negro Playwrights Company, emerged with his *Big White Fog* and *Our Lan'*. Richard Wright's *Native Son* was adapted for the stage and was greeted with critical acclaim as well as controversy as it went on national tour. A group called the Committee for the Negro Arts produced William Branch's *Medal for Willie* in 1951; Roger Furman's Negro Art Players and Maxville Glanville and Julian Mayfield's the Group were formed in 1952. Greenwich Mews Theatre, in Manhattan, supported African American theater by producing William Branch's *In Splendid Error* (1954) and Loften Mitchell's *Land Beyond the River* (1957). The period was one of integration: Actors Equity and other groups refused to return to segregation in the theater.

Radical dramaturgy

The 1960s were a turbulent period in American history. The turbulence found much expression in revolutionary or protest theater. The period witnessed the activities of playwrights Ossie David (*Purlie Victorious*) and Adrienne Kennedy (*Funnyhouse of a Negro*), but it is mostly remembered for such radical plays as *The Slave, Dutchman*, and *The Toilet*, by Imamu Amiri Baraka (formerly LeRoi Jones); Lonne Elder III's *Ceremonies in Dark Old Men*; Charles Gordone's *No Place to Be Somebody*; Ed Bullins's *Gentleman Caller*; and James Baldwin's *Blues for Mister Charlie*. In an abrasive, frightening manner, these playwrights exposed the tensions and anger building up in American society as no one had ever dared before. Baraka, with his Black Arts Theater, was the foremost leader of the period. Douglas Turner Ward's *Days of Absence* and *Happy Ending* expressed similar feelings in a humorous, satirical manner.

The 1970s maintained the gains of an earlier decade while extending the African American theatrical domain. The Negro Ensemble Company produced, with artistic grace, Gus Edwards's *Offering* and Lennox Brown's *Twilight Dinner*. The New Federal Theater was established by African American producer Woodie King, Jr., in Manhattan; it was there that Ed Bullins's *Taking of Miss Janie* premiered. The pacesetter in this decade, as he was in the previous decade, was Imamu Amiri Baraka. He dazzled the theater world with *Slaveship, Experimental Death Unit #1, The Motion of History, Junkies Are Full of (Shhh . . .)* and *A Recent Killing*.

The 1970s also witnessed the birth of a new form of African American theater known as rituals. Rituals combined revolutionary ideology, African American Christian liturgy, music, dance, and life experiences. Most of these plays were produced at the New Lafayette Theater. Two of the most popular rituals were *A Ritual to Bind Together and Strengthen Black People So That They Can Survive the Long Struggle That Is to Come* and *To Raise the Dead and Foretell the Future*.

Recent theater

The hallmark of recent African American theater is successful playwriting that has brought with it much recognition. Charles Fuller's *Soldier's Play* won the Pulitzer Prize for Drama and Ron Milner struck Broadway with his *Checkmates*. But the one American playwright who dominated the 1980s is an African American named August Wilson. Never since the days of Eugene O'Neill, Arthur Miller, and Tennessee Williams had a playwright been so critically acclaimed. Each of his four plays—*Ma Rainey's Black Bot-tom*; *Fences*; *Joe Turner's Come and Gone*; and *The Piano Les-son*—received the New York Drama Critics Circle Award for best play of the season, while *Fences* and *The Piano Lesson* additionally won the Pulitzer. His most recent plays are *Two Trains Running* (1992) and *Seven Guitars* (1996).

Other male playwrights, while not achieving Wilson's height, also gained prominence. George C. Wolfe's *Colored Museum*, Bill Gun's *Forbidden City*, Garland Thompson's *Tutankh-amon, the Boy King*, Lonne Elder III's *Splendid Murmur*, and Steve Carter's *House of Shadows* were successfully produced. The Crossroads Theatre of New Brunswick, New Jersey, joined the New Federal Theatre and the Negro Ensemble Company as the most active theaters of the period. All bodes well for African American theater practice at the end of this millennium and the beginning of the next.

FILM

One may better appreciate the contributions of African American males to the film industry by a cursory look at the history of American cinema. From Thomas Edison's photographic experiments in 1893 through D. W. Griffith's *Birth of a Nation* in 1915, there were black characters in films, but those characters were not played by African Americans but by white Americans in blackface. On only rare occasions were African Americans used, and of these only Sam Lucas played a leading role in the fourth version of *Uncle Tom's Cabin*. After protests by the NAACP over the blackfaced and unfavorable depiction of African Americans in *The Birth of a Nation*, African Americans were gradually allowed to portray insignificant and stereotyped roles: the "coon triumvirate" of the pickaninny, Rastus, and Uncle Remus; the Uncle Tom; the tragic mulatto; the mammy; the brutal black buck; the jesters; and the servants (Bogle 1994, 8).

The level of art that African Americans brought to these lowly characters and their determination to rise above and to challenge the stereotypes opened new vistas for the true depiction of the African American. African American males were the first to rise to the challenge of forging a new filmic image for African Americans in the roles in which they were cast, as actors in their own right, as independent filmmakers, and as directors and producers. African American male stars and superstars of the film industry—Oscar Micheaux, Sidney Poitier, Ossie Davis, Jim Brown, Paul Robeson, Melvin Van Peebles, Richard Pryor, Eddie Murphy, Denzel Washington, Morgan Freeman, Gordon Parks, Sr., Gordon Parks, Jr., Charles Burnett, Rex Ingram, John Singleton, Bill Cosby, Laurence Fishburne, Wesley Snipes, and Spike Lee—whether as actors, screenwriters, directors, or producers, have given a respectable name and recognition to the African American. By their hard work and dedication, they and numerous others, both male and female, have laid a solid foundation and set an example for posterity.

Pioneers

The formation of the Lincoln Motion Picture Company in Los Angeles in 1916 by a group of African American entrepreneurs led by George and Noble Johnson laid the foundation for the participation of African Americans in film production. With the Lincoln Company in place, films in which African Americans became featured performers were made. In the 1920s, many more African American film companies emerged—Renaissance Film Company, Lone Star, and Democracy Photoplay Corporation, to name a few. But it is the Micheaux Film and Book Company that was the pacesetter. Its proprietor, Oscar Micheaux, played an influential role in the direction that the African American film industry would take in future years.

The 1930s witnessed mass distribution of sound films. It also brought into prominence such performers as Stepin Fetchit and Daniel Haynes. With James Weldon Johnson of the NAACP working as a film consultant, African American musicals were introduced. Eubie Blake, Noble Sissle, and Cab Calloway became box office names. Outside musicals, Paul Robeson starred in *The Emperor Jones*, while Clarence Brookes took on the role of a respectable physician of stature in *Arrowsmith*. The Great Depression and World War II adversely affected the growth of the African American film industry.

Postwar film

After World War II, a more tolerant view of the African American male became visible in films. Sidney Poitier, Harry Belafonte, Gordon Parks, Sr., and Sammy Davis led the way in playing prominent roles. Of these, Poitier's *Guess Who's Coming to Dinner* became memorable. Not even the agitations of the 1960s could hold back African Americans from furthering their film talent. The desire for an African American hero soon led to the production of films such as Melvin Van Peebles's *Sweet Sweetback's Baadasss Song*, Gordon Parks, Sr.'s *Shaft*, and Gordon Parks, Jr.'s *Superfly*. But soon this desire led to the production of unrealistic films referred to as "blaxploitation" in which violence, pimps, and drug dealers were extolled. These films include *Black Caesar*, *Black Samson*, *Boss Niger*, and many others. The 1970s, however, also offered male superstars, some old in the business and some newcomers: Ossie Davis, Poitier, and Richard Pryor. These latter Hollywood personalities were successful in entertaining a broad segment of the society.

Box-office attractions since the 1980s

The 1980s opened with two prolific filmmakers: Richard Pryor and Eddie Murphy. Pryor's *Brewster's Millions* and *Richard Pryor Here and Now* and Eddie Murphy's *Beverly Hills Cop*, *Trading Places*, and *Coming to America* were pacesetters in comedy. Independent filmmakers began to make their mark, and two of these—Spike Lee and Robert Townsend—received critical acclaim for *She's Gotta Have It* and *Hollywood Shuffle*, respectively. Along with these directors came a host of actors such as James Earl Jones (*Patriot Games*), Danny Glover (*Lethal Weapon* and *Lethal Weapon II*), Louis Gosset, Jr. (*An Officer and a Gentleman* and *Iron Eagle II*), Denzel Washington (*Glory* and *Malcolm X*), and Morgan Freeman (*Lean on Me* and *The Power of One*). As the end of the millennium approaches, younger African American film stars have begun to make their impact, thus ensuring the continuity of excellence. Among them are Samuel L. Jackson, Martin Lawrence, and Will Smith.

CONCLUSION

Both the contributions African American males have made to entertainment and the impact of these contributions on African American males in general have been positive. The impact in most instances is part of the positive contributions.

The conceptualization of African American entertainment as "counter-hegemonic cultural production" (hooks 1991, 351) has led to a true depiction of African Americans on the screen and in theater productions. The artists continue to portray deep emotional and intellectual probings of the black experience.

Discourses on race have been opened up. Racial stereotypes were introduced and challenged; African characters such as kings, powerful warriors, and nobility have been included in shows. The racial definition of good and evil, with their attendant color association, was artistically interrogated. A didactic element was introduced to show that things may not be as they appear, that black is no more evil than white is good.

Job opportunities opened up, and younger African American males have begun to pursue careers in the entertainment industry. There has been a realization, too, that entertainment serves as a commercialization and advertising of one's culture. African Americans have helped to show that in the production of black entertainment, politics and aesthetics merge. The black aesthetic school has emerged to argue that a "specific world view, an ethos, a sensitivity exist in the black community and have resulted in a specific creative tradition both in the arts and in everyday life" (Long 1989, 130).

In addition to being an instrument of survival under harrowing economic, social, and political circumstances, entertainment has been directed to show that African American culture thrives. Its presence has made all Americans more aware than ever before of African American creativity and ingenuity. It also helped to challenge African Americans to rise beyond mental obstructions to their development. It has brought the awareness that when properly accessed, "the European/African duality of the African American could . . . serve as a powerful vehicle for the loftiest of black musical and dramatic expressions" (Stewart 1998, 102). Black entertainment is a contribution of African Americans to the cultural development of the United States. As James Haskins points out, African Americans have been "one of the primary sources of . . . innovations" in entertainment since the late eighteenth century (Haskins 1990, 215).

African American male entertainers affirm the connection between Africa and black America, which to them is unseverable. They bring a reverence and a deep appreciation of African history and culture in opposition to what in the past was despised by Euro-American consciousness. It was the philosopher Hegel who speculated that Africa had no history. As if to counter this and to express appreciation of pan-Africanism, most African American entertainers have generally turned to African history and culture for metaphors and symbols of empowerment. Even in a most ludicrous manner, Eddie Murphy's *Coming to America* aspires to this.

I am an invisible man. No, I am not a spook like those who haunted Edgar Allan Poe; nor am I one of your Hollywood-movie ectoplasms. I am a man of substance, of flesh and bone, fiber and liquids—and I might even be said to possess a mind. I am invisible, understand, simply because people refuse to see me. (Ellison 1995, 3)

African American male entertainers have made it possible for African Americans to be visible and recognizable to all. They used the entertainment industry to disrupt the hitherto acceptable conditions of African American presence or absence (Ward 1971, 315), visibility or invisibility, and by so doing made the African American male a visible man whose presence is felt. This is their greatest legacy.

References

Bogle, Donald. 1994. *Toms, Coons, Malattoes, Mammies, and Bucks*. New York: Continuum.

Ellison, Ralph. 1995. *Invisible Man*. New York: Vintage.

Emery, Lynne Fauley. 1988. *Black Dance from 1619 to Today*. Princeton, NJ: Dance Horizons.

Haskins, James. 1990. *Black Dance in America*. New York: HarperCollins.

hooks, bell. 1991. Micheaux: Celebrating Blackness. *Black American Literature Forum* 25(2):351-60.

Long, Richard A. 1989. *The Black Tradition in American Dance*. New York: Rizzoli.

Roach, Hildred. 1992. *Black American Music: Past and Present*. Malabar, FL: Krieger.

Southern, Eileen. 1997. *The Music of Black Americans*. New York: Norton.

Stewart, Earl L. 1998. *African-American Music*. New York: Shirmer Books.

Ward, Douglas Turner. 1971. Day of Absence. In *Contemporary Black Drama*, ed. Clinton F. Oliver and Stephanie Sills. New York: Charles Scribner.

ANNALS, *AAPSS*, **569**, May 2000

Incarcerated African American Men and Their Children: A Case Study

By GARRY A. MENDEZ, JR.

ABSTRACT: Many studies have been directed toward incarcerated women and their responsibilities in raising their children despite their incarceration. This same concern has not been forthcoming in the case of incarcerated men and parenting programs or other responsibility programs for them. Male responsibility programs have, for the most part, not included incarcerated men, a large and growing segment of the population. It has been suggested that incarcerated men have no interest in their children and that, in fact, they have been and continue to be bad fathers. This article reports on a study that was conducted by the National Trust for the Development of African-American Men to try to determine the attitudes of incarcerated men toward fatherhood while they are incarcerated. The study found that incarcerated men were interested in improving their relationships with their children and families and that they would be willing to participate in a program that would help them do so.

Garry A. Mendez, Jr., is currently the founding president of the National Trust for the Development of African-American Men. The organization concentrates on solving problems through the use of African and African American values. Prior to founding the Trust, Mendez was a visiting fellow at the U.S. Department of Justice, National Institute of Justice, where he worked on developing and evaluating a program that he designed, Crime Is Not a Part of Our Black Heritage. He earned his doctorate at the University of Michigan.

NOTE: This study was funded by the National Institute of Justice, U.S. Department of Justice.

I MPRISONMENT is a big enterprise in the United States. More than 1.5 million are locked up on any one day (U.S. Bureau of Justice Statistics 1997b, 2). Over 10 million Americans will see the inside of a prison or jail in any one year (U.S. Bureau of Justice Statistics 1997a, 6). Imprisonment is also a growing enterprise. In 1996 there were more than three times as many prisoners as there were in 1980 (Maguire and Pastore 1995, 548). Incarceration has been referred to as the "prison-industrial complex" (Schlosser 1998); a huge amount of money is involved in incarceration outside of the departments of correction themselves. Such diverse industries as telephone companies and architectural firms have a vested interest in the continued growth of incarceration in America.

Perhaps the most striking aspect of prisons in the United States is the racial composition of the population. Six percent of the population of the United States is African American and male. Almost half of all the men in prison are African American. African American men are imprisoned at a rate more than six times higher than white men. Of every 100,000 white Americans, 306 are in prison. The figure for African Americans is 1947 per 100,000 (Donziger 1996, 102). According to the Sentencing Project, on an average day in America, one of every three African American men aged 20 to 29 is in prison or on parole (Mauer and Huling 1995, 1). A national study conducted in 1990 showed that more than 4 of every 10 African American men aged 18 to 35 were in prison, on probation, on parole, on bail, or being sought by the police with a warrant (Mauer 1990). Official statistics suggest that nearly 3 of 10 black men face the prospect of going to prison during their lifetimes. This figure does not include the likelihood of going to jail (U.S. Bureau of Justice Statistics 1997a).

Many of the social problems confronted by the African American community have been attributed to the lack of fathers in the daily family setting. In response to this problem, a number of African American male responsibility programs and networks have been established across the country. These programs focus on such areas as parenting, mentoring, role modeling, and the general development of positive relationships between African American men and their families.

Dr. Jeffery Johnson, director of the National Center for Strategic Nonprofit Planning and Community Leadership, an organization that addresses the needs of fragile families, indicates that the problem is absent fathers and that these fathers are absent for a variety of reasons that are never really examined. Instead, it is simply assumed that the fathers are irresponsible, and they are categorized as deadbeat dads.

The discussion around absent fathers has given little attention to the absent father who is incarcerated. The organizations that have developed programs to prepare men to be more responsible note that they have ex-offenders in their programs, but they do not work with the men until they are released. Furthermore, they make no special effort to seek out ex-offenders to motivate and mobilize them to become responsible fathers.

The role of incarcerated men regarding responsibility and fatherhood has been virtually overlooked by communities and correctional program staff around the country. The relationship between children and parents has been viewed as a mother-child issue, with little concern given to the relationship between children and their fathers.

There are nearly 85,000 women incarcerated in the United States—compared to 1.8 million men (U.S. Bureau of Justice Statistics 1999). It is estimated that over 60 percent of these men have at least one child (Lanier 1995, 34-36), which means that at a minimum there are at least 600,000 children whose fathers are incarcerated. If the multitude of social problems of inner-city communities, and specifically youths, are related to absent fathers, then it would seem that attention should be given to ensuring that incarcerated fathers be assisted in assuming their responsibility of parenting their children.

It has been assumed that because incarcerated men have been involved in criminal behavior, they have not been good fathers and do not care about their children and their families. Consequently, when policymakers and administrators plan programs for the incarcerated, they completely overlook the possibility that incarcerated men should or would care to be a part of the development of their children. As more attention is given to the issue of responsible parenting and fatherhood, however, it would seem that programs should emerge in prisons.

Do incarcerated men care about their families and children, and, if so, can we develop programs that will allow them to assume this responsibility while they are incarcerated? The National Trust for the Development of African-American Men conducted a study, funded by the National Institute of Justice, to determine the attitudes of incarcerated men toward responsible fatherhood, with the intent of moving toward building stronger communities and reducing the flow of individuals into the corrections system.

STATEMENT OF THE PROBLEM

Many inner-city communities are suffering multiple problems because fathers are absent. A large and growing number of these absences are the result of incarceration. In realizing this, responsible fatherhood programs will seek to expand their programs by making a conscious effort to include ex-offenders in their current work.

There is reason to believe that fatherhood programs will want to address the huge problem of the growth of prisons, prison reform, and all of the related issues. While prison reform issues are being debated, there are thousands of children in need of fathers right away. Therefore, it is critical to ascertain whether or not absent fathers, in prison, can become responsible for their children while they are incarcerated.

In order to make this determination, we must first understand the attitudes and perceptions of incarcerated men toward parenting their children. Then programs can be developed that either address these attitudes or build upon them. The present study attempts to focus on describing these attitudes and perceptions, with the intent of assisting in the development of future programs. The main hypotheses of the study were that incarcerated fathers are interested in their children and families, that they would like to assist in child rearing, and that they would participate in a program to learn how to assist.

Interest in children and families

A standard training exercise that is used by the National Trust in its work around the country is to ask participants to list the adjectives that best describe African American men. Inevitably, the list will consist of all negative descriptors. The response transcends race, gender, age, socioeconomic status, and the current incarceration status of the people responding. The image of an African American male is negative, and no African American male seems to escape that portrayal.

As a result of this perception, when community problems such as those involving families are addressed, most interventions tend to focus on supporting African American women without including the men. Instead of working with the fathers, the focus has been on mentoring and role modeling. The assumption is that the men simply do not care and will not assume responsibility for their families and children.

This negative perception is exacerbated by the problem of incarceration. If a man is incarcerated, it is automatically concluded that he could not be a good father because he is in prison. This suggests that the act of committing a crime makes a person less concerned or loving in the family construct. Little if anything is known about the concerns or interests of the men before they are incarcerated, and once they are incarcerated, no one seems to care. The present inquiry will attempt to understand the attitudes of incarcerated men and their families.

Desire to assist in child rearing

Much attention has been given to the issue of failure to pay child support, and in many cases payment of child support has surfaced as the true indicator of how responsible and concerned the fathers are with respect to their children's welfare.

According to Jeffery Johnson, there are any number of reasons why fathers do not make support payments, and they are not related to concern for or love of their children. He indicates that, in many cases, the men do not have the money or they are not given access to the children. Failure to provide money does not mean lack of concern, interest, or love.

When men are incarcerated, they have no control over access to their children. This is completely in the hands of the person who has custody of the children. Furthermore, it might be unclear to both the inmate and the family as to the role that the father may play in the family, given his situation.

Participation in
  child-raising programs

If, in fact, inmates have not been responsible fathers in the past, it seems that, now that they are incarcerated, there is an opportunity to work toward making them responsible fathers for the future. For this to happen, they would need help in developing the necessary skills to assume the role of a responsible father and family member. There is no need to wait until the man returns to the community for him to assume his responsibilities. A willingness to participate in a structured program to assist him in changing his previous behavior would serve both his family and the community. The issue of responsible fatherhood may be more convoluted than simply determining that the father does not care about his children and family.

SAMPLING PROCESS

The individuals included in the study were incarcerated in prisons in New York State. Like most New York State prisoners, they tended to be from large metropolitan or urban areas, with the majority coming from New York City and the surrounding suburbs. Initially, it was thought that all of the participants would be selected from Green Haven Prison because the National Trust was known in that prison. Since the prison was familiar with the organization, it would be easier to work with the administration and the inmates. The plan was to use the men who were members of the Green Haven Trust to encourage the other inmates to participate in the study. It was anticipated that this process would yield hundreds of men in Green Haven alone.

Fishkill and Mid-Orange Correctional Facilities would serve as additional sites because several inmates who were members of the Green Haven Trust had been transferred to those two prisons. Since there were plans to expand the program into each of these facilities, the men believed that they would be able to convince fellow inmates to join the study. It was decided to pursue this approach, and a request was made to the administration at each of these facilities to allow the National Trust to conduct the survey. In all three cases, the administration agreed to allow the study to be conducted, but the process would have to be worked out with each prison because each operated in its own manner.

It was emphasized that the participants in the study would have to be volunteers. In addition, it would be the responsibility of the National Trust to conduct the study because the prisons did not have the labor to handle the task.

The original plan was to have the men in the National Trust inform the population that the study was going to be conducted and that inmates were encouraged to participate. Names would be collected, and those men would be taken to an area where the survey would be completed. The questions would be read aloud to make sure that men who had difficulty reading could still participate. The Trust inmates also identified Spanish-speaking inmates who would function as interpreters for men who either did not understand English or had some problems with the language.

A visit was made to each of the facilities to train the Trust inmate volunteers in how to assist in conducting the survey; the logistics of conducting the survey required that the Trust survey team have the assistance of the men. The major concern that was raised by the Trust volunteers was the amount of time it took to complete the survey. Given the reading level of the population, it was thought that participants would take longer than the projected time (45 minutes) to complete the survey, despite the fact that we had field-tested the survey at another facility. It should be noted that inmates generally will not participate in studies because they are suspicious of how the data will be used and by whom. The Trust was warned by all three administrations that the men probably would not complete the surveys and that the administrators would not in any way get involved in convincing participants to finish them. Each facility presented the investigators with a different series of problems in getting participants and conducting the survey.

GREEN HAVEN

Green Haven is a maximum-security prison housing long-term offenders. The men in the Trust program informed the population of the dates that the survey was to be conducted, and arrangements were made for the team to begin work. The first group of respondents comprised individuals who attended the computer literacy program conducted by the Trust participants.

The principal investigator was taken to areas of the prison where large numbers of men were present, and he was allowed to explain the study to the men and ask them to participate. Although large numbers of men agreed to participate, they were not allowed to respond to the survey at that point because doing so would interfere with the normal operation of the prison. Anyone wishing to participate would have to sign up at another time and make arrangements to do the survey on their own. They could not be brought together in any other way because of security concerns.

The next strategy was to go to the school area, where the men were in classes, and try to convince them to complete the survey. The teachers had been instructed to allow anyone who desired the time to do the survey. For security reasons, the survey had to be completed during the regular class time because the men would have to return to their cells for the count.

With the help of the Trust inmates, a number of surveys were completed in this manner, but due to the time constraints, most of the men took the surveys back to their cells, and for the most part these surveys were never completed. Finally it was decided that surveys would have to be distributed on an individual basis and the Trust team would have to keep reminding the men to return them.

Obviously, this seriously reduced the responses by the men. Surveys were distributed to over 1500 men, and we were able to get 278 to respond. Prison security issues made it impossible to get as many responses as had been anticipated, however.

MID-ORANGE

Mid-Orange is a medium-security prison and has a much more relaxed environment. The initial step to get participants was to have the two Trust members who had been transferred to Mid-Orange from Green Haven talk to the population about the study. The administration arranged for inmates to sign up to participate, and dates for conducting the survey by the National Trust team were established.

Upon arrival at the facility it was noted that approximately 20 men had signed up to be included in the study. Those men had been notified to come to the school area to complete the survey. At the scheduled time, however, none of the men came to the designated room.

It was decided that the Trust team should visit the various areas of the prison and encourage the men to participate in the study. The team moved from one area to another distributing Trust materials and explaining not only the nature of the study but the nature and purpose of the organization. The two Trust members from Green Haven had established a committee that would spend the balance of the next day and a half encouraging the men to participate. As in the case of Green Haven, the Trust members identified several Spanish-speaking men to act as interpreters for any men who had

difficulty with English. The Trust survey team was set up in one room that accommodated approximately 25 men at a time. In another room, the principal investigator spoke with potential participants, encouraging them to be part of the study. Members of the committee moved around the facility and encouraged the men to come in and listen to the principal investigator explain the nature of the study and its intended purpose. The main concern that was expressed was that the New York State Department of Corrections had hired us and that the study was a method of getting more information to be used against them. Despite this concern, 200 men completed the survey at Mid-Orange.

FISHKILL

As in the other two prisons, at Fishkill it was left to the five Trust members, who had participated in the program, to begin talking to the men concerning their becoming respondents to the survey. They posted notices in various sections of the prison, and they moved through the population using various opportunities to talk with men about the Trust and the work that had been done at Green Haven.

However, as the Trust members stated, they were new to Fishkill, and although Fishkill was classified as a medium-security prison, the rules there were often more restrictive than in Green Haven, which is a maximum-security prison. (The staff explained that although it was officially a medium-security institution, some special units on the grounds required a stricter security approach.) Recruiting participants was therefore more difficult.

The sign-up process produced only 19 names on the list. We suggested to the administration that experience had told us that signing up the men would not be the best method of getting them to be part of the study. We requested that the principal investigator be allowed speak to the men and try to persuade them to participate. It was decided that one day would be set aside for anyone who desired to do so to take the survey, and taking the survey would be done in the school area because that location would provide access to the most men. The men were to come to their normal classes or program activities in the education area, and the principal investigator would be allowed to talk to them and try to get them to volunteer for the study. There were approximately 10 classrooms, with a total number of at least 300 men in the area. The plan was to explain the study and have the volunteers complete administration of the survey after the presentation. During morning class time, a number of the men agreed to complete the survey, but the majority opted to leave once they found that not only was it optional but they could leave the area and use the time as free time. It was considered a day off from school, and they decided to leave the school.

The same process was followed with the afternoon classes, but by then the word had spread that inmates did not have to come to the education area, so the turnout was vastly reduced.

Furthermore, some inmates were spreading the word that the study was going to be used by the Trust in a negative manner. It was decided that the Trust men would approach other prison organizations and ask them to participate in the study. With this technique, over a thousand surveys were distributed to the population, and 358 surveys were completed and returned to the Trust.

Normal sampling methods are difficult to apply in a prison situation. Researchers are therefore usually forced to rely on volunteer participation, with all its accompanying selection problems. Under the circumstances, however, this is the best that we could do.

It should be noted that the racial breakdown for the respondents was 62 percent African American, 20 percent Latino, 5 percent white, and 6 percent other. This is similar to the racial breakdown of the prison population of New York State prisons overall.

SUMMARY

The analysis revealed that the responses of the survey participants seemed to support the three main hypotheses of the study. Incarcerated fathers are interested in their children and families; incarcerated fathers would assist in child rearing; and incarcerated fathers would participate in a program to help understand how to assist in raising children.

Interest in children and families

The common thought is that incarcerated men do not care about their children and families. The children of incarcerated parents have been viewed as a problem for the mother, with little attention given to the father. This bias carries over into the prison community, where parenting education has focused on the responsibility of the mother despite her situation. The children are the woman's responsibility regardless of the circumstances.

Despite the concern about the absence of fathers in urban communities, few if any parenting programs are directed at absent fathers who are incarcerated; yet 92 percent of the men in this study indicated that they wanted to improve their relationship with their children. As enlightened as our society may be, children of incarcerated parents are still considered the responsibility of the mother regardless of which parent is incarcerated.

It should be noted that although only 29 percent of the men in our study indicated that they were married, 75 percent indicated that they had children. Furthermore, 51 percent indicated that they had three or more children. This raises the question of how many children are involved in the issue of incarcerated fathers. This also raises the issue of how many spouses and families are involved.

The men indicated that they were still an important part of the family despite their incarceration. Furthermore, they also indicated that they felt guilty about their separation from the family. (Although the men feel guilty, it is unknown at this point how much of a positive contribution they were making to the family before they were incarcerated.) Both of these responses, however, would seem to indicate that intervention programs could be built that utilize the feeling of guilt and perceived family importance to motivate the men.

The families might not see the men as important to the family as the men see themselves. Stated another way, the men's perceived importance to their families may be driven by the families' attempt to assist them when they are incarcerated rather than by need on the part of the family. There may be willingness on the part of the men to play a greater role in the family, but there are usually issues within the family that the men have to address in order to normalize the relationship. Men who have been in prison for long periods of time, such as the men in this study, often develop a memory that tends to exclude many of the problems that they have brought to their families. Family members, especially mothers, continue to support inmates while they are incarcerated, but this does not mean that prior to incarceration they were positive contributors to the family. In fact, either directly or indirectly, they have victimized their families as they have victimized their communities.

Further indication of the interest of the men in their children is reflected in the finding that 69 percent of the men write to their children at least once a month. In addition, 56 percent of the men speak to their children at least once a month by telephone. It could be argued that the men have time on their hands and therefore they write to their children less out of interest in the children than to ward off boredom. Nonetheless, the fact remains that they use that time to try to maintain contact with their children. Although the data are not available as to whether the children respond to the men's letters, it seems that the men would discontinue writing if their children did not respond. In either event, the men make the effort on their own.

With the telephone calls, the situation changes. All calls from prison are collect. The men are allowed to call only a limited number of people, and they are allowed only a specific number of calls per month. It is entirely up to the person receiving the call as to whether the inmate can make the contact. In other words, the access is controlled by the family, not the inmate, yet over half of the men speak to their children at least once a month. Spouses or guardians control the contact; however, it is clear that they agree to have the men interact with their children.

There are other factors that should be considered with respect to telephone access. The first is the cost of collect calls from prisons in New York State. The charge is $3.33 for the first minute and $0.33 for each additional minute. These fees are not the same as the telephone fees incurred by citizens who are not involved with incarceration, and they are charged to a segment of the population that can least afford the cost. This means that families have to make financial sacrifices to maintain telephone contact between children and fathers.

A factor that may mask the true number of telephone contacts that are made is the absence of telephones in the homes of many inner-city poor families. According to the U.S. Department of Commerce, telephone penetration in the United States is 98 percent. It is not known whether this penetration holds true in inner cities and rural communities.

Although telephone contact is fairly high, the cost of the telephone calls and the extent of telephone penetration indicate what the situation would be like if circumstances were more normal. The combination of the men's writing and the families' accepting collect calls at the current rate suggests that the families are attempting to maintain a relationship between the men and their children.

There is a third method by which the men can maintain contact with their children, and that is through visits. A question about visits was not included in the survey because not only are visits completely controlled by the family but they are a great financial hardship on them. The three prisons in this study are fairly close to the New York metropolitan area, where most of the men lived before their incarceration. Yet a trip to any of the prisons is at least two hours each way, and there is no public transportation to any of the three. There are several private businesses that have emerged that charge people to transport them to the prisons in the state. Some of these trips require that families travel from the early hours of the morning to the late hours of the night. Some prisons are as far as eight hours away from the New York metropolitan area. Under these conditions, visits to the prison are extremely expensive and time-consuming; therefore, this method of contact has far greater limitations than writing and telephone calls.

In spite of these access issues, the men reported that they maintain warm and intimate relations with their children and that they had affectionate feelings toward their children. This seems to contradict the perception that because the men are incarcerated they are uncaring and lack fatherly feelings. In addition, 70 percent of the men indicated that they were strongly concerned about how their children were doing emotionally. This seems like another indicator that the men may be ready for an intervention that helps them address the emotional condition of their children.

Desire to assist in child rearing

Our second hypothesis, that incarcerated fathers would like to assist in child rearing, was supported by the results of our study. In addition, 68 percent of the men indicated that they were responsible for the raising of their children in spite of their incarceration, and that same percentage indicated that they were responsible for the education of their children. Both of these responses are of special interest because so much

has been said about inner-city men's not taking responsibility for their children. In this case, we have incarcerated men indicating that they are responsible for the children not only in general but specifically for their education. For many years, education has been considered the method by which poor people can elevate themselves out of poverty, and these men feel that they have the responsibility for ensuring that this happens.

Given their circumstances, it would be easy for the men to take the position that they can be responsible for neither the raising nor the education of their children; however, they have said just the opposite. This would seem to indicate that incarcerated men have a different attitude from what might be expected toward their children and their responsibility.

Furthermore, over 80 percent of the men indicated that they encourage their children to do their best. This seems to reflect an older school of thought in the African American community that argued that one had to do one's best regardless of racism or other outside forces. In actuality, doing one's best was encouraged because of racism.

Child raising in our society has begun to be viewed as the responsibility of both the mother and the father, with the more progressive thinkers discussing the roles and circumstances that guide who is responsible for what within a family. A noted exception to this thinking deals with incarcerated people.

It has been said that since the inmates were not responsible before they were incarcerated, they would not assume any responsibility while they are locked up. There are two ways that this might be viewed: it can be accepted that the men were not good fathers; or it can be accepted that they may not have been good fathers on the outside but, since they are incarcerated, we should make them better fathers now. Furthermore, the assumption that they were or are not good fathers is made simply because they are in prison, yet we really know very little about these men and their fathering role. The circumstances surrounding their fathering is unknown and presumed. Nonetheless, if indeed they were not good fathers before incarceration, their current situation gives society the ability to create good fathers in the prison setting. They are under the control of the state, and they also have the time to reflect upon themselves and their role in the family.

Sixty-five percent of the men indicated that they respected their fathers, and another 42 percent strongly disagreed with the statement that their fathers were bad examples. It has been said that the men have ended up in prison because their fathers were absent or did a poor job of parenting. But the men themselves do not blame their fathers. In fact, they seem to have high opinions of their fathers. In the group sessions that the National Trust conducts in the prison, it has been noted that the men often report that their incarceration has nothing to do with their parents or family but instead reflects choices that they have made on their own. Their parents taught them right from wrong,

but the parents also never knew what the men were doing because the men hid the behavior from their parents. This seems to indicate that although society and perhaps even their spouses thought of the men as bad and contributing to the antisocial behavior of their children, the majority of the men in this study disagree.

Further support for this is reflected in the number of times after a young man is killed in the community the mother comes forth and claims that her son never did anything wrong. Yet, the entire neighborhood is aware of the criminal behavior of the young man in question. Parents come to the prison and question their sons about how they can be involved with the criminals who are in the prison. They see their sons as different from the other men in the prison.

These responses suggest that the heavy emphasis on painting the males as negative fathers may be open to question and that at least the incarcerated men in this study do not perceive males as such.

The study also revealed that 33 percent of the men contributed money to their families. Obviously, the sums given cannot amount to what they would be expected to contribute if they were in the outside community because they are limited in how much they are able to earn while they are incarcerated. An inmate normally earns about $5 a week. Some men are employed in prison industry, which allows them to earn as much as $2000 in a year; however, these jobs are limited. Given the very small amount of income available to the inmates, their financial contributions to their families are all the more significant and meaningful. They are willing to assist in the raising of their children to the point of sacrificing their very limited income, income that is critical to their lives in prison. This sacrifice confirms that these men would like to assist in the raising of their children.

Ninety-one percent of the men reported that their families wanted them to come back home, and 73 percent indicated that their families had forgiven them for their past behavior. These responses seem to indicate that the men would be able to play a role in the raising of their children despite having been incarcerated. It would also suggest that it is important to get the family involved in the plans that the state makes for working with the men while they are incarcerated and when they return to the community.

In addition, the men also reported that their families trusted them and listened to them to some degree. If this is in fact true, then working with the men and their fathering role could have an impact on the family and the community. Skills and attitudes developed in a program within the prison would easily be transferred to the family, thus creating a situation where the children have the advantage of having a father with skills.

With over 50 percent of the children's mothers and guardians encouraging them to write to their fathers, it would seem that the communication structure is in place for the fathers to assume their role.

Participation in
  child-raising programs

The results of our study supported our third hypothesis, namely, that incarcerated fathers would participate in a program to help understand how to assist in raising children. Eighty-seven percent of the men indicated that they would like to participate in a program that would assist them in improving their relationship with their children.

Our society has identified the absence of fathers in the family as the primary reason for the breakdown of the African American family, yet, as mentioned previously, the nearly 1 million African American men who are incarcerated are ignored when it comes to ways of saving the family. In spite of this attitude, the large majority of these inmates want to be involved with their children and will participate in a program. Furthermore, as also mentioned, they have demonstrated that they are attempting to assume the role of the father, with limited to no existing formal support.

Eighty-three percent of the inmates reported that their families support them and continue to maintain contact and support. Although society may have written these men off, their families and children have not. It seems that we have the men and their oftentimes impoverished families trying to maintain the family structure with all the constraints of an incarcerated father who is at least two hours away by car.

Sixty-two percent of the men have a good relationship with the people who are raising their children, including the children's mothers. As mentioned earlier, the custodial party has encouraged the children to write to their fathers.

Although the men are willing to participate in a program, 43 percent indicated that their spouses or guardians would not participate, and the same 43 percent indicated that the spouses or guardians would not allow the children to participate. Only 5 percent indicated that the spouses and children would definitely participate. None of these responses is unexpected. They might be attributed to the fact that the men realize that the program would be conducted primarily in the prison and, as mentioned, travel to the prison is an additional hardship on the family. Another explanation might be that although the families support the men, there are still some issues that need to be addressed by the men with their spouses before the family can participate. It must be understood that, in many cases, the men have brought a great deal of hardship and stress on their families, and issues related to that are not resolved.

For his part, the inmate might be ready to move into the father role, but the families still have a memory of his behavior before he was incarcerated. Any program designed to develop these fathers would have to take that into consideration. When men go to prison, they often make claims about how they have changed, but when they return to the community, they return to old habits. There may be any number of reasons for this return to former behavior; regardless of the reason, it comes back to haunt the family.

With the ever growing concern about violence in the community, special attention should be paid to the attitude of the inmates toward violence and their children. When asked about disciplining their children, 65 percent of the inmates strongly opposed the use of physical punishment. Over half of the men indicated that rewards and praise were better than punishment for getting children to behave. These responses are of particular interest because of the popular misconception that poor people, especially poor African American and Latino parents, are physically abusive of their children. The thinking is that these groups rely on spanking as the primary method of controlling children's improper behavior. However, in this study we have a collection of men who have been incarcerated for many kinds of crimes—many for murder—who nonetheless believe that physical punishment is inappropriate for disciplining their children.

Continuing along this line, 72 percent of the men reported that they encouraged their children to resolve problems by talking rather than resorting to violence. The men modeled this behavior in that they reported that they talk things over with their children when they misbehave. Obviously, they are unable to conduct physical punishment in their current situation, but we have no reason to doubt that they handled similar situations in the same manner when they were in the community.

These attitudes would seem to be building blocks for a program that helps the men understand how to improve their relationship with their families and community. These findings seem to indicate that incarcerated men are concerned about their children and families and would participate in a program that would help them in improving their relationships with them. The findings also seem to indicate that the attitudes of the men concerning warmth, discipline, encouragement, and aggressive behavior are similar to those that would be expected of individuals in the general society.

IMPLICATIONS AND RECOMMENDATIONS

Incarcerated men have been basically overlooked with respect to their ability to assume a major role in the raising of their children. The findings from this study, however, suggest that the following recommendations should be considered by the major stakeholders involved in the future of incarcerated men and their families:

1. Programs that teach incarcerated men how to participate in the raising of their children should be required of all of the men. Just as school is mandatory for youngsters, human development classes that include fatherhood, parenting, and social development should be mandatory for inmates. Training should be mandatory because, as was found in this study, 75 percent of the inmates had children, and all of them

have the potential to have children whether they are married or not. Society cannot afford to allow these men to return to the community without educating them about their responsibilities to their children and their families.

2. The families of the men continue to maintain contact with them over the years. Therefore, human development programs should attempt to include the men's children and the children's mothers in the training that the men receive. The focus of the programs should be on family counseling as opposed to marriage counseling because the focus of the work should primarily be directed toward developing the children and only when appropriate toward the saving of a husband-wife relationship between the parents.

3. Incarceration rates are so high in African American communities that there is a danger that incarceration will become a part of the culture. It is therefore recommended that partnerships be developed between correctional facilities and the African American community. These partnerships would be designed to create a cooperative working relationship between corrections and community. The community has a vested interest in having its men return to the community as productive citizens, and the prison could use the influence of the community to assist in minimizing conflict between the inmate population and the staff. In other words, the community would function as a stabilizing force in the prison setting.

4. Connecting the men to their children or to children in their communities has the potential to reach at-risk children. It has been stated that the children of incarcerated men are the most at risk of getting involved in crime. By bringing the families together to work on problems, the men will be able to persuade their children to avoid activity that would result in incarceration. In other words, there would be an expectation that the men participate in the breaking of the cycle of young people's entering the criminal justice system.

5. The standard of appropriate or acceptable fatherhood has centered around the issue of child support. Although financial support is important, it is clear that incarcerated men are quite limited in their ability to provide much in this area. The issue of fatherhood is becoming clarified in society. It is becoming evident that nurturing and emotional support of children is just as critical. Incarcerated men can be taught to provide nurturing and emotional support through telephone communication, written communication, and regular family visits.

6. Building upon the interest of the men to father their children, it is recommended that they formally establish paternity for all of their children. In doing so, they will ensure that their children receive any benefits that they will have accrued in their lives. Furthermore, the children will have access to the father's side of the family, which is critical for such matters as health records. The historical health records of the family are important for the maintenance of a health program for the children.

The common impression is that incarcerated men have little to offer their children. The findings of the present study, however, indicate that these men want to nurture their children. Even from prison, a man can be a positive influence in the lives of his sons and daughters.

References

Donziger, Steven R., ed. 1996. *The Real War on Crime*. New York: HarperPerennial.

Lanier, C. S. 1995. Incarcerated Fathers: A Research Agenda. *Forum on Corrections Research* 7(2):34-36

Maguire, Kathleen and Ann L. Pastore, eds. 1995. *Sourcebook of Criminal Justice Statistics*. Washington, DC: Department of Justice, Bureau of Justice Statistics.

Mauer, Marc. 1990. *Young Black Men and the Criminal Justice System: A Growing National Problem*. Washington, DC: Sentencing Project.

Mauer, Marc and Tracy Huling. 1995. *Young Black Americans and the Criminal Justice System: Five Years Later*. Washington, DC: Sentencing Project.

Schlosser, Eric. 1998. The Prison-Industrial Complex. *Atlantic Monthly*, Dec., 51-77.

U.S. Bureau of Justice Statistics. 1997a. *Lifetime Likelihood of Going to State or Federal Prison*. Washington, DC: Department of Justice.

———. 1997b. *Prison and Jail Inmates at Midyear 1996*. Washington, DC: Department of Justice.

———. 1999. *Prisoners in 1998*. Washington, DC: Department of Justice.

African American Men in the American West, 1528-1990

By QUINTARD TAYLOR

ABSTRACT: The first black men to enter the West were Spanish-speaking settlers from central Mexico. They were followed by free English-speaking fur traders and by slaves primarily in Texas. Some males arrived in California during the 1850s, initiating a voluntary migration of farmers, miners, soldiers, and cowboys through the nineteenth century. In the early twentieth century, black men settled mainly in the cities and worked in unskilled nonunion occupations. By World War II, far more migrants had arrived in response to wartime work opportunities. War work allowed both newcomers and old residents access to skilled unionized employment for the first time. Discrimination continued, however, prompting a civil rights movement in the West in the 1960s that paralleled activities in the South. That movement opened new opportunities for the skilled and educated. However, postwar deindustrialization moved many unskilled African American men to the margins of the Western urban economy.

Quintard Taylor, the Scott and Dorothy Bullitt Professor of American History at the University of Washington, is the author of In Search of the Racial Frontier: African Americans in the American West, 1528-1990 *(1998) and* The Forging of a Black Community: A History of Seattle's Central District from 1870 Through the Civil Rights Era *(1994). He has written forty articles on African American history in the West.*

THE saga of African American men in the West began in November 1528 with the experiences of an African male slave, Esteban, who along with 15 other men washed ashore on a sandbar near present-day Galveston, Texas, the survivors of an ill-fated expedition of 260 men that had begun in Havana, Cuba, eight months earlier. Born half a world away, in Azamor, Morocco, Esteban was the first African to set foot in what would become Texas and the western United States (Bandelier 1905, 53-65).

The stranded men endured a Gulf Coast winter and then were enslaved for the next five years by the Capoques Indians. By September 1534, Esteban and three remaining survivors escaped, crossed the Rio Grande, and straggled over Chihuahua and Sonora, finally reaching Mexico City in July 1536. Three years later, the viceroy of New Spain organized another expedition into the North American interior, led by Franciscan friar Marcos de Niza but which included Esteban as guide and interpreter. The expedition ended tragically at the Zuni town of Hawikah (just east of the present Arizona–New Mexico border) when, against the instructions of town elders, Esteban attempted to enter the town and was killed (Bandelier 1905, 72-108, 180-84; Hallenbeck 1987, 15-32).

Esteban played a crucial role in Western history. The de Niza expedition strengthened Spanish claims in the North, encouraging additional exploration and the eventual founding of towns such as Santa Fe, Los Angeles, and El Paso, and initiated the tripartite meeting of Indian, Spanish, and Anglo cultures that would shape much of the Southwest's history. It also opened this northern frontier to subsequent dark-skinned settlers. For the next three centuries, persons of African ancestry more likely moved north from Mexico rather than west from the Atlantic slope (Weber 1982, xvi).

Men of African ancestry moved to northern New Spain to escape the discrimination they faced in central Mexico. Two men, Sebastian Rodríguez Brito and José Antonio, are typical. Rodríguez, the Angolan-born free son of African slaves, rose from servant to landholder in the late seventeenth century and eventually married Isabel Olguin, an *española* widow, in 1692. Antonio, a Congo-born slave brought to El Paso in 1752, married Marcela, an Apache maid in a neighboring household, eight years later (McDonald 1995, 1-34).

As the marriage of Rodríguez to Olguin suggests, Spanish colonial policies promoted upward social and political mobility among men of African ancestry. The Mexican War of Independence enhanced that mobility by abolishing slavery and declaring the equality of all Mexican citizens before the law. Fugitive slaves and free black men "from the states" soon took note of those promises. Beginning in the 1820s, a small number of African American men arrived in Texas, the Mexican province most accessible to people from the United States. Among those immigrants was Samuel H. Hardin, who wrote that he and his wife had moved to Texas because Mexico's laws "invited their emigration" and guaranteed their right to own property (Woolfolk 1976, 22-37, 153-55). William Goyens, a North Carolinian, settled near Nacogdoches in 1820 and became a blacksmith, freighter, trader, land speculator, and slave owner. At his death in 1856, he had amassed nearly 13,000 acres in four east Texas counties (Prince 1967, 1-30).

A smaller number of English-speaking African Americans entered California between 1821 and 1848. One of them, West Indian–born William A. Liedesdorff, became a successful merchant captain in New York and New Orleans before arriving in San Francisco in 1841. Liedesdorff sailed his commercial schooner, the *Julia Ann*, on regular voyages between Honolulu and California and operated the *Sitka*, the first steam-powered vessel in San Francisco Bay. As one of the most prominent businessmen in the city, Liedesdorff was elected to the town council in 1847 and helped establish its school system (Savage 1953; Lapp 1977, 9-11).

THE ANTEBELLUM WEST

Much of the pre-1846 exploration and early settlement in western North America took place on Mexico's northern frontier. However, after 1788, some English-speaking African Americans entered the Rocky Mountains and Pacific Northwest. Like their more numerous white counterparts, African Americans chose this region primarily for the profits derived from trading or trapping. But the frontier afforded freedom from racial restrictions typically imposed by "settled" communities (Hafen 1965, 21-72).

The life of James Beckwourth, who lived and worked in the West for nearly 60 years, symbolized that freedom. Born in Virginia in 1798 of a slave mother and white father who brought his family to St. Charles, Missouri, in 1810, Beckwourth worked as a hunter until he joined the Ashley fur trapping expedition in 1824. He lived twice with the Absaroka Indians in Montana and during that time took two Native American wives. Later he married Louisa Sandoval, a "young Spanish girl" in Santa Fe in 1840, and Elizabeth Lettbetter, an African American woman, in Denver in 1860 (Bonner 1972, 98-99, 122-41; Oswald 1965, 37-60).

Beckwourth trapped at the foot of the Rocky Mountains in 1826 and two years later along the Snake River in Idaho and Wyoming. By the mid-1830s he supervised trading operations at Fort Vasquez, New Mexico, and in 1845 he joined the rebel forces of Juan Bautista Alvarado in an abortive attempt by *californios* to gain independence from Mexico. By 1847, he had returned to New Mexico in time to help the Americans defeat Mexican forces in the region (Weber 1982, 101-2; Bonner 1972, 456-65; Oswald 1965, 50-55).

In 1849, Beckwourth reappeared in California and discovered the pass through the Sierra Mountains that now carries his name. He then took a land claim on the California side of Beckwourth Pass and built a combined hotel and store that sold supplies to California-bound emigrants. This business anchored the town eventually named after him. Sixty-one-year-old Beckwourth moved to Denver in 1859 during the Pike's Peak Gold Rush, and he managed a trading store. He died quietly of natural causes a month after returning to the Crow Indian country in 1866 (Bonner 1972, 518-20; Hafen 1928, 138-39; Oswald 1965, 43-46).

Few historians link African bondage with the West. Yet on the eve of the Civil War, 182,556 slaves composed 30 percent of the total population of Texas, while the Indian Territory's 7367 black slaves comprised 14 percent of the total population (U.S. Bureau of the Census 1864, xv; Doran 1975, 501-2). Black men in Texas and Indian Territory did the heavy work of plowing, felling trees, and digging ditches and occasionally developed some special skills, as in Indian Territory, where they were ferrymen and stevedores, and Texas, where they became cowboys (Campbell 1989, 55-56, 251).

California adopted an antislavery constitution in 1849. Yet state officials were unable or unwilling to challenge slaveholders who continued to bring their bond servants to the state until the outbreak of the Civil War. By 1852, 300 slaves were working in the gold fields, and an undetermined but sizable number were house servants in California cities. California had, by far, the largest number of bond servants west of Texas (Lapp 1977, 65).

Slavery was short-lived in the other states and territories of the West. Indeed, one state, Kansas, came to symbolize freedom for African Americans held in bondage in neighboring states. Twelve thousand blacks took advantage of the Civil War to gain their liberty through flight. Henry Clay Bruce, the brother of future Mississippi senator Blanche K. Bruce, recounted how he and his fiancée escaped from Missouri to Kansas in 1863. Bruce strapped around his waist "a pair of Colt's revolvers and plenty of ammunition" for the run to the western border. "We avoided the main road and made the entire trip at night . . . without meeting anyone. . . . We crossed the Missouri River on a ferry boat to Fort Leavenworth, Kansas. I then felt myself a free man" (Taylor 1998, 97).

Free blacks sought out the Far West for economic opportunity and refuge from racial restrictions. Yet white Western state and territorial governments rapidly constructed familiar racially based proscriptive legislation that denied voting rights, prohibited African American court testimony, and banned black homesteading, jury service, and marriage with whites. Some black men challenged these restrictions. Missouri farmer George Washington Bush, who led his wife and six children and four other families on an eight-month, 2000-mile journey to the Pacific Northwest in 1844, declared en route that "if he could not have a free man's rights [in Oregon], he would seek the protection of the Mexican Government in California or New Mexico" (Minto 1901, 212). The Bush party eventually reached Oregon, but, unlike the majority of white settlers who spread out over the Willamette Valley south of the

Columbia, they chose the sparsely populated area north of the river, a decision that initiated subsequent migration into the area and organization of Washington Territory.

Economic gain motivated black migration to antebellum California as much as racial refuge. For the intrepid, the effort seemed well worth the dangers. In 1851, Peter Brown described his new life as a gold miner to his wife, Alley, in St. Genevieve City, Missouri. "I am now mining about 25 miles from Sacramento City and doing well," he wrote. "I have been working for myself for the past two months . . . and have cleared three hundred dollars. California is the best country in the world to make money. It is also the best place for black folks on the globe. All a man has to do, is to work, and he will make money" (Taylor 1998, 84).

Such reports prompted additional migration. By 1852, the black population in California had doubled to 2000 women and men. As with all mining frontiers, it was overwhelmingly male. Of the 952 blacks counted in 1850, only 9 percent were women. Ten years later, when black California numbered 4086 inhabitants, black women comprised only 31 percent of the total population (U.S. Bureau of the Census 1853, xxxiii; 1864, 33).

California's antebellum urban black men pursued a range of occupations similar to those available in eastern cities. A few fortunate African Americans in San Francisco became wealthy business owners. John Ross operated Ross's Exchange, a used-goods business, while James P. Dyer, the West's only antebellum black manufacturer, began the New England Soap Factory in 1851. Although Mifflin W. Gibbs arrived in San Francisco in 1850 with ten cents, within a year he formed a partnership with fellow Philadelphian Peter Lester, the Pioneer Boot and Shoe Emporium, a store that eventually had patrons from Oregon to Baja California (Gibbs 1968, 44-45; *Proceedings* 1855, 18).

THE POST–CIVIL WAR ERA

In February 1863, while eastern America fought the Civil War, and the Emancipation Proclamation was less than two months old, black San Francisco newspaper owner Peter Anderson wrote an editorial that envisioned a great march of freed people westward, urged on by "our leading men in the east," and "our white friends who have been battling in the cause of freedom" (*Pacific Appeal* [San Francisco], 14 Feb. 1863, 2). That great march would come, however, only after black men and women were convinced their rights would be respected. The most important of those rights was suffrage. In 1866, a convention of black men meeting in Lawrence, Kansas, challenged the widely held idea that black voting was a privilege that the white male electorate could confer or deny at its pleasure. Then the convention issued this warning to the Euro-American majority in the state: "Since we are going to remain among you, we believe it unwise to . . . take from us as a class, our natural rights. . . . We must be a constant trouble in the state until it extends to us equal and exact justice" (*Kansas Tribune* [Lawrence], 28 Oct. 1866, 2).

The campaign for suffrage in Colorado Territory had national implications. Between 1864 and 1867, Colorado Territory's 150 African Americans, including Lewis Douglass, son of the national civil rights leader Frederick Douglass, waged a relentless campaign to press Congress to delay statehood for the territory until their suffrage rights were guaranteed. William J. Hardin, who had arrived in Denver in 1863 from Kentucky, assumed the leadership of this effort, contacting Massachusetts senator Charles Sumner by telegram to outline the grievances of the territory's African Americans. Senator Sumner declared his opposition to Colorado statehood after reading the telegram from the black leader before the U.S. Senate. The debate over black suffrage restrictions in Colorado prompted Congress to pass the Territorial Suffrage Act in January 1867; the act gave black men the right to vote months before similar rights were extended to African Americans in the South and three years before the Fifteenth Amendment ensured similar rights for African American males in Northern and Western states (Berwanger 1981, 144-45).

In Texas, mostly ex-slave men attempted to guarantee their voting (and other civil) rights through the Texas Republican Party. On 4 July 1867, approximately 20 white and 150 black delegates met in Houston to form the new party. They were led by George T. Ruby of Galveston and Matthew Gaines of Washington County, both of whom were elected to the state senate in 1869 and thus were the highest-ranking black elected officials in Texas during the Reconstruction period. By 1898, 42 black men had served in the legislature at different times (Taylor 1998, 110).

The Seminole, Creek, and Cherokee Nations allowed their former slaves to participate fully in tribal government. In all, 68 men were elected to the Seminole, Creek, and Cherokee legislatures. The Creek Nation had the largest and most consistent black political representation anywhere in the West during the last three decades of the nineteenth century. Creek freedmen were elected judges and district attorneys in tribal courts, and district officials for the tribal government. One freedman, Jesse Franklin, was elected justice of the tribal Supreme Court in 1876 (Debo 1941, 185-237). Nine other African American men were elected to other Western state and territorial legislatures in Colorado, Kansas, Nebraska, Oklahoma Territory (which was separated from Indian Territory in 1867), Washington, and Wyoming.

After the Civil War, tens of thousands of African American men headed west toward a thousand-mile frontier extending from North Dakota to Oklahoma. Sometimes these homesteaders followed promoters such as Kansas emigration leader Benjamin Singleton and created thriving communities such as Nicodemus, Kansas; Boley, Oklahoma; and Dearfield, Colorado. More often than not, however, they came on their own, like future scientist George Washington Carver in Ness

County, Kansas, in 1886, and future filmmaker Oscar Micheaux in Gregory County, South Dakota, in 1904. A fortunate few homesteaders such as Robert Ball Anderson in Nebraska generated their own success stories on the plains. Born a Kentucky slave, Anderson was 41 years old when he took his first homestead claim in Box Butte County, Nebraska, in 1885. By 1918, Anderson owned 2000 acres and was the largest black landholder in the state (Taylor 1998, 137-55; Anderson 1967, 58).

Cattle herding and soldiering were the two Western occupations that remained almost exclusively male. Black cowboys, who were more numerous in Texas than in any other Western state or territory, nonetheless comprised only 4.0 percent of the total of Texas herders in 1880 and 2.6 percent in 1890. Overall, 1200 black cowboys were about 2.0 percent of the total in the West. Black cowboys may have been few in number, but they worked throughout the West, as recounted in numerous newspapers, journals, biographies, and histories that briefly mention their activities (U.S. Bureau of the Census 1897, 532-626; 1918, 513-16).

Typical of such accounts was J. Frank Dobie's description of Pete Staples, a former Texas slave, who after the Civil War worked along the Rio Grande with *vaqueros* (cowboys), both in northern Mexico and west Texas (Dobie 1924, 52-53). Mississippi-born slave Bose Ikard was lifted from anonymity by the praise given him by his employer, Texas cattleman Charles Goodnight. "Ikard . . . was my detective, banker, and everything else in Colorado, New Mexico, and the other wild country I was in. . . . [He] was the most skilled and trustworthy man I had" (Haley 1949, 242). On rare occasions, men such as Daniel Webster "80 John" Wallace in Texas and James Edwards in Wyoming rose from cowboys to cattlemen. Each owned 10,000-acre ranches in their home states by 1910 (Webb 1957, 1-35; Guenther 1989, 21-24).

Twenty-five thousand black men served in the 9th and 10th Cavalry and the 24th and 25th Infantry of the United States Army between 1866 and 1917. Black soldiers fought the Kiowa and Cheyenne in Kansas in 1867, the Comanches in Texas in 1869, and the Apache in New Mexico in 1880 and participated in the Ghost Dance campaign against the Sioux in 1890-91. They also protected Indian Territory reservations from white encroachment throughout the 1880s, defended Kiowa women and children from attack by Texas Rangers in 1879, and protected Ute Indians from Colorado militiamen in 1887 (Taylor 1998, 169-74).

Buffalo soldiers performed police duty throughout the West, pursuing desperados and Mexican political revolutionaries in the Rio Grande border region, including Francisco "Pancho" Villa in 1916. On other occasions, buffalo soldiers stood between whites and Chicanos, as in the El Paso Salt War of 1879, and between clashing cattle ranchers in Lincoln County, New Mexico Territory, in 1878 and Johnson County, Wyoming, in 1890. By the 1890s, black troops were most frequently utilized to preserve the peace in Western labor disputes such as the mining strikes of 1892 and 1899 in the Coeur d'Alene valley of northern Idaho (Taylor 1998, 174-90).

THE URBAN WEST

While some nineteenth-century black men trailed cattle from Texas to Dodge City, grew wheat on the high plains, or mined gold in the Black Hills of South Dakota, a larger number of African American males moved to Denver, San Francisco, Seattle, and Los Angeles and smaller cities such as Salt Lake City, Topeka, and Helena, Montana, seeking employment in the expanding urban economy. These men founded and supported churches, fraternal organizations, and social clubs that helped shape the pattern of black city life well into the twentieth century (Taylor 1998, 192-96).

Regardless of the city, African American men performed similar work. They were personal servants in wealthy households, hotel waiters, railroad porters, messengers, cooks, and janitors. In ports such as Seattle, Portland, and San Francisco, they were sailors, ship stewards, and dock workers. Some entrepreneurial black men operated barbershops, restaurants, saloons, drugstores, and hotels. By the 1890s, most Western urban black communities had a few doctors and lawyers and newspaper editors and ministers (Cox 1982, chap. 4; Taylor 1994, chap. 1).

A handful of African American males became remarkably successful. San Franciscans Richard Barber, William E. Carlisle, Peter H. Joseph, George Washington Dennis, and Henry M. Collins had acquired modest fortunes in real estate by the 1870s (Daniels 1980, 29-30). Colorado's most prominent African American male settler, Barney Ford, built Denver's largest hotel, the Inter-Ocean, in 1874. Later in the decade, Ford accepted the invitation of Cheyenne businessmen to build a hotel in the Wyoming territorial capital (Hall 1895, 4:440-41). In 1905, Robert C. Owens, grandson of Los Angeles black community leader Bridget "Biddy" Mason, constructed a six-story, $250,000 building, earning him the designation "the richest Negro west of Chicago" (Crumbly 1905; Bunch 1988, 17-19).

Few black Western newspaper editors matched the wealth of Barney Ford or Robert C. Owens, but they often ranked as both prosperous businessmen and community leaders. Among the most prominent in the region were San Franciscans Peter Anderson and Philip Bell, who edited the region's oldest African American newspapers, the *Pacific Appeal* and the *Elevator* (Broussard 1977, 49-54). Other newspaper men included Joseph D. D. Rivers, editor of the Colorado *Statesman*; Joseph Bass of the Montana *Plaindealer*; William L. Eagleson, owner and editor of *Colored Citizen* in Topeka; and Horace Cayton, who organized the Seattle *Republican*. Los Angeles's *California Eagle* served the community from 1879 to 1966 (Fisher 1971, 163; Taylor 1994, 19-20). Salt Lake City's small African American community supported two newspapers between 1895 and 1910. The larger, the *Utah Plain Dealer*, edited by William W. Taylor, ran from 1895 to 1909, while its rival, the *Broad Ax*, was published by Julius Taylor from 1895 until 1899 (Coleman 1980, 89-103).

Politics attracted African American urban males regardless of their wealth or occupation. By all indications, black men eagerly voted in city, state, and federal elections, usually supporting the Republican Party despite meager patronage rewards and few opportunities to campaign for office. Topeka, Kansas, proved an exception with respect to patronage and campaign opportunities. Between 1879 and 1881, nearly 3000 migrants to Topeka expanded the existing community of 700. The new citizens turned to politics, electing black Republican Topekans to numerous local offices. Alfred Kuykendall, for example, was elected constable in 1879, a post he held for 10 years, while Wesley I. Jameson was justice of the peace in 1888 and "Colonel" John Brown became Shawnee county clerk in 1889. Beginning in 1897, Fred Rountree represented the Fifth Ward in the Topeka City Council. Black Topeka's crowning achievement in this area came in 1891 when President Benjamin Harrison appointed local attorney and political activist John L. Waller U.S. consul to Madagascar (Woods 1981, 104, 120; Cox 1982, 82-83, 123-24, 145).

Nineteenth-century urban employment patterns for African American males continued virtually unchanged until World War II. C. L. Dellums, vice president of the Brotherhood of Sleeping Car Porters, recalled work opportunities soon after he came to the San Francisco Bay Area from Texas in 1923: "I had been around here long enough to realize there wasn't very much work Negroes could get." They could either "go down to the sea in ships or work on the railroads" (Broussard 1993, 40).

Despite their poverty, working-class black men supported a growing number of professionals and entrepreneurs. By 1915, black Houston had nearly 400 businesses (SoRelle 1992, 103-15). Black Los Angeles had fewer but more high-profile businesses along Central Avenue. Businesses on "the Avenue" included the Golden State Mutual Life Insurance Company and the Hotel Somerville, built by dentist J. Alexander Somerville, and the Hudson-Liddell Building, owned by Dr. H. Claude Hudson and designed by black architect Paul Williams (Bunch 1988, 31).

By the early 1930s, black voters had turned to the Democratic Party. Los Angeles's black voters epitomized this shift when, in 1934, Republican Frederick Roberts, who had served 16 years in the state assembly, was defeated by a 27-year-old Democrat, Augustus Hawkins. Hawkins represented the south-central Los Angeles assembly district until 1962, when he became the first African American congressman from California. With his ties to unions and left-wing politicians, Hawkins personified an emerging political nexus of liberals, labor, and blacks in the Roosevelt coalition (Fisher 1971, 228-35).

San Antonio blacks in the 1930s supported Charles Bellinger, an African American political boss who in the 1920s forged a deal with San Antonio's Latinos and the white-led political machine. In exchange for increased public services—parks, water lines, and street paving—Bellinger delivered a bloc of approximately 8000 votes. Unique in Texas at the time when most of the state's African American voters were disfranchised, Bellinger's machine demonstrated how blacks and Latinos could exert leverage in a hostile political system (Sapper 1972, 36-69, 102-3; Mason 1994, 184-91).

Black men also developed a Western literary tradition, which began when Texas author Sutton E. Griggs wrote *Imperium in Imperio*, an 1899 novel that urged economic and political autonomy for black Texans. It continues with contemporary Western writers such as Berkeley author Ishmael Reed and Seattle playwright August Wilson. Three 1920s-era writers, Langston Hughes, Wallace Thurman, and Arna Bontemps, attempted a Los Angeles renaissance before moving on to Harlem in 1925. Hughes, Thurman, and Bontemps worked with lesser-known writers at the 28th Street YMCA, near Central Avenue. These artists were supported by Thurman's short-lived *Outlet* magazine and its successor, *Flash Magazine*, two of the earliest black literary journals in the West (Taylor 1998, 245).

Western African American jazz musicians fared better than writers. These black men thrived in Kansas City, Los Angeles, Seattle, Dallas, Oklahoma City, and Denver and, in the process, helped shape the evolving national jazz culture of the 1920s and 1930s. By the 1920s, Kansas City had emerged as a vital center of jazz. Black musicians from Kansas, Oklahoma, Texas, and Colorado made their way to Kansas City's nearly 500 nightclubs, taverns, and cabarets, creating a dynamic music scene rivaling Harlem and Chicago's South Side (Stowe 1992).

Black Houston, Dallas, San Antonio, Fort Worth, El Paso, Oklahoma City, Denver, and Omaha provided the first audiences for little-known but ambitious jazz artists. Dallas's Deep Ellum, for example, "swarmed with blues singers, boogie woogie pianists and small combos" who constantly formed and dissolved acts that played the clubs and bars of the city. Jazz bands also went on the road. The Troy Floyd Orchestra in San Antonio, the Blues Syncopaters of El Paso, and the Oklahoma City–based Blue Devils, which at various times included Count Basie, Jimmy Rushing, and Lester Young, traveled a circuit through Kansas, Nebraska, Missouri, Wyoming, Texas, Colorado, South Dakota, and New Mexico (Rice 1996, 108-10; Stowe 1992, 66).

WORLD WAR II

World War II changed forever the African American West. The region's black population grew by 443,000 (33 percent) during the war decade and redistributed itself toward the West Coast. Most of these newcomers concentrated in five major metropolitan regions: Seattle-Tacoma and Portland-Vancouver in the Pacific Northwest; the San Francisco Bay Area, comprising San Francisco, Oakland, and smaller cities such as Berkeley and Richmond; the Los Angeles–Long Beach area; and San Diego. The numbers were less dramatic in Denver, Omaha, Phoenix, Tucson, and Honolulu, but these cities also saw surging black populations (U.S. Bureau of the Census 1943, tab. 35; 1952, tab. 53).

The population grew because of expanding work opportunities. After decades of menial labor, thousands of black men entered the region's factories and shipyards. Migrants came west for work in shipbuilding and aircraft production, initially lured by recruiters. Between 1942 and 1943, Kaiser Shipyards brought nearly 38,000 workers on "liberty" trains that originated as far east as New York City. Another 60,000 paid their way to the West Coast. Wartime migration soon assumed a momentum independent of Kaiser's recruiting efforts. By 1943, black workers were writing home about the high wages, the mild climate, and greater freedom (Johnson 1993, 38, 52-54; Moore 1989, 78).

Wartime labor demands guaranteed that black men would work; they did not guarantee equitable treatment. Throughout the war, black workers, shipyard and aircraft plant managers, and union officials engaged in a triangular struggle over workplace segregation and worker assignments. Black workers, for example, could build ships but not repair them, or they could clean ships but not paint them. Eventually labor shortages and production demands broke down this racial classification, but most black workers remained in unskilled work for the rest of the war (Kesselman 1990, 41-43; Archibald 1947, 60-84; Johnson 1993, 63-75).

The International Brotherhood of Boilermakers (American Federation of Labor) accounted for much of the black workers' difficulty. After years of complete exclusion, the union in 1937 reversed its policy and created all-black "auxiliary" locals. Four years later, the Boilermakers negotiated a closed-shop agreement with West Coast shipbuilders guaranteeing jurisdiction over 65 percent of the U.S. shipyard workers and all of those in West Coast yards except in Seattle. By 1944, 32,000 black employees had been forced into A-26 in Oakland, A-32 in Portland, A-92 in Los Angeles, and A-41 in Sausalito (Harris 1981; Hill 1977, 192-200; Smith and Taylor 1980).

When black workers protested their status in the summer of 1943, the Boilermakers compelled the shipyards to fire black workers for protesting the auxiliary scheme. In rapid succession, 200 workers were dismissed at Marinship in Sausalito, 100 at Moore Drydock in Oakland, 300 workers at Cal Ship in Los Angeles, and 350 at the three Kaiser shipyards in Portland. Among the dismissed Marinship workers was Joseph James, president of the San Francisco chapter of the National Association for the Advancement of Colored People (NAACP). Shipyard workers in each community immediately mounted legal challenges. Joseph James's suit against Marinship near San Francisco reached the California Supreme Court in 1944. The court ruling in *James* v. *Marinship* ordered the Boilermakers to dismantle their auxiliary structure in the state. A U.S. district court in

Portland ruled much the same, and in 1946 the California Supreme Court in *Williams* v. *International Brotherhood of Boilermakers* reaffirmed and extended the earlier *James* opinion (Taylor 1998, 260)

Thousands of African American men came west in uniform. Fort Huachuca, in the Arizona desert, had the largest concentration of black soldiers in the nation after the Army combined the 25th, 368th, and 369th Regiments to create the U.S. 93rd Infantry Division. Fort Huachuca, once a base for buffalo soldiers, now expanded to accommodate 14,000 soldiers, who constituted the only all-black division. However, unlike the buffalo soldiers, who were led by white officers, the 93rd had nearly 300 black officers (Jefferson 1995, 231-43).

Other African American soldiers were also stationed at military facilities remote from any communities. The men of the 93rd, 95th, 97th, and 388th engineers regiments worked in temperatures as low as 70 degrees below zero while building the Alcan Highway through Alaska and the Canadian Northwest (Twichell 1992, chaps. 7, 9, and 10; Morgan 1992, 1-6). Black soldiers and sailors patrolled ammunition depots at Hawthorne, Nevada, and Hastings, Nebraska. At other times, however, African American soldiers were located at military bases near African American communities. The 5000 soldiers and sailors stationed at Seattle's Fort Lawton, Fort Lewis near Tacoma, or the naval base at Bremerton visibly increased the black presence in the Puget Sound region. Comparable concentrations

of servicemen in the San Francisco Bay Area, Los Angeles, San Diego, Denver, and San Antonio all had a similar effect (Nash 1985, 105-6; Russell 1995, 76-80).

Western African American men shared the nation's joy on V-J Day, but the celebration soon ceased. By war's end, Western industrialists were scaling back war-related production and employees. Kaiser shipyards in Richmond shrank their workforce from 47,000 in December 1944 to 9000 in March 1946, a pace matched by other defense plants and shipyards. By 1947, thousands of unemployed black men who had been "essential workers" during the war now roamed the streets of Los Angeles, Oakland, and Portland. In 1947, black Oaklanders composed half of those applying for indigent relief, although they comprised only 10 percent of the city's population. Nearly half of the 4000 blacks in Vallejo, California, were unemployed. The prospects for postwar employment in Portland were so dismal that the black population declined by 50 percent (11,000) between 1944 and 1947 (Taylor 1998, 273-74).

Those African American communities that were larger in size became more politically visible and active. In 1943, an African American named Earl Mann, of Denver, was elected to the Colorado legislature. Five years later, Berkeley pharmacist W. Byron Rumford went to the California Assembly, where he joined Los Angeles assemblyman Augustus Hawkins. In 1950, attorney Charles Stokes who had arrived in Seattle only in 1944, became the first African American from his city to serve in the

Washington state legislature, while Hayzel Daniels and Carl Sims were elected to the Arizona legislature. A postwar political coalition of San Antonio blacks and Latinos elected Gus García and George Sutton to the local school board in 1948. Sutton was the first black elected official in Texas since the nineteenth century (Taylor 1998, 275).

Black Western popular culture soon brought changes to literature and music. Chester Himes's novel *If He Hollers, Let Him Go* was the first to capture the wartime migrant experience. But the greatest impact could be heard in bars and clubs and eventually on radios and in concert halls. Los Angeles's Central Avenue became the fountainhead of new jazz music styles such as bebop, pioneered by newcomers Charlie Parker, Dizzy Gillespie, and Coleman Hawkins, or the "cool jazz" of Nat King Cole, who teamed with local musicians such as Dexter Gordon, Charles Mingus, and Eric Dolphy. Central Avenue's numerous nightclubs and after-hours bars stretched seven miles from downtown to Watts, rivaling New York's famed 52nd Street (Marmorstein 1988; Cox 1996, 65-70).

THE STRUGGLE
FOR CIVIL RIGHTS

One half of the Double V campaign to defeat the Axis ended with V-J Day. The other half, the struggle for civil rights, continued virtually without interruption. Western black men confronted job discrimination, housing bias, and de facto school segregation through legal challenges and direct-action protests such as sit-ins and other public demonstrations. The legal effort reached its apogee with the 1954 U.S. Supreme Court decision *Brown* v. *Board of Education of Topeka*. However, direct action preceded and followed the *Brown* decision (Taylor 1998, 278-80).

On Saturday, 19 July 1958, Ron Walters, a Wichita State College freshman and head of the Wichita NAACP Youth Council, led 10 African American high school and college students in a four-week sit-in at the Dockum drugstore lunch counter. The students won their battle, preceding by almost two years the more famous sit-ins in Greensboro, North Carolina. The Wichita campaign also marked the beginning of seven years of direct-action protests in a dozen Western cities from San Antonio to Seattle. One of the largest protests, a challenge of the discriminatory hiring practices at the Sheraton Palace Hotel in San Francisco in 1963, involved 1500 demonstrators, including a young attorney, Willie Brown, and became the single largest civil rights action in the Far West (Taylor 1998, 285-92).

On 11 August 1965, in a predominately African American neighborhood near Watts, California Highway Patrolman Lee Minikus stopped 21-year-old Marquette Frye and in the process touched off the Watts riot, the largest African American civil uprising in the nation's history. When the conflict was over, 34 people were dead—29 blacks, 3 Latinos, 1 Asian, and 1 white. After 1965, the name "Watts" symbolized poverty, anger, alienation, resentment, and a disturbing future for urban America (Horne 1995, 96).

Although the cry "black power" was first heard during a Canton, Mississippi, speech by Stokely Carmichael, its major manifestation evolved in the West. Within a year of the Watts uprising, Maulana Ron Karenga founded United Slaves (US) and soon emerged as the most prominent black nationalist in Los Angeles. In February 1966, he organized the first Watts Summer Festival, to honor the dead and recast the riot as a revolt. The festival attracted 130,000 people. Karenga also supported Freedom City, a proposal to allow Watts to secede from Los Angeles (Tyler 1983, 45, 221-22; Horne 1995, 200-201).

Karenga promoted his views in a series of interviews with national newsmagazines in 1966. In an interview with John Gregory Dunne, Karenga dismissed the civil rights movement's goals. "Why integrate? Why live where we are not wanted?" And to Andrew Kopkind he reported, "Blacks should control their own communities. . . . We are free men. We have our own language. . . . Only slaves and dogs are named by their masters." Karenga soon eclipsed all rivals except Imamu Amiri Baraka of Newark, New Jersey, as the leading black nationalist in the United States (Taylor 1998, 303-4).

The origins of the Black Panther Party in Oakland reveal a similar repudiation of the civil rights struggle. Black Panthers founders Huey P. Newton and Bobby Seale conducted their first meeting at a West Oakland clubhouse on 15 October 1966. Newton and Seale had histories much like those of thousands of black Oakland residents, whom the new party vowed to defend. Born in Monroe, Louisiana, Newton came west to Oakland with his family in 1945, when he was 3. Seale was born in Dallas, Texas, in 1936 but grew up in Codornices Village, the sprawling housing project that straddled the Berkeley-Albany border. Newton and Seale were members of the generation of black Westerners who, unlike their shipbuilding parents, could not secure a place in the postwar Bay Area economy. In 1961, Newton and Seale met at Oakland City College, drawn together by their mutual admiration for Malcolm X, "street brothers," and socialist theories (Newton 1973, 11-72, 105-9; Seale 1968, 4-8).

The Panthers called for armed self-defense of black communities, urged African Americans to embrace Marxism, and espoused alliances with other U.S. radicals and with revolutionary governments throughout the world. Moreover, the Panthers believed that direct confrontation with police across the United States would hasten the revolutionary struggle they and their allies were destined to win (Pearson 1994, 112-13).

The Panthers never found common ground with Maulana Ron Karenga's US. Both the Panthers' Southern California chapter and US operated in South Central Los Angeles and drew from the same constituency of impoverished, alienated black youths. To appeal to these youths, many of whom had gang backgrounds, both organizations promoted their streetwise bravado, which quickly devolved into a series of street confrontations culminating in the bloody 1969 shoot-out on the University of California at Los Angeles campus that left Los Angeles Panthers Alprentice "Bunchy" Carter and John Huggins dead in a dispute over the first director of the campus's new Afro-American Studies Center (Brown 1992, chap. 8; Tyler 1983, 227-34).

Despite the evidence of racism all around them, many African American men continued to believe the West offered a chance for both economic opportunity and political freedom. Economic opportunity propelled hundreds of free blacks to enter Mexican Texas in the 1820s and thousands to come to Gold Rush California in the 1850s. In the 1890s, tens of thousands came to homestead in Oklahoma Territory for "the last chance for a free home." Seeking similar opportunity, 200,000 African Americans migrated to West Coast shipyards and aircraft plants during World War II. Indeed, the desire for freedom seemed centuries older than the quest for land. Ironically, the words of a deposition by a black woman, Isabel de Olvera, in anticipation of her move north in 1600 from central Mexico to what would become New Mexico, best summarized the views of black men. Expressing concern that she might face racially inspired discrimination, Olvera said, "It is proper to protect my rights. . . . I demand justice," and thereby illustrated a determination to challenge that discrimination. In their own way, black male Westerners who fought segregated Kansas schools from the 1870s to the 1950s, who

refused to accept the Boilermakers' discriminatory union plan during World War II, or who confront racial discrimination today through the courts or in direct-action protests continue the legacy of Olvera; they, too, demand justice ("Gordejuela Inspection" 1953, 562).

References

Anderson, Robert. 1967. *From Slavery to Affluence: Memoirs of Robert Anderson, Ex-Slave*. Steamboat Springs, CO: Steamboat Pilot.

Archibald, Katherine. 1947. *Wartime Shipyard: A Study in Cultural Disunity*. Berkeley: University of California Press.

Bandelier, F., ed. 1905. *The Journey of Alvar Nunez Cabeza de Vaca*. New York: A. S. Barnes.

Berwanger, Eugene. 1981. *The West and Reconstruction*. Urbana: University of Illinois Press.

Bonner, Thomas D., ed. 1972. *Life and Adventures of James Beckwourth*. Lincoln: University of Nebraska Press.

Broussard, Albert. 1977. The New Racial Frontier: San Francisco's Black Community: 1900-1940. Ph.D. diss., Duke University.

———. 1993. *Black San Francisco: The Struggle for Racial Equality in the West, 1900-1954*. Lawrence: University Press of Kansas.

Brown, Elaine. 1992. *A Taste of Power: A Black Woman's Story*. New York: Pantheon Books.

Bunch, Lonnie, III. 1988. *Black Angelenos: The Afro-American in Los Angeles, 1850-1950*. Los Angeles: California Afro-American Museum.

Campbell, Randolph B. 1989. *An Empire for Slavery: The Peculiar Institution in Texas, 1821-1865*. Baton Rouge: Louisiana State University Press.

Coleman, Ronald. 1980. A History of Blacks in Utah, 1825-1910. Ph.D. diss., University of Utah.

Cox, Bette Yarbrough. 1996. *Central Avenue—Its Rise and Fall (1890-c.1955)*. Los Angeles: Beem.

Cox, Thomas C. 1982. *Blacks in Topeka: A Social History*. Baton Rouge: Louisiana State University Press.

Crumbly, F. H. 1905. A Los Angeles Citizen. *The Colored American Magazine* 9(Sept.):482-85.

Daniels, Douglas Henry. 1980. *Pioneer Urbanites: A Social and Cultural History of Black San Francisco*. Philadelphia: Temple University Press.

Debo, Angie. 1941. *The Road to Disappearance*. Norman: University of Oklahoma Press.

Dobie, J. Frank, ed. 1924. *Legends of Texas*. Austin: Texas Folklore Society.

Doran, Michael F. 1975. Population Statistics of Nineteenth Century Indian Territory. *Chronicles of Oklahoma* 53(4):501-2.

Fisher, James A. 1971. A History of the Political and Social Development of the Black Community in California, 1850-1950. Ph.D. diss., State University of New York at Stony Brook.

Gibbs, Mifflin W. 1968. *Shadow and Light: An Autobiography*. New York: Arno Press and the New York Times.

Gordejuela Inspection: Inspection Made by Don Juan de Onate and Juan de Sotelo by Order of Gaspar de Zuniga y Acevedo, Count of Monterrey, Governor and Captain General of New Spain, August, 1600, The. 1953. In *Don Juan de Onate: Colonizer of New Mexico, 1595-1628*, ed. George P. Hammond and Agapito Rey. Vol. 5. Albuquerque: University of New Mexico Press.

Guenther, Todd. 1989. "Y'all Call Me Nigger Jim Now, But Someday You'll Call Me Mr. James Edwards": Black Success on the Plains of the Equality State. *Annals of Wyoming* 61(2):20-40.

Hafen, LeRoy R. 1928. The Last Years of James P. Beckwourth. *Colorado Magazine* 5(4):134-39.

———. 1965. A Brief History of the Fur Trade of the Far West. In *The Mountain Men and the Fur Trade of the Far West*, ed. LeRoy Hafen. Vol. 1. Glendale, CA: Arthur H. Clark.

Haley, James Evetts. 1949. *Charles Goodnight, Cowman and Plainsman*. Norman: University of Oklahoma Press.

Hall, Frank. 1895. *History of the State of Colorado*. Chicago: Blakely Printing.

Hallenbeck, Cleve, ed. 1987. *The Journey of Fray Marcos de Niza*. Dallas: Southern Methodist University Press.

Harris, William H. 1981. Federal Intervention in Union Discrimination: FEPC and West Coast Shipyards During World War II. *Labor History* 22(3):325-47.

Hill, Herbert. 1977. *Black Labor and the American Legal System*. Vol. 1, *Race Work and the Law*. Washington, DC: Bureau of National Affairs.

Horne, Gerald. 1995. *Fire This Time: The Watts Uprising and the 1960s*. Charlottesville: University Press of Virginia.

Jefferson, Robert Franklin. 1995. Making the Men of the 93rd: African American Servicemen in the Years of the Great Depression and the Second World War, 1935-1947. Ph.D. diss., University of Michigan.

Johnson, Marilyn. 1993. *The Second Gold Rush: Oakland and the East Bay in World War II*. Berkeley: University of California Press.

Kesselman, Amy. 1990. *Fleeting Opportunities: Women Shipyard Workers in Portland and Vancouver During World War II and Reconversion*. Albany: State University of New York Press.

Lapp, Rudolph. 1977. *Blacks in Gold Rush California*. New Haven, CT: Yale University Press.

Marmorstein, Gary. 1988. Central Avenue Jazz: Los Angeles Black Music of the Forties. *Southern California Quarterly* 70(4):415-26.

Mason, Kenneth. 1994. Paternal Community: African Americans and Race Relations in San Antonio, Texas, 1867-1937. Ph.D. diss., University of Texas at Austin.

McDonald, Dedra S. 1995. Slavery and Freedom in the Southwest: African Descendants in Spanish Colonial New Mexico. Manuscript.

Minto, John. 1901. Reminiscences of Experiences on the Oregon Trail in 1844. *Oregon Historical Quarterly* 2(3):209-54.

Moore, Shirley Ann. 1989. The Black Community in Richmond, California, 1910-1963. Ph.D. diss., University of California, Berkeley.

Morgan, Lael. 1992. Writing Minorities out of History: Black Builders of the Alcan Highway. *Alaska History* 7(2):1-13.

Nash, Gerald D. 1985. *The American West Transformed: The Impact of the Second World War*. Bloomington: Indiana University Press.

Newton, Huey P. 1973. *Revolutionary Suicide*. New York: Harcourt Brace Jovanovich.

Oswald, Delmont R. 1965. James P. Beckwourth. In *The Mountain Men and the Fur Trade of the Far West*, ed. LeRoy Hafen. Glendale, CA: Arthur H. Clark.

Pearson, Hugh. 1994. *The Shadow of the Panther: Huey Newton and the Price of Black Power in America*. Reading, MA: Addison-Wesley.

Prince, Diane Elizabeth. 1967. William Goyens, Free Negro on the Texas Frontier. M.A. thesis, Stephen F. Austin State College.

Proceedings of the First State Convention of the Colored Citizens of the State of California. 1855. Sacramento, CA: Democratic State Journal Printer.

Rice, Marc. 1996. Frompin' in the Great Plains: Listening and Dancing to the Jazz Orchestras of Alphonso Trent, 1925-44. *Great Plains Quarterly* 16(2):107-15.

Russell, Beverly. 1995. War II Boomtown: Hastings and the Naval Ammunition Depot. *Nebraska History* 76(2-3):75-83.

Sapper, Gary. 1972. A Survey of the History of the Black People of Texas, 1930-1954. Ph.D. diss., Texas Tech University.

Savage, W. Sherman. 1953. The Influence of Alexander Liedesdorff on the History of California. *Journal of Negro History* 38(3):322-32.

Seale, Bobby. 1968. *Seize the Time: The Story of the Black Panther Party and Huey P. Newton*. New York: Vintage Books.

Smith, Alonzo N. and Quintard Taylor. 1980. Racial Discrimination in the Workplace: A Study of Two West Coast Cities During the 1940s. *Journal of Ethnic Studies* 8(1):35-54.

SoRelle, James M. 1992. The Emergence of Black Business in Houston, Texas: A Study of Race and Ideology, 1919-45. In *Black Dixie: Afro-Texan History and Culture in Houston*, ed. Howard Beeth and Cary Wintz. College Station: Texas A&M University Press.

Stowe, David W. 1992. Jazz in the West: Cultural Frontier and Region During the Swing Era. *Western Historical Quarterly* 23(1):53-73.

Taylor, Quintard. 1994. *The Forging of a Black Community: Seattle's Central District from 1870 Through the Civil Rights Era*. Seattle: University of Washington Press.

———. 1998. *In Search of the Racial Frontier: African Americans in the American West, 1528-1990*. New York: W. W. Norton.

Twichell, Heath. 1992. *Northwest Epic: The Building of the Alaska Highway*. New York: St. Martin's Press.

Tyler, Bruce. 1983. Black Radicalism in Southern California, 1950-1982. Ph.D. diss., University of California at Los Angeles.

U.S. Bureau of the Census. 1853. *Seventh Census of the United States: 1850.* Washington, DC: Robert Armstrong.

———. 1864. *Eighth Census of the United States, 1860.* Washington, DC: Government Printing Office.

———. 1897. *Population of the United States, 1890.* Part II. Washington, DC: Government Printing Office.

———. 1918. *Negro Population in the United States, 1790-1915.* Washington, DC: Government Printing Office.

———. 1943. *Sixteenth Census of the United States, 1940, Population.* Vol. 2, *Characteristics of the Population.* Washington, DC: Government Printing Office.

———. 1952. *Seventeenth Census of the United States, 1950, Census of the Population.* Vol. 2, *Characteristics of the Population.* Washington, DC: Government Printing Office.

———. 1953. *Census of Population, 1950.* Vol. 2, *Characteristics of the Population.* Washington, DC: Government Printing Office.

Webb, Hertha Auburn. 1957. D. W. "80 John" Wallace: Black Cattleman, 1875-1939. M.A. thesis, Prairie View A&M College.

Weber, David J. 1982. *The Mexican Frontier, 1821-1846: The American Southwest Under Mexico.* Albuquerque: University of New Mexico Press.

Woods, Randall B. 1981. *A Black Odyssey: John Lewis Waller and the Promise of American Life, 1878-1900.* Lawrence: Regents Press of Kansas.

Woolfolk, George Ruble. 1976. *The Free Negro in Texas, 1800-1860: A Study in Cultural Compromise.* Ann Arbor: University Microfilms International.

The Media and the Black Response

By LEWIS DIUGUID and ADRIENNE RIVERS

ABSTRACT: African American men have played a role in all aspects of the media in the United States, but their participation has not always been welcomed or come easily. The dominant media have either excluded African Americans or portrayed them in such a bad light that some black people may have preferred exclusion. But over the years African Americans have used adversity to motivate them to create opportunities for themselves. Racist editorial attacks on black people motivated Samuel Cornish and John Russworm to found the country's first black newspaper. Years later, Percy Sutton purchased his first station, WLIB radio (New York), as a means of marshaling political power for the city's black and Hispanic communities. As the twentieth century comes to a close, African American men work in all areas of the media in positions ranging from technicians to owners. The level of their authority and their images vary, but they have a definite presence.

Lewis Diuguid serves as the Kansas City Star's *vice president for community resources and serves on the paper's editorial board. He writes two weekly columns in the paper's opinion section and cochairs the diversity initiative at the paper.*

Adrienne Rivers, an associate professor of journalism at the University of Kansas, teaches a course on minorities and the media. The former television news producer's research interests include the development of private media in Africa.

T HE media have not been kind to African American males. Throughout America's history, black men, teenagers, and boys too often have been depicted as buffoons, criminals, or oversexed animal-like creatures who lust after white women. That followed a design in this country to maintain an inferior, second-class status for black people, dating from slavery on through the twentieth century. The aftermath of the civil rights movement brought about some change, but the media first had to be shown what they had done wrong. As Jannette L. Dates and Edward C. Pease (1994) wrote,

The Kerner Commission, established by President Lyndon B. Johnson after the civil disorders of the mid-1960s, severely criticized the nation's media for failing to transmit information adequately about race relations and ghetto problems and urged the media to "bring more Black people into journalism" in order to make that possible. (90)

The Kerner Commission (officially called the National Advisory Commission on Civil Disorders) and others pointed out that the media were viewing the diverse and multicultural news and events in this country through the lens of a monoculture—the culture of white males. What appeared in newspapers, magazines, television, and radio were distorted images of people who were different. Andrew Hacker (1994) wrote that African Americans know that the dominant media are white: "To their eyes, the mainstream media speak for a white nation, which expects all citizens to conform to its ways. Nor do they see that much has changed since the Kerner Commission remarked, 'The media report and write from the standpoint of a white man's world'" (84). That lack of diversity remains a problem in the media. The National Association of Black Journalists reported in June 1999 that black journalists hold only 2955, or just 5.36 percent, of the nation's newsroom jobs. By 1998, minorities held a total of 11.55 percent of U.S. newsroom jobs. The American Society of Newspaper Editors (ASNE) in 1978 (when minorities held only 4.00 percent of newsroom jobs) set a deadline of the year 2000 to have the percentage of minorities holding professional newsroom jobs equal the percentage of minorities in the population. The percentage of minorities in the population is rapidly approaching 30 percent today; African Americans make up 13 percent of the total U.S. population. ASNE decided to push back to 2025 its goal of parity with the population. Vernon Stone reported in his latest study that minorities made up 18 percent of the television news workforce and 11 percent of the radio news workforce in 1994 (Stone 1999a, 1999b).

Here is what shows up when diversity in media jobs goes begging. The November 1998 issue of *The Freedom Forum and Newseum News* reported that a Women and Men and Media study of sound bites from experts on network newscasts showed definite bias toward white men. The study, "Who Speaks for America? Sex, Age and Race on the Network News," showed that 87 percent of the experts on network newscasts were males, 92 percent of whom were white. The sound bites from the people on the street showed more diversity. About 41 percent of them came from women, and 14 percent were from people of color. The impression that these findings give the public is that only white males are educated, competent, and qualified to speak authoritatively. Clint C. Wilson II and Felix Gutierrez (1985) wrote, "Blacks, Latinos, Native Americans, Asians and other people of color were treated as fringe audiences, not important enough in numbers to dictate the content that would be directed to the mass audience" (39, 41, 42). The authors noted,

The technique developed by the mass media in dealing with racial minorities and others outside the mainstream involved symbols and stereotypes. The mass media, because they dealt with a wide audience, came to rely on symbols and stereotypes as a shorthand way of communicating through headlines, characters and pictures. . . .

Racial minority groups were among the groups portrayed by symbols and stereotypes in the entertainment and news media. Whites might be seen in a wide range of roles in a movie ranging from villains to heroes. In contrast, blacks were seen only as comical mammys, wide-eyed coons, or lazy, shuffling no-goods. There were no alternative portrayals to counter the stereotype. (41-42)

The news media also are guilty of using media stereotypes to define African American males. As Katheryn K. Russell (1998) wrote,

The public representation of Blackness is a distorted one. The media as well as the academic community are largely responsible for this caricature. Blacks are rou-

tinely portrayed as marginal, deviant members of society. The exceptions to these portrayals have been insufficient to alter the public's perception. These deeply rooted images are clearly holdovers from slavery. Our public language on race and crime makes it difficult to combat these stereotypical images. (149)

Russell wrote that the media images that criminalize black men are responsible for racial hoaxes as crimes. She cited the Susan Smith case as her first example. Smith, a white South Carolina mother, in October 1994 told police that a black man had carjacked her vehicle, which contained her two sons, aged 3 years and 14 months. She appeared on national television along with a composite drawing of the suspect. Russell (1998) wrote, "Nine days after an extensive federal and state manhunt for the fictional Black carjacker, Smith confessed to murdering her sons" (69).

Russell found 67 racial hoaxes nationwide between 1987 and 1996. She found that 70 percent were perpetrated by whites who fabricated crimes against blacks. A hoax is "when someone fabricates a crime and blames it on another person because of his race or when an actual crime has been committed and the perpetrator falsely blames someone because of his race" (Russell 1998, 70).

The prevalence of racial hoaxes leads to bigger societal problems and a cycle that perpetuates stereotypes and a criminal image of African American males.

Racial hoaxes that target Blacks create a distinct, more acute social problem than hoaxes that target people of other races. Blacks in general and young Black men in particular are saddled with a deviant image. In fact, crime and young Black men have become synonymous in the American mind. . . . These images have combined to create the "criminal black-man." (Russell 1998, 71)

Racial hoaxes are devised, perpetrated, and successful precisely because they tap into widely held fears. The harm of the racial hoax is not limited to reinforcing centuries-old deviant images of blacks. Hoaxes also create these images for each new generation.

THE OVERALL EFFECT OF NEGATIVE MEDIA PORTRAYALS

The media have left this country with a misimpression of crime and of who commits most of the illegal acts, wrote Ray Suarez (1999). The result is continuing white flight from urban cores and a fear of African American males. According to Suarez, the media, especially television news, have led white, middle-class people to develop a heightened sense of becoming a victim of crime.

The exaggerated feelings of vulnerability to crime among the white middle class has helped remake the urban landscape in the last 50 years. But that feeling of vulnerability does not square with who really suffers from crime. In a country in which 70 percent of the people call themselves white, only 49 percent of crime victims are actually white. The black population of the United States floats around 12 to 13 percent; crime victims are black 49 percent of the time. (244)

Suarez reasoned that the faulty perception of many white people that they were likely to be a crime victim nurtured the "scare talk of crime, dangerous urban youth, and dangerous communities" (244).

It is the media, then, that implant the stereotype of African American males' being criminal. Television programs such as *PJs*, *Sparks*, and others also show black men as skirt chasers, athletes, and clowns. Those are likely the only images many white people will have of African Americans because this country is still very segregated. Those media stereotypes subconsciously come to the fore whenever people have to face African Americans who are seeking an education, housing, goods or services, or jobs or promotions. Those negative images act like chains and shackles holding African Americans back and making it harder for them to be seen as just as competent and committed as anyone else. Unlike their white colleagues, African Americans have to overcome long chains of media stereotypes. What is worse are the low expectations that these media stereotypes create for African American males. Media images of what being black is include foul language, poor performance in school, criminal behavior, athletic prowess, buffoonish conduct, bad attitudes, and skirt chasing. The stereotypes hold adult African Americans back. Young African Americans who witness that internalize those limitations and create for themselves a generation-wide barrier to achievement. Pushing ever upward since slavery has been what being black truly is.

It is no wonder that nearly half of the 1.8 million people in prison in the United States are black. Law enforcement suspects and then captures people based on believing the stereotype of bad behavior by black people. The institutions of society have programmed this capture to occur. In turn, too many African American males fall into the trap of thinking that acting criminally is what being black is, when in fact it is all part of a historical lie.

It would be easy to walk away from all of this distressful news with feelings of despair and hopelessness. However, many media companies are training their staffs to value diversity and to appreciate the richness of America's multicultural population. The aim is to tell the truth and give the public a fuller and more accurate picture of all the people of this nation. Perhaps more important is that more print and broadcast media are training, recruiting, hiring, and promoting more African Americans and other people of color. This will enable the media to do a better job of telling the stories of African Americans from the historical perspective of being black in America. Dr. Carter G. Woodson (1990) wrote years ago, "As an English abolitionist said more than a century ago, 'The portrait of the Negro has seldom been drawn but by the pencil of his oppressor, and the Negro has sat for it in the distorted attitude of slavery' " (180). The start of the black press in 1827 with *Freedom's Journal* was the beginning of black people's telling their own story—the truth. The

growth in the number of African Americans in mainstream media jobs has increased the opportunity for more diversity of media coverage and more truth being known about African American males.

AFRICAN AMERICAN
MALES AND THE MEDIA

The media industry in the United States has a racist history. Whether one examines the newspaper industry, the radio industry, the film industry, or the television industry, the history of each includes segments where those in control enforced policies or practices to exclude or denigrate anyone who was not a white male. This disdain often did not, however, stop those in power from appropriating the work or creativity of those who were not white. Despite such obstacles, black men have played a role in all the media of the United States; their contributions have helped shape all aspects of the print and broadcasting industries, especially the arenas of news and entertainment. Some of the results of their and others' work is that today's media environment includes magazines such as *Emerge* and *Essence*, the cable network BET, the Burrell Advertising Agency, and media associations such as the National Black Media Coalition and the National Association of Black Journalists. These organizations are here today because African Americans had the foresight and energy to fight for ways to control how the United States and the world view the African American. Not all African Americans agree with all of the images created by African Americans, but the fact that there are images that vary and that black people create some of these images is an achievement worth noting.

THE BLACK MALE AND THE PRINT MEDIA

The tradition of black people's publishing challenges to the lies told about them began when Samuel Cornish and John Russworm started the first black newspaper, *Freedom's Journal*, in 1827. They clearly stated their purpose in one of their first editorials: "We wish to plead our own cause. Too long have others spoken for us" (Dates 1990, 346).

Lionel C. Barrow, a former dean of the Howard University School of Communications, wrote that *Freedom's Journal* was the first of 42 black periodicals published in the United States before Emancipation (Barrow 1977). According to Barrow, the black press played four basic functions. It served as a watchdog for the black community; it provided a platform for responding to attacks against blacks published in white newspapers; it provided a different viewpoint, "even from that of liberal whites" (35); and it transmitted and preserved black culture. Willis Hodges's *Ram's Horn* and Frederick Douglass's *North Star* (both of which began publication in 1847) illustrate these functions perfectly. Hodges began publishing the *Ram's Horn* after the editor of the *New York Sun* refused to run Hodges's retort to some of the *Sun's* anti-black editorials. The editor told Hodges he would run the piece as a $15 ad, which the editor would modify. "When Hodges protested, he was told 'The Sun shines for all white men and not for colored men.' If he wanted the Afro-American cause advocated, he should found his own paper" (Barrow 1977, 34). Hodges, described as a militant, free black whitewasher, ran his paper until it closed in 1848. By that time, it had reached a circulation of 2500, which was par with the circulation figures of white newspapers of the day.

Douglass began publishing the *North Star*, Barrow (1977) wrote, "not only to prove that Blacks could . . . but also because of differences in opinion with Garrison and other abolitionists" (35). Whereas some abolitionists called for dissolving the union between the slave and nonslave states, Douglass opposed this idea vehemently.

Vociferous opposition to slavery characterized much of the writing in the black periodicals during the first era of the black press (1827-65). However, while the number of publications grew dramatically between 1865 and 1890 (from 42 to 575), the stridency of the writing cooled down dramatically. Dates (1990) wrote that the black codes in the South and lynchings by whites did a lot to temper black newspapers. She added that the accommodationist stance staunchly advocated by Booker T. Washington also contributed to the development of a virtually muted black press. But in the 1900s, a new era of the black press began with the publication of papers such as the *Boston Guardian* by William Monroe

Trotter and the *Chicago Defender* (1905) by Robert S. Abbott.

The outspokenness of these and other black publications helped bring attention to the irony of black soldiers' fighting a war to protect rights that they did not enjoy at home. Editorials, commentaries, and articles in these publications also contributed to the black migration to the North and to national discussions about how blacks were portrayed in the media.

The period of 1900-1954 was the heyday of the black press. Black newspapers enjoyed wide circulation and were clearly instrumental in bringing about social change, some of which had a negative impact on the black press. The end of legal segregation thanks to cases like *Brown* v. *Board of Education of Topeka* opened up doors at some of the mainstream publications for talented journalists of the black press. The civil unrest of the 1960s had the mainstream press actively pursuing these journalists.

The black press still exists today, albeit with nowhere near the vibrancy or clout it maintained in the early 1900s. The positive side of this is that some of the country's leading newspapers include the names of black men. A check of employee directories of the late 1990s shows that Harry Williams is an editor at the *St. Louis Post-Dispatch*, Gromer Jeffers is a reporter at the *Kansas City Star*, and Calvin Lawrence is a copyeditor at *Newsday*. Some of these black newspapermen have also received national recognition for their work. Angelo Henderson at the *Wall Street Journal* won the Pulitzer Prize for feature reporting in 1999. Clarence Page won a Pulitzer in 1989 for his commentaries while at the *Chicago Tribune*, and William Raspberry received the award in 1994 for commentaries in the *Washington Post*.

Samuel Adams and the late Robert C. Maynard are examples of men who have made significant contributions to the industry by serving as mentors in addition to their work as journalists. Adams earned recognition for the series of articles he produced for the *Atlanta Constitution* while he traveled in the South testing the newly enacted civil rights laws. But he has had even more impact as a mentor and teacher at the University of Kansas School of Journalism. Maynard nurtured a number of journalism careers at the *Oakland Tribune*, the paper he owned and published, and helped ensure that this practice would continue by establishing the Maynard Institute of Journalism Education.

The newspaper journalists noted here constitute only a small fraction of the number of African American men who have contributed to the newspaper industry. They accomplish this task while demonstrating excellence and while maintaining a sense of how far the industry has come since the day in the 1800s when a newspaper editor said his paper published for everyone but black people. Many of today's black newspapermen continue to hone their skills while remaining mindful of the changes the newspaper industry must make to reflect the diversity that is America.

The history of magazine publishing by blacks dates back as far as the first black newspaper. "New-England born militant black abolitionist" David Ruggles was the editor of *Mirror of Liberty*, which was published in New York in 1838 (Lee 1997, 565). This quarterly had anti-slavery as its main theme. Thomas Hamilton began publication of the *Anglo-African Magazine* in 1859. It became a weekly and ran until 1885.

Other magazines also came and went during this period. One of the struggles all of the publications faced was the limited readership the publishers could expect in the black community. The proscription against enslaved blacks' learning to read meant that even among freed black people, who might be able to afford the publications, the literacy rate was still low. Nevertheless, this challenge did not stop the publication of magazines. Later publications included *Small's Illustrated Monthly* (1905), *Paul Jones Monthly Magazine* (1907), and the *Colored American Magazine* (1900-1909). Writers of the Harlem Renaissance—Countee Cullen, Claude McKay, James Weldon, Arna Bontemps, and others—found outlets for their creativity in black magazines such as these and in W.E.B. Du Bois's *Horizon* (1907-10) and *The Crisis*, which is still published today by the National Association for the Advancement of Colored People.

Other black magazines today include John Johnson's *Ebony* and *Jet* magazines. *Ebony* is widely read here in the states and abroad and serves as a good resource for keeping up with the famous and nearly famous black people in the United States. The format has proven so successful that Johnson has begun publishing *Ebony South Africa*. *Emerge*, owned by Robert Johnson, bills itself as black America's newsmagazine. It offers a look at national and international political issues as well as the arts. Earl Graves's *Black Enterprise* takes a no-fluff approach to economic issues and opportunities and is targeted to African American entrepreneurs and executives.

Of course, part of the appeal of newspapers and magazines lies in the photographs that grace their pages. Again, historically, black people did not fare well in the photographs of the early days of the newspaper and magazine industries. Photographers James VanDerZee and Prentice Herman Polk helped change that. These men were among some of this country's first black photographers. Both produced portrait photographs of African Americans in the late nineteenth century that portrayed their subjects in kinder terms than what typically appeared in general publications. Of course, world-renowned photographer, writer, and screenwriter Gordon Parks has received recognition for his black-and-white photographs of life in the United States—photographs that offer commentary on the impact of race and poverty in this country.

In the late 1980s, a group of 50 black photojournalists offered a dramatic look at the United States with the publication of their photo essay, *Songs of My People: African-Americans, a Self Portrait* (Easter, Cheers, and Brooks 1992). Some of the men who worked on this project include D. Michael Cheers, Dudley M. Brooks, and Eric Easter.

While black men were establishing a newspaper and magazine tradition, they were also publishing books. Dates and Barlow (1990) wrote that it was the stereotypical portrayal in popular books of the African in America as a contented slave or as the ever smiling Sambo that helped give rise to the publication of slave narratives. According to William Andrews (1997), some of these narratives appeared as early as 1760 "in the periodical press in England and the United States" (667). These earlier published narratives were short, but the narratives published by the likes of Frederick Douglass, Williams Wells Brown, and Henry Bibb often ran hundreds of pages. Dates and Barlow (1990) wrote that these narratives depicted defiant slaves who took their lives into their own hands "and were the first instances of African American voices reaching the outside world, moving beyond the black oral tradition and the slave community" (11).

Douglass wrote his slave narrative, *Narrative of the Life of Frederick Douglass, an American Slave, Written by Himself*, in 1845 (Douglass [1845] 1968). Not long afterward, some of the first African American novels appeared. According to literature scholar Maryemma Graham (1997), William Wells Brown, Frank J. Webb, and Martin Delany wrote three of the four best-known earliest black novels. These works, like so much of the writing by blacks during this period, reflected on the cruelty of slavery and the need for it to come to an end. Again, they had a black man speaking for himself.

Black writers also contributed to the media by challenging the stereotypes that were prevalent in the mainstream media. Dates and Barlow (1990) credited African American writers such as William Still and his novel *The Underground Railroad* and Charles Chestnutt and his novel *The Conjure Woman* as leading the charge in providing true descriptions of black people. According to Dates and Barlow, in *The Conjure Woman*, the character "Uncle Julius is the antithesis of Uncle Remus; this wily raconteur is more interested in preserving his integrity and surviving in the postbellum era than in glorifying antebellum slavery and remaining loyal to his former masters" (12).

By the late 1800s and early 1900s, some newspaper and magazine publishers also began publishing books. These multimedia publishers tended to publish books periodically, and they "generally published books by local authors or on subjects of regional interest" (Joyce 1997, 607). One such publisher was the Fortune and Peterson Company of New York, which also published the black newspaper *New York Age*. The company published a volume of poetry, *Dreams of Life*, by T. Thomas Fortune (1905), one of the company's owners.

Magazine publisher Thomas Hamilton, Sr., published *A Pilgrim-*

age to My Motherland: An Account of a Journey Among the Egbas and Yorubas of Central Africa, which was written by Robert Campbell (1861). Campbell wrote this book after accompanying black newspaper owner Martin Delany on a trip to Africa in 1859.

As noted throughout this article, the significance of the work of men like the novelists Martin Delany and Frank J. Webb and the men of letters who followed them was that they provided a look at the United States, and even the world, from their perspectives. Undoubtedly, the authors' race influenced their views, but so did their individual life experiences. The result was writing that reflected a variety of ways of thinking that provided readers with a more balanced view of life.

BLACK MEN AND THE BROADCAST MEDIA

While the history of broadcasting technically begins with radio, from a programming point of view, the industry's history begins with the minstrel shows. Dates and Barlow (1990) wrote that the minstrel shows of the late 1800s were, among other things, where African Americans attempted to challenge the stereotypes perpetuated by whites. Unfortunately, the black actors were not very successful in their endeavors. Derogatory depictions of blacks in minstrel shows carried over to radio almost intact. The prime example of this was the *Amos 'n' Andy* show. Barbara Dianne Savage (1999) noted that the show's popularity among radio listeners came from its use of "shared stereotypes of black men and women" (7).

Amos 'n' Andy functioned for whites in much the same way that minstrelsy and other popular depictions of racial stereotypes had in the nineteenth century. It worked to reinforce a sense of whiteness by its contrivance of blackness. . . . The show's theme of "cultural incompetence" was used to cast blacks as the "ultimate outsider" against which whites could find a unifying sense of privilege and superiority. (7)

Barlow (1990) wrote that while the depiction of African Americans was bad, their employment opportunities were worse. Radio shows during the 1920s and 1930s featured programs such as *Plantation Nights*, a "variety show set on a southern plantation, with African Americans cast as slaves singing, dancing, and joking for 'massa' and 'missus'" (182). Meanwhile, black actors found themselves having to study black dialect in order to secure employment. "Wonderful Smith, an African American comic with the 'Red Skelton Show,' was dropped from the series . . . because he had difficulty sounding as Negroid as they expected" (183).

Despite such hurdles, African Americans did have a role in radio's early days, although the role appeared to be more ad hoc than ongoing. One example was the production of *Freedom's People* in 1941-42, which came about in response to the government's fear of racial unrest in the early 1940s. The series, which aired on NBC, explored black history and culture. According to Savage (1999), "an alliance between black federal officials, prominent black intellectuals such as Alain Locke and Sterling Brown, black performing artists such as Paul Robeson, and racially moderate whites" produced the programs (15).

While Robeson frequently appeared on radio programs as a guest performer, neither he nor any of the other people Savage listed in the foregoing made their living primarily by working in radio. However, there were other blacks who did during this period. One even became a millionaire. In 1927, Jack L. Cooper began a radio show called *The Negro Hour* on Chicago station WGBC. Cooper featured the latest recordings of black artists and was the only announcer in Chicago to do so at this time. He further developed his innovation by offering the first regular black newscasts, featuring news from the *Chicago Defender* (Barlow 1990, 184). Other black men working in commercial radio at the time were "Ed Baker and Van Douglas in Detroit, Eddie Honesty and Jack Gibson in Chicago, Hal Jackson in Washington, D.C., and Norfley Whitted in Durham, North Carolina. Together they set the stage for the unusual postwar ascendancy of the African American disc jockey" (186).

It could be said that African Americans and black-oriented programming helped save the radio industry in the 1950s when television threatened its existence. By the 1950s, advertisers and radio station programmers had begun to appreciate that the African American market had not been tapped and that it would be profitable to do so. This

realization was prompted by the rise of television at the expense of the radio industry. Radio station owners who could not turn to television as a source of revenue reformatted their stations to black-oriented music instead. These black-oriented music stations and their talented African American disc jockeys made the airwaves more representative of the United States while educating the majority of the population about a segment of society that so many tried to dismiss and ignore.

The popularity of the black-formatted stations helped strengthen the presence and power of African Americans in radio. By 1972, John Johnson of *Ebony* magazine fame and Percy Sutton and his Inner City Broadcasting corporation had become the first two black owners of radio stations. That same year, the Mutual Black Network came into existence. This network provided affiliated stations with sports and news from a black perspective. It became the Sheridan Broadcasting Network in the early 1980s when the black-owned Sheridan Broadcasting Corporation purchased it. Sheridan expanded the network's offerings "to feature live broadcasts of black college sports events and public affairs shows that highlighted African American journalists and political leaders" (Barlow 1990, 227). One year later, the National Black Network formed. It, too, offered news, sports, and public affairs programming from a black perspective. The drawback to this otherwise positive development is that it filled a void that the mainstream broadcasters then became less inclined to fill. In

1986, blacks owned 150 radio stations. In 1999, African Americans owned 165 radio stations.

Television was supposed to hold a bright future for African Americans as far as inclusion and portrayals were concerned. A cursory glance would suggest that it has lived up to this expectation. Viewers saw images of black people from the earliest days of the industry. However, the quality of those images was another matter. J. Fred MacDonald (1988) noted that black musicians such as Duke Ellington, Louis Armstrong, and Cab Calloway made appearances on variety shows during television's early days. However, so did an updated version of *Amos 'n' Andy*, this time featuring black men in the roles of the main characters, who were black, instead of featuring white actors, as had been the case when the program aired on the radio. MacDonald also noted that during this period African Americans had other roles besides buffoons, singers, and dancers. "Blacks were among the nonprofessional cast on *The Black Robe*, an NBC series that in 1949 reenacted the drama of night court. A black couple was among those married on KLAC-TV's (Los Angeles) *Wedding Bells*. . . . And in 1954, explorer Matthew Henson discussed his Arctic adventures on NBC's *Today* show" (15). While these roles were not stereotypical portrayals, they were not particularly strong portrayals either.

In television news, the 1950s were an interesting period. Independence movements in Africa and domestic calls for racial justice in America resulted in African Americans' appearing on the news as subjects. Their appearance as newscasters, however, would have to wait until the next decade.

By the 1960s, African American men had begun to have stronger roles in television entertainment and television news. Bill Cosby costarred with Robert Culp in *I Spy*. Ossie Davis, Sammy Davis, Jr., and Greg Morris had roles on popular dramas. Harry Belafonte won an Emmy award in 1960, and James Earl Jones received an Emmy nomination in 1963. On the news front, ABC hired Mal Goode in 1962, making him the first black network correspondent. On the local level, African American newsmen got their breaks in the 1960s as well. Gil Noble (1981) wrote in his memoir that he got his job at the New York ABC affiliate shortly after the Kerner Commission forced the networks to hire blacks. According to Noble, black men such as Bill McCreary, Ed Williams, Clarence Rock, and Roy Davis joined him in finding employment at some of New York and New Jersey's major television and radio stations.

Black men continued to have a strong presence on television through the end of the 1960s. The 1970s, however, repeated the programming practices of the 1950s. Black men appeared on television but in stereotypical roles, epitomized by Jimmy Walker in *Good Times*. However, from the late 1970s to the mid-1980s, there was a rise in the number of black writers and producers in television. Thanks to the work of men such as Alex Haley (*Roots*),

Tim Reid (*Frank's Place*), Bill Cosby (*The Cosby Show*), and Quincy Jones (*Fresh Prince of Bel Air*), the images of black people improved and became more diverse.

The 1990s were a mixed bag as far as black men in television are concerned. The ascendancy of the Fox Network and Black Entertainment Television's cable channel along with the advent of the WB and UPN networks provided more outlets for programming featuring black actors, writers, producers, and directors. Some of the programs, such as the *Wayan's Brothers* and *Martin*, relied heavily on the stereotypical portrayal of African American men as unrefined and loud-talking. Meanwhile, programs such as *Roc* and *E.R.* provided vehicles for black men to appear in strong comedic and dramatic roles. However, a survey of 1998 movie and television roles published May 1999 in the *Kansas City Star* showed African Americans made up only 13.4 percent of the total job base, down from 14.1 percent in 1997. This trend appeared to continue in 1999. Of the 38 new television shows introduced as the lineup for the final television season of the 1990s, only two programs were built around black stars. Twenty-nine of these shows had no minority characters at all. (Several of the networks did adjust some of the programs after receiving heavy criticism from critics and advocacy groups.)

In the news industry, the presence of black men at the end of the twentieth century is mixed as well. A study cited in the *New York Daily News* (Huff 1999) reported that minorities got more air time than ever before on the Big Three evening newscasts. According to the article, minority reporters covered 15 percent of the stories in 1998, up from 7 percent in 1991. The report said minorities comprised 20 percent of the network corps, up 100 percent from 1991. But researcher Vernon Stone (1999b) reported in his latest survey of the broadcast news industry workforce that black men equaled 5.6 percent of the television news workforce and only 1.9 percent of the nation's television news directors. According to Stone, these figures represented a plateauing of the number of African American men in image-shaping and decision-making positions in television news. Be that as it may, the men who are in these positions include Ed Bradley, a long-time correspondent on CBS's *60 Minutes*; Bernard Shaw, the main anchor on CNN; long-time *ABC News* correspondent George Strait; and *NBC News* correspondent Joe Johns.

On the local level, African American men work as general managers, news directors, anchors, reporters, producers, editors, and cameramen. While Stone's research (1999b) indicates that black men will not be found in news or news management positions in every market of the United States, they will be found in most of the major markets.

CONCLUSION

Farai Chideya (1995) wrote,

Pointing out times when the media has misrepresented the African-American community can only make the media better. Pointing out issues and problems facing the African American community, no matter how painful, can only make the community better. The media belongs to all of us. If we want it to work, we have to work. (11)

In the end, all of these efforts will push the truth in front of America, showing the country the real image of African American males as mostly hard-working, taxpaying citizens with the same hopes and dreams as everyone else.

References

Andrews, William L. 1997. Introduction. In *The Oxford Companion to African American Literature*, ed. William L. Andrews, Frances Smith Foster, and Trudier Harris. New York: Oxford University Press.

Barlow, William. 1990. Commercial and Noncommercial Radio. In *Split Image: African Americans in the Mass Media*, ed. J. Dates and W. Barlow. Washington, DC: Howard University Press.

Barrow, Lionel C. 1977. Role of the Black Press in Liberation Struggle. In *Sesquicentennial 1827-1977: Black Press Handbook 1977*. Washington, DC: National Newspaper Publishers Association.

Campbell, Robert. 1861. *A Pilgrimage to My Motherland: An Account of a Journey Among the Egas and Yorubas of Central Africa*. New York: T. Hamilton.

Chideya, Farai. 1995. *Don't Believe the Hype: Fighting Cultural Misinformation About African Americans*. New York: Penguin Books.

Dates, Jannette L. 1990. Print News. In *Split Image: African Americans in the Mass Media*, ed. J. Dates and W. Barlow. Washington, DC: Howard University Press.

Dates, Jannette L. and William Barlow. 1990. Introduction: A War of Images. In *Split Image: African Americans in the Mass Media*, ed. J. Dates and W. Barlow. Washington, DC: Howard University Press.

Dates, Jannette L. and Edward C. Pease. 1994. Warping the World—Media's Mangled Images of Race. *Media Studies Journal* 8(Summer):89-96.

Douglass, Frederick. [1845] 1968. *Narrative of the Life of Frederick Douglass, an American Slave, Written by Himself*. New York: New American Library.

Easter, Eric, D. Michael Cheers, and Dudley M. Brooks, eds. 1992. *Songs of My People: African Americans, a Self-Portrait*. Boston: Little, Brown.

Fortune, T. Thomas. 1905. *Dreams of Life*. New York: Fortune & Peterson.

Graham, Maryemma. 1997. Novel. In *The Oxford Companion to African American Literature*, ed. William L. Andrews, Frances Smith Foster, and Trudier Harris. New York: Oxford University Press.

Hacker, Andrew. 1994. Are the Media Really White? *Media Studies Journal* 8(Summer):81-88.

Huff, Richard. 1999. More Women, Minority TV Reporters Gaining Airtime. *New York Daily News*, 17 Feb. Available at http://straightline.net/stories/1999/Feb/17/S532649.asp.

Joyce, Donald Franklin. 1997. Publishing. In *The Oxford Companion to African American Literature*, ed. William L. Andrews, Frances Smith Foster, and Trudier Harris. New York: Oxford University Press.

Lee, A. Robert. 1997. Black Periodical Press. In *The Oxford Companion to African American Literature*, ed. William L. Andrews, Frances Smith Foster, and Trudier Harris. New York: Oxford University Press.

MacDonald, J. Fred. 1988. *Blacks and White TV: Afro-Americans in Television Since 1948*. Chicago: Nelson-Hall.

Noble, Gil. 1981. *Black Is the Color of My TV Tube*. Secaucus, NJ: Lyle Stuart.

Russell, Katheryn K. 1998. *The Color of Crime: Racial Hoaxes, White Fear, Black Protectionism, Police Harassment and Other Macroaggressions*. New York: New York University Press.

Savage, Barbara Dianne. 1999. Introduction. In *Broadcasting Freedom: Radio, War and the Politics of Race 1938-1948*. Chapel Hill: University of North Carolina Press.

Stone, Vernon. 1999a. Minorities and Women in Radio News. Available at http://web.missouri.edu/~jourvs/raminw.html.

———. 1999b. Minorities and Women in Television News. Available at http://web.missouri.edu/~jourvs/gtvminw.html.

Suarez, Ray. 1999. *The Old Neighborhood: What We Lost in the Great Suburban Migration, 1966-1999*. New York: Free Press.

Wilson, Clint C., II and Felix Gutierrez. 1985. *Minorities and Media: Diversity and the End of Mass Communication*. Thousand Oaks, CA: Sage.

Woodson, Carter G. 1990. *The Mis-Education of the Negro*. Lawrenceville, NJ: African World Press.

Foreign-Born African American Males: Turning Barriers into Opportunities

By FESTUS E. OBIAKOR, SUNDAY O. OBI, and PATRICK GRANT

ABSTRACT: African Americans, both U.S. and foreign born, confront multidimensional problems that range from prejudicial perceptions to illusory generalizations. For many foreign-born African American males, problems include difficulty adjusting to a new cultural environment, xenophobia, and miscategorization. Despite such problems, they are able to succeed and excel in their chosen professions. In this article, case studies are used to reveal how foreign-born African American males turn barriers into opportunities. Additionally, the authors discuss implicit and explicit motivational factors that assist them in maximizing their fullest potential in mainstream American society.

Festus E. Obiakor is a professor in the Department of Exceptional Education, University of Wisconsin–Milwaukee. A teacher, scholar, and consultant in the field of special education, he is the author or coauthor of more than 100 publications.

Sunday O. Obi is an associate professor in the Division of Education and Human Services at Kentucky State University. His research interests include school reform and multicultural education.

Patrick Grant is an associate professor in the Department of Special Education at Slippery Rock University of Pennsylvania. He was instrumental in setting the stage for special education in Jamaica.

A FRICAN American males, whether born in the United States or in foreign countries, confront multidimensional problems. These problems range from misperceptions to illusory generalizations because of negative attributions to their race or skin color. Shelby Steele, an African American scholar with conservative viewpoints, agreed that

the condition of being Black in America means that one will likely endure more wounds to one's self-esteem than others and that the capacity for self-doubt born of these wounds will be compounded and expanded by the Black race's reputation of inferiority. . . . Black skin has more dehumanizing stereotypes associated with it than any other skin color in America, if not the world. When a Black presents himself in an integrated situation, he knows that his skin alone may bring these stereotypes to life in the minds of those he meets and that he, as an individual, may be diminished by his race before he has a chance to reveal a single aspect of his personality. (Steele 1990, 36)

Steele's statement has psychological, educational, socioeconomic, and political ramifications for African American males, whether they are U.S. or foreign born. In other words, African American males have the added pressure of proving themselves despite circumstances and situations that others do not encounter.

While the foregoing assertions are correct, one cannot downplay the fact that many African American males have been successful at different educational, socioeconomic, and political levels. For instance, for many foreign-born African Ameri-

cans, misperceptions on the basis of race and skin color have had little devastating effect on how they view and tackle successes and failures. It is logical to argue that other personality and motivational variables contribute to how they internalize or externalize misperceptions and biased generalizations. More than two decades ago, John Ogbu, a leading scholar on minority group issues, addressed this interesting phenomenon (Ogbu 1978). He noted that different minority groups respond to school success and failure differently. To a large extent, that response affects how these group members confront society's trials and tribulations. In this article, we use cases to analyze implicit and explicit motivational factors responsible for successes of foreign-born African American males in mainstream American society in spite of prejudicial expectations and gross generalizations.

ENDEMIC PROBLEMS CONFRONTING AFRICAN AMERICAN MALES

As indicated, African American males face a myriad of problems. As a result, many scholars (for example, Bell 1985, 1992; Staples 1984) have been critical of the ideology of equal opportunity in the United States because of racial and class stratifications. "The ideology of equal opportunity masks the reality of a country stratified along racial, gender, and class lines" (Staples 1984, 2). Staples decried the complex web of informal rules and processes that impedes achievements, opportunities, and choices for African Americans. He added that African Americans who attempt to take advantage of opportunities (for example, in colleges) experience intellectual racism. He noted, for instance, that there is a pervasive perception that African American students and faculty are unqualified and intellectually inferior to their peers and colleagues. As a consequence, affirmative action regulations designed to facilitate the recruitment and retention of minority faculty are now abused, counterproductive, and even unworkable (Staples 1984, 1986). It has been acknowledged that "no college has lost a contract because of failure to comply with affirmative action regulations nor does the government follow-up on how well schools implement their promises to remedy racial and gender imbalances in their work force" (Staples 1984, 5). Also acknowledged is the huge presence of the old-boy network and of what he calls the "new racism," which (1) tends to deny the existence of racism or the responsibility for it; (2) opposes quotas and affirmative action regulations; (3) calls for reduction in welfare, food stamps, and public housing; (4) defends phony meritocracy; and (5) relies heavily on standardized tests that are not valid predictors of quality performance (Staples 1986). Currently, race still matters in American society, and because it matters, proactive efforts must be made to alleviate its devastating effects (Banks 1999; Grossman 1998; Obiakor 1994, 1999; West 1993).

Many of the aforementioned problems have been acknowledged, in some measure, by many conservative African American scholars (for example, Loury 1985, 1992; Sowell 1993; Steele 1991); however, how these problems can be resolved has been usually the bone of contention. The belief that racism is the only impediment to opportunities and choices in all facets of American life has been long held by many, and "the pride and self-respect valued by aspiring peoples throughout the world cannot be the gift of outsiders—they must derive from the thoughts and deeds of the peoples themselves. Neither the guilt nor the pity of one's oppressor is a sufficient basis upon which to construct self-worth" (Loury 1985, 11). While Loury does not condone racism and discrimination in the provision of opportunities and choices, he castigates the African American community for what he calls the "enemy without" and the "enemy within." The enemy without includes implicit and explicit racism at all levels; the enemy within includes black-on-black crime, self-destructive tendencies, drug abuse, teenage pregnancy, and excessive reliance on government support. Like many African Americans, Loury recognizes the role of the government in resolving the critical problem of the underclass in society; he nevertheless advocates the building of constructive, internal institutions that could integrate efforts of African American business, academic, and political elites. As he has succinctly pointed out, "No people can be genuinely free so long as they look to others for their deliverance" (Loury 1985, 11).

Many foreign-born African American males find themselves entangled in the web of racism, prejudicial perceptions, xenophobia, discriminatory generalizations, and problems of adjustment to their new environment. For instance, our experiences and interactions with people have exposed us to negative assumptions about Africa, its diaspora, and its descendants, most of whom are black.

These assumptions include (a) Africa is a "dark" continent, (b) Africans are dark-skinned, (c) Africans are cannibals who live on trees and in huts, (d) Africans do not have roads, streets, and lights, (e) Africans are short, (f) African men are chauvinists, (g) African men have two or more wives, and (h) African women are not free. (Obiakor 1990-91, 3)

There are other sad examples. A few years ago, efforts were made by some scientists in the medical field to attribute the origin of the acquired immunodeficiency syndrome (AIDS) virus to Haiti. Today, in the news, high-powered efforts are also made to attribute the origin of AIDS to African monkeys. These sad notions have far-reaching implications regarding how men from these places are viewed as they socially interact in mainstream American society. The leading misconception about Africans has long been that "if you know one African, you know them all." Is it any surprise that some people view Africa as one nation with a monolithic viewpoint? Similarly, there exists a dangerous supposition that all African Americans respond to societal problems in the same fashion—this supposition treats all African Americans as one.

SAMPLE CASES AND REVELATIONS

Foreign-born African Americans, like other minorities in America, appear to confront a myriad of problems that range from implicit misconceptions to explicit xenophobia. Consider the case of the brutal beating of Rodney King by some members of the Los Angeles Police Department and the case of the brutal beating and abuse of Abner Louima or the case of the shooting and killing of Amadou Diallo by some members of the New York Police Department. These cases reveal similar trends of racial abuse, brutality, and domination of black persons by overzealous white police officers. Though these problems are similar, not all African Americans respond to issues of race and discrimination in the same way. Like other immigrant minorities, foreign-born African Americans respond to societal imperatives differently (see Ogbu 1978).

To properly explore the multidimensional problems that foreign-born African American males confront and their techniques for dealing with them, we have used cases. Our attempt is to "create experiences that embody cultural meanings, and cultural understandings that operate in the 'real' world" (Denzin 1995, 8). These cases reveal experiences and self-stories that make up important events in people's lives. They open "a parallax of discordant voices, visions, and feelings" and "yield to a cacophony of voices demanding to be heard" (14-18). In addition, they provide powerful means of learning through experiences and "represent an interesting paradox in that they are deeply personal, evolving out of an individual's experiences" (Colbert, Trimble, and Desberg 1996, xiii).

Based on the cases presented in this article, we intend to illuminate data necessary for furthering research and policy. These cases resulted from personal interactions and telephone interviews with people who immigrated to the United States from different predominantly black nations. These individuals live in different locations in the United States and are engaged in different professional careers. They were asked similar open-ended questions, namely:

1. What is your name?
2. Where are you originally from?
3. When did you come to the United States?
4. What problems did you encounter?
5. How did you tackle your problems?
6. What is your profession right now?

To get detailed information, each interview session lasted 45-60 minutes. Participants were given leeway to share their views. To respect confidentiality, in this article we did not use the real names of those interviewed. We also felt that it was unnecessary to give the exact work locations of those interviewed. We wanted to avoid fears that could prejudice subjects' responses.

Case 1

Subject 1 came originally from Nigeria to the United States in 1979, more than 20 years ago. He indicated that he has consistently endured discrimination since coming to the United States. He related, "I faced xenophobia and racism when I was working on my master's and doctoral degrees." He noted that his professors looked down on him and refused to provide him with opportunities to grow. This lack of support continued when he graduated. He was unable to get jobs in his area of expertise (geological sciences). Subject 1 did not give up despite his predicaments. He noted that perseverance, persistence, hard work, and his family values have been instrumental to his survival. At present, he is an associate professor at a university in Texas.

Case 2

Subject 2 came originally from Ghana to the United States in 1976, more than 23 years ago. As he pointed out, "I have suffered from discrimination, subtle racism, lack of networks, identity crisis, and adjustment problems." However, he noted, "I have survived because I am pragmatic, I work hard, and I am self-assured." He also added that his family values from Ghana have been useful ingredients for his success. Subject 2 indicated that he has an internal locus of control—for instance, he designs internal means to overcome his problems. Right now, he is an associate professor at a college in Mississippi.

Case 3

Subject 3 came originally from Mali to the United States in 1978, more than 21 years ago. He indicated that he lacks networks and opportunities. He also noted that he has experienced implicit and explicit racism and tremendous job discrimination and xenophobia. He has been surprised by the fact that all his peers who earned engineering degrees at the same time he did got steadier, better-paying jobs than he did. Though Subject 3's problems seem to be multidimensional, he explained that his assertiveness, perseverance, self-assured behavior, and hard work have been beneficial to him. He added that his family values have also been very helpful. At present, he is an engineer for a private company in the District of Columbia.

Case 4

Subject 4 came originally from Jamaica to the United States in 1969, more than 30 years ago. As he indicated, "I have been through so many trials and tribulations." He acknowledged that great opportunities have come his way since coming to the United States but added, "I will never forget my negative experiences in my job at a vacuum cleaning company in Illinois when a colleague referred to me as a second-class citizen or when my wife and I experienced housing discrimination." He also recounted not being allowed to swim in the swimming pool of his apartment complex. In spite of his problems, Subject 4 believes the United States is a great country that has given him the opportunity to maximize his potential. In his words, "My secrets to survival include personal confrontation, assertiveness, perseverance, and educational training." Right now, he is a successful subcontractor in Florida.

Case 5

Subject 5 came originally from Trinidad to the United States in 1976, more than 23 years ago. He noted that he has experienced overt racism and discrimination. According to him, "It is difficult to solidify friendships in the U.S. It's like no one gives a damn." He has, however, managed to survive in spite of all the odds. Subject 5 noted that he has succeeded because of individual initiative, persistence, family values, and what he calls "inner" perseverance. At present, he is an accountant for a *Fortune* 100 company in New Jersey.

Case 6

Subject 6 came originally from Nigeria to the United States in 1984, more than 15 years ago. As he indicated, "I have experienced job discrimination, financial problems, lack of opportunities, xenophobia, and psychological problems of 'not belonging' and not being accepted by whites or blacks." He felt that he was getting tired of proving himself to people since coming to the United States. Despite his problems, Subject 6 has succeeded in his endeavors because of his persistence, perseverance, hard work, and family values.

He is proud that he has been able to maximize his potential. As he says, "I have achieved a lot." At present, he is a respiratory therapist in Georgia.

Case 7

Subject 7 came originally from Ethiopia to the United States in 1975. He explained that he has experienced racism, job discrimination, lack of support, and what he calls the "white superiority complex." He added that people seem to be indifferent in the United States. For instance, he complained that many people never take him seriously. To a large extent, this has been responsible for his inability to secure employment in his field of study. Subject 7 has been able to earn his doctorate degree and establish his own business. He credits his success to his belief in himself and God, individual initiative, persistence, and hard work. As he pointed out, "I return favors and love people regardless of race, religion, political affiliation, or place of origin." Currently, he is an entrepreneur who operates his business in Kansas.

Case 8

Subject 8 came originally from Nigeria to the United States in 1989, more than 10 years ago. He had lived in Romania for many years, so he understood what culture shock was all about. In the United States, he indicated that he has experienced discrimination, linguistic problems, job-related problems, and negative perceptions. He experienced severe discrimination as a student; this discrimination had forced him to

redirect his area of study in his doctoral program. Today, Subject 8 is a certified school teacher in Illinois. He credits his survival and success to his perseverance, persistence, family values, and hard work.

Case 9

Subject 9 came originally from Jamaica to the United States in 1954, more than 45 years ago. He noted that he has experienced all forms of racism, job discrimination, housing discrimination, lack of support, and indifference of people. He remembered losing his employment in one workplace because his boss did not like the kind of book that he was reading. Another experience that remains with him is the racism he experienced as a doctoral student. He remembers, "When I was a doctoral student, some of my professors told me bluntly that I would not graduate from the program." Currently, Subject 9 is an associate professor at a university in Pennsylvania. His secrets to survival include hard work, dedication, strong belief in self, family values, a good wife and children, individual initiative, and understanding and valuing of his "blackness."

Case 10

Subject 10 came originally from Nigeria to the United States in 1977, more than 22 years ago. He recalled being treated differently by his peers and professors. He indicated, "I have experienced subtle racism by the questions that I am asked about my accent. I have also experienced the lack of support that makes me feel a little strange." In spite of his problems, Subject 10 is a successful certified public account with a master's degree in business administration. At present, he is a senior tax manager at an accounting firm in California. His success is due to his desire to make something of himself, good education, and the determination to be as good as others. He also credits his success to family values, self-awareness, and self-responsibility. As he concluded, "I try to take advantage of the unique opportunities that I have had."

Case 11

Subject 11 came originally from Haiti to the United States in 1991. In his opinion, he has experienced mild racism. In his words, "People comment on my accent. I do not go looking for racism, but I know I have experienced mild discrimination, and Black skin carries with it some form of prejudice." Subject 11 observed that he increased his potential for success in the United States through hard work, good education, perseverance, and determination. According to him, "I set high goals for myself." At present, he is a software engineer at a *Fortune* 500 company in Illinois.

Case 12

Subject 12 came originally from South Africa to the United States in 1993. In his few years in this country, he has experienced racism, job discrimination, and xenophobia. He indicated that he went to several job fairs that were fruitless. At first, he felt like giving up in the face of adversity. Although Subject 12 encountered multidimensional problems, he has been able to survive. He credits his success to perseverance, dedication, determination, and his ability to relate cross-culturally to others. At present, he is a financial analyst for an international engineering company in Kansas.

Case 13

Subject 13 came originally from Zimbabwe to the United States in 1965, more than 34 years ago. He indicated that he has experienced ethnocentrism and chauvinism in scholarship, and closed mindedness while in school. At work, his problems included lack of professional respect and recognition, and racism in faculty promotion. Sometimes he felt unwanted and resented by his peers and colleagues. Subject 13 has been able to tackle his myriad problems through perseverance, hard work, dedication, and family values. He has never believed in giving up. Right now, he is an associate professor at a university in Pennsylvania.

Case 14

Subject 14 came originally from Guyana to the United States in 1964, more than 35 years ago. While in school, he encountered professors who doubted his intelligence and ignored whatever he said. He had problems adjusting to the educational system (for example, the great emphasis on multiple-choice tests). At work, he had employers who did not expect him to be as smart as they were or who talked down to him. Those individuals apologized after the fact and made statements such as "You are different from other blacks in America." Subject 14 has encountered people who smiled at him but meant no good. On one occasion, he was promised an apartment over the telephone only to be denied the apartment when it was found that he was black. He was also shocked to learn, on several occasions, that some white people whom he called friends talked negatively about him in his absence. In his words, "Whites think you should be subservient to them even when you are more qualified than they will ever be." At present, Subject 14 is a teacher in a junior high school in Florida. In addition, he is an adjunct professor at a junior college in the same state. He credits his success to working twice as hard, learning to adjust to the system, support from friends and family members from his home country, strength of character, refusing to give up or be subordinate, refusing to allow people to let him feel less than he is, and never allowing people to make him think they are better than he.

Case 15

Subject 15 came originally from Haiti to the United States in 1986, more than 13 years ago. He indicated that he had never encountered adjustment or racist problems. In school, everyone was great. He found it easy to get jobs. As he pointed out, "I was in the union and I did not have any confrontations with my supervisors. I am a great worker and I take my work seriously." He never had interpersonal problems. He added,

I have great friends. My friends come from all over the world. They love me, and I love them, too. They helped me a lot, and they support me. Since I am a friendly person, I try to make everybody comfortable around me. I do not form my life on negative behaviors. The best way to survive in the United States is to be positive and know where you are coming from and what you want.

At present, Subject 15 is unemployed. He is a full-time student who is doing exceedingly well in his studies. His secret to survival is prayer. In his words,

I am a spiritual person. I pray a lot, and my faith in God helps me to deal with my problems. I keep a positive mind all the time. Before I face any obstacle, I ask God to show me the way before I make any decision. My ultimate weapon is prayer. I do not allow problems to take the first priority in my life.

Case 16

Subject 16 came originally from Barbados to the United States in 1969, more than 30 years ago. He indicated that his first experience with education in the United States was positive because he was recruited for his doctoral degree by the chairperson of the department. In his words, "My first negative experience was with African Americans. Now I can understand their frustration. I never experienced housing discrimination. However, my children while playing in the streets were called 'niggers' a time or two. I also found feces on my doorstep." Subject 16 has been able to survive and succeed. At present, he is a full professor at a university in Virginia. He credits his success to working twice as hard, learning to adjust to the system, support from family in his home country, strength of character, refusing to give up in the face of adversity, and developing relationships with core people.

MOTIVATIONAL FACTORS RESPONSIBLE FOR SUCCESS

From the subjects' responses, it can be said that foreign-born African American males experience racist and prejudicial patterns of behavior similar to those experienced by other African Americans or minorities in American society. Sometimes they have the added burden of proving themselves not just to the dominant whites but also to African Americans born in the United States. Subject responses reveal that all of the subjects have endured implicit and explicit racism, prejudicial expectations, and illusory generalizations. Some of the subjects recalled specific traumatic experiences (such as being fired from a job because of the kind of book read or being told bluntly by professors that graduation in particular programs was impossible). In other words, they have all endured some form of adjustment problem or identity crisis. In spite of the problems, subject responses reveal high motivational levels for all foreign-born African American males. Many have credited their survival to hard work, perseverance, self-assurance, and family values. Many have developed intrinsic motivational techniques to tackle their predicaments, and some even attribute their successes to belief in God. Based on subject responses, they all seem to be self-aware, self-responsible, and self-empowered as they created opportunities and choices for themselves (see Obiakor 1993, 1994).

As immigrant minorities, foreign-born African American males appear to reject offensive definitions of their status, which they sometimes consider better than it was in their countries of origin. In addition, they appear to devote less time to internalizing the effects of discrimination (see Ogbu 1978). As a consequence, the promises of wealth, opportunity, and sometimes political freedom are motivational forces that influence their survival strategies. It is logical to assert that foreign-born African American males overcome socioeconomic, cultural, and linguistic problems that they face by quickly adapting to new cultural challenges in their host society (Ogbu 1988, 1990). To a large degree, they begin to define "quality" from the perspective of the dominant white society.

Foreign-born African American males seem to depend a lot on their family values. For many of them, "the family is a cultural entity that will be difficult to drastically change because of its role as the cornerstone of the African culture. It is the dominant connecting force which provides a source of socio-cultural continuity. The African family unifies the delicate rough edges of the community" (Obiakor 1990-91, 3). In a nutshell, the African family focuses on reproduction, child care, socialization, economic support, collective responsibility, and status replacement. Embodied in the traditional African family is traditional education, which prepares individuals to

develop latent physical skills, inculcate respect for elders and those in position of authority, develop character, acquire specific vocational training and develop a healthy attitude toward honest labor, develop a sense of belonging and to participate actively in family and community affairs, and to understand, appreciate and promote the cultural heritage of the community at large. (Fafunwa 1975, 20)

These principles of traditional African life seem to be comparable with traditional American principles of survival and uplift.

Foreign-born African American males appear to succeed in mainstream American society because of the strong sense of character imparted to them by their respective families. Their rough edges are usually smoothed before they come to the United States. With this background, they are prepared to tackle all kinds of problems and make themselves and their families proud. Unquestionably, "the home has a great impact on children's development. The home cannot be divorced from values, symbols and cultures that students bring to school programs" (Obiakor 1992b, 7). Though there are some foreign-born African American males who abuse drugs and commit crimes, many of them are dedicated and committed to tasks. In fact, many rely on their family values to succeed in their education, job, and advancement despite endemic problems associated with immigrating to a society where race continues to matter.

Another important motivational factor responsible for the success of foreign-born African American males is their self-knowledge of who they are. They do not view themselves as victims; rather, they tend to have an accurate understanding of their personal characteristics. They also tend to have accurate self-esteem (that is, a self-descriptive behavior that reflects self-love or self-evaluation). Finally, because of the traditional respect for honest labor in their cultural upbringing, they develop an accurate self-ideal (that is, self-empowerment, or an ability to expend efforts to achieve goals). Since foreign-born African American males are able to self-analyze, they make functional goal-directed decisions (Obiakor 1992a, 1995, 1996). Their personal survival is remarkable because they do not feel hopeless, they have high expectations, and they understand the importance of effort or the importance of succeeding in the face of failure (Graham 1997).

Foreign-born African American males do not internalize prejudicial judgments with great intensity, as their U.S.-born counterparts do. Their immigrant status creates different contexts and circumstances. They try to have realistic expectations, avoid unnecessary assumptions, and create rewarding environments. They do not wait for ready-made governmental answers—they sometimes create their own answers to their fundamental problems. They are usually information seekers who see no boundaries. It is no surprise that they live in areas that U.S.-born African Americans might find uncomfortable. This does not necessarily mean that they condone retrogressive behaviors; it means only that they are willing to collaborate, consult, and cooperate with individuals whose behaviors they find repulsive. In general, foreign-born African American males tend to be success oriented. They tend to know who they are, learn the facts when they are in doubt, change their thinking, use resource persons, build self-concepts, learn and teach with a variety of techniques, make the right choices, and continue to learn (Obiakor 1994, 1998, 1999).

PERSPECTIVES

In this article, we have used cases to reveal how foreign-born African American males turn their barriers into opportunities. Although there might be problems in generalizing from these cases across subjects or even settings, they unveil real persons, real problems, real situations, and real solutions. Like other African Americans, foreign-born African American males encounter multidimensional problems that range from misperceptions to illusory generalizations due to negative attributions to their race or skin color. But, as immigrant minorities, they solve their myriad problems proactively and consistently. Their goals usually are to better themselves and free themselves from the socioeconomic and political shackles sometimes imposed on them by their home countries. It seems that foreign-born African American males view education not as white people's prerogative but

as an instrument for societal survival and advancement. They do not belabor the issue of racism but find innovative ways to deal with it. The core of their strength is family values—they do not want to disappoint their families. For most of them, their families have invested a great deal in their education; as a result, it behooves them to educate themselves to increase cultural and socioeconomic continuities.

Based on the cases that we analyzed, it is reasonable to conclude that foreign-born African American males develop accurate self-knowledge, self-love, and self-empowerment that assist them in making functional goal-directed decisions. In an era when many African American males are in jail or otherwise in trouble with the criminal justice system, policymakers and policy implementers must make efforts to tap into the talents and energies that foreign-born African American males bring into mainstream America. The African American community must also employ their talents in their struggles for equal opportunity and racial equality. Collaboration, consultation, cooperation, discourse, and dialogue must be fostered to include multiple voices—they are forces of a developing social struggle. When they are buried beneath the visible surface, they tend to explode like time bombs in unexpected fashions. We must all come to the realization that

economic consciousness, social consciousness and political consciousness should not be divorced from each other in American society. The dominant society should play its role in proving (not just saying) that racism is repugnant. Measurable efforts should be made to understand the different minority groups. The assimilationist view and the "melting pot" philosophy will be unworkable in the 21st century. . . . Mere tokenism will not work. Only measurable efforts will. (Obiakor 1993, 41)

References

Banks, James. 1999. *An Introduction to Multicultural Education.* 2d ed. Boston: Allyn & Bacon.

Bell, Derrick. 1985. *And We Are Not Saved: The Elusive Quest for Racial Justice.* New York: Basic Books.

———. 1992. *Faces at the Bottom of the Well: The Permanence of Racism.* New York: Basic Books.

Colbert, Joel, Kimberly Trimble, and Peter Desberg. 1996. *The Case for Education: Contemporary Approaches for Using Case Methods.* Boston: Allyn & Bacon.

Denzin, Norman K. 1995. The Experiential Text and the Limits of Visual Understanding. *Education Theory* 45(Winter):7-18.

Fafunwa, Babatunde. 1975. *History of Education in Nigeria.* London: Macmillan.

Graham, Sandra. 1997. Using Attribution Theory to Understand Social and Academic Motivation in African American Youth. *Educational Psychologist* 32:21-34.

Grossman, Herbert. 1998. *Ending Discrimination in Special Education.* Springfield, IL: Charles C Thomas.

Loury, Glenn C. 1985. The Moral Quandary of the Black Community. *Public Interest* 79:9-22.

———. 1992. Why Steele Demands More of Blacks Than of Whites. *Academic Questions: A Publication of the National Association of Scholars* 5:19-23.

Obiakor, Festus E. 1990-91. Family Life in Africa: Revisiting the Mismeasured Custom. *Minority Voices* 13-14:3-5.

———. 1992a. Self-Concept of African American Students: An Operational Model for Special Education. *Exceptional Children* 59(Oct.-Nov.):160-67.

———. 1992b. Self Image and Fatherhood. *Vision Chattanooga: A Publication of the Chattanooga Resource Foundation* 2(Winter):7.

———. 1993. Opportunity and Choice in Higher Education: Perspectives for African American Scholars. *SAEOPP Journal: Journal of the Southeastern Association of Educational Opportunity Program Personnel* 12(Fall):31-44.

———. 1994. *The Eight-Step Multicultural Approach: Learning and Teaching with a Smile.* Dubuque, IA: Kendall/Hunt.

———. 1995. Self-Concept Model for African American Students in Special Education Settings. In *Effective Education of African American Exceptional Learners: New Perspectives,* ed. Bridgie A. Ford, Festus E. Obiakor, and James M. Patton. Austin, TX: Pro-Ed.

———. 1996. Self-Concept: Assessment and Intervention for African American Learners with Problems. In *African American Adolescents and Adults with Learning Disabilities: An Overview of Assessment Issues,* ed. Noel Gregg, Rebecca Curtis, and Stacia Schmidt. Athens: University of Georgia, Roosevelt Warm Springs Institute for Rehabilitation, Learning Disabilities Research and Training Center.

———. 1998. Make Your Own Destiny. *Emporia State University Bulletin* 8(Aug.):17.

————. 1999. *Beyond the Steps: Multicultural Study Guide*. Dubuque, IA: Kendall/Hunt.

Ogbu, John U. 1978. *Minority Education and Caste*. San Francisco: Academic Press.

————. 1988. Human Intelligence Testing: A Cultural Ecological Perspective. *National Forum: The Phi Kappa Phi Journal* 68(Spring):23-29.

————. 1990. Understanding Diversity: Summary Statements. *Education and Urban Society* 22(Aug.):425-29.

Sowell, Thomas. 1993. *Inside American Education: The Decline, the Deception, the Dogmas*. New York: Free Press.

Staples, Robert. 1984. Racial Ideology and Intellectual Racism—Blacks in Academia. *Black Scholar* Mar.-Apr.: 2-17.

————. 1986. The Dwindling Black Presence on Campus. *New York Times Magazine*, Apr., 46-62.

Steele, Shelby. 1990. The "Unseen Agent" of Low Self-Esteem. *Education Week*, 36.

————. 1991. *The Content of Our Character: A New Vision of Race in America*. New York: HarperPerennial.

West, Cornel. 1993. *Race Matters*. New York: Vintage Books.

The Health of African American Men

By JOHN A. RICH

ABSTRACT: The health of African American men and the role of African American men in the health care system constitute a complex story of historical oppression combined with incredible resilience and dedication. Social forces of racism and discrimination coupled with economic disadvantage have worked against the health of black men for centuries. Yet throughout the history of black people in America, black men and women have been the principal providers of care to one another, relying upon training at segregated yet proud medical institutions of higher learning. African American physicians and scientists have made substantial yet unappreciated contributions to medical science and practice. Still, the health status of African Americans lags behind that of whites, and the health of African American men in particular has reached crisis proportions. Future improvement in the health status of African American men will depend upon improving access to effective medical insurance, eliminating biases in the health care system that alienate black men from health care, increasing the representation of people of color as medical providers, and developing health education approaches that address health risks that are unique to men.

John A. Rich is the medical director of the Boston Public Health Commission and associate professor of medicine and social and behavioral sciences at Boston University School of Medicine and Public Health. He founded the Young Men's Health Clinic at Boston City Hospital (now Boston Medical Center) in 1992 and currently serves as its director. He conducts research into the health of young urban men and particularly the social context of violent victimization.

A FRICAN American men in the United States suffer a disproportionate burden of preventable morbidity and mortality. According to 1997 data from the National Center for Health Statistics, black males had the highest age-adjusted death rate of any group, at 921 deaths per 100,000, a rate that is 60 percent higher than the death rate for white males and 90 percent higher than the overall death rate. While the life expectancy at birth for black males increased 1.1 years between 1996 and 1997 and reached a record high of 67.2 years in 1997, it still lagged 7.1 years behind the life expectancy for white males and 9.3 years behind the overall life expectancy for all groups. The difference in life expectancy between black males and white males was primarily due to higher death rates in black males for five conditions: heart disease, cancer, homicide, human immunodeficiency virus (HIV) infection, and perinatal conditions (Centers for Disease Control and Prevention 1999b).

Men between the ages of 15 and 44 also have a high death rate from preventable diseases. However, young black men suffer a greater burden of preventable causes of death than white men in the same age group. In 1997, the three leading causes of death for all males between the ages of 15 and 24 were, in order, accidents, homicide, and suicide. However, the leading cause of death for young black men aged 15-24 was homicide, followed by accidents and suicide. The death rate from homicide for these men was five times the rate for white males. For 25- to 44-year-old males of all races, accidents, heart disease, and suicide ranked as the top three causes of death. Among black men between the ages of 25 and 44, HIV stands as the leading cause of death, followed by heart disease, accidents, and homicide. The death rate from HIV in this group is four times the rate among similarly aged white men (Centers for Disease Control and Prevention 1999a).

Black men also suffer higher rates of preventable illness such as sexually transmitted diseases. Nationally, gonorrhea rates among black males aged 15-19 are 77 times the rates for similarly aged white males. Syphilis and chlamydia rates show similar disparities (Centers for Disease Control and Prevention 1997). Despite this disproportionate burden of disease, young men in this age group are the least likely to have health insurance and the least likely to seek preventive health services. Data from the National Ambulatory Medical Care Survey show that men aged 15-24 have lower physician visit rates than any other gender and age group and that black patients aged 15-24 have the lowest rates of any race-age group. However, black patients in this age group are more likely to seek care in an emergency room (McCraig 1999).

The reasons for increased risk of preventable disease among African American men are multifactorial. Black men have higher rates of poverty and unemployment than any other group. Current mortality data clearly demonstrate that all cause mortality and disease rates are inversely related to socioeconomic status. Courtenay and others have documented the relationship between unhealthy behaviors and constructions of manhood. They argue that risk-taking behavior provides a way in which marginalized men attempt to establish themselves as men, in the absence of more mainstream ways to demonstrate power. African American men, perceiving themselves as powerless, may more likely think to engage in risk behavior as an assertion of manhood. Yet when data on the health status of black men are reported in the popular media, important explanatory factors are rarely included, leading to the further propagation of negative stereotypes of black men (Courtenay 1998, in press). Larger structural barriers such as racism and class bias further alienate men of color from health care resources that might affect unhealthy behaviors (Williams and Collins 1995; Williams, Lavizzo-Mourey, and Warren 1994). In the sections that follow, I examine several specific health issues and their disproportionate prevalence among black men.

VIOLENCE

Homicide is the leading cause of death for young black men aged 15-34. In 1996 in the United States, 5626 black men in this age group died as homicide victims. In 1989, the lifetime chances of a black man's dying as a result of homicide were 1 in 27, compared to 1 in 205 for white men. In 1992, despite making up only 1.3 percent of the nation's population, black males aged 16-24 experienced 17.2 percent of the nation's homicides. This is equivalent to a homicide rate of 114.9 per 100,000 for this group. Black males in 1992 were nearly 14 times more likely to be victims of homicide than the general population (Bastian and Taylor 1994).

The impact of nonfatal violence among young black men is much less appreciated. Nonfatal injury accounts for significant morbidity and occurs 100 times more frequently than fatal violence. In 1992, among young black males aged 12-24, there was one violent victimization for every eight black males. These episodes of nonfatal violence have serious consequences. Some young men are left with crippling disabilities that remove them from the workforce and destroy their chances for future meaningful work. Others are left with significant emotional disability due to post-traumatic stress disorder.

The truth of young black men as victims of violence is often overshadowed by depictions of their roles as perpetrators. Most young black male victims are injured by other young black men; U.S. Justice Department statistics show that the vast majority of interpersonal violence for blacks and whites is intraracial. In 1992, among the victims of violence aged 16-24 who could determine the characteristics of their assailants, 82 percent of the victimizations of black males and 71 percent of the victimizations of white males involved an offender or offenders of the same race (Bastian and Taylor 1994).

Post-traumatic stress disorder is a trauma-related syndrome, characterized by extreme hyperstimulation, nightmares, depression, hypervigilance, and flashbacks to the traumatic experience. It has been little studied in young men in the inner city but may contribute to significant disability, substance use, and possibly even recurrent violence (Breslau et al. 1991; Campbell and Schwarz 1996; Fitzpatrick and Boldizar 1993). Young men who are injured in the inner city may be left feeling vulnerable when they return to their neighborhoods. Plagued by symptoms of anxiety and hyperstimulation even in environments that previously seemed safe to them, some may feel compelled to arm themselves with guns or knives, doubting the ability or desire of the police to protect them or to apprehend their assailants. Others may turn to alcohol or other drugs such as marijuana in an attempt to self-treat their anxiety. The combination of these reactions related to the symptoms of trauma has the potential to increase a young man's risk of violence.

Victims of violent injury are more likely to suffer a recurrent violent injury. In a study of victims of violence in Detroit, Sims et al. (1989) found that 44 percent of patients suffered a recurrent injury within a five-year period. Over that same period, 20 percent died, due to both violence and substance abuse. Goins, Thompson, and Simpkins (1992) found a recurrence rate of 48 percent in a Baltimore study. They also found an association between unemployment and recurrent violence, suggesting that efforts aimed at reducing the rate of unemployment might help to lower episodes of violent injury.

While some have suggested that this increased rate of reinjury is due to the return of these young men to illicit or dangerous activities or their attempting to exact revenge upon their assailants, our own work suggests something more complex. Young men who live in economically hostile environments and who are injured may feel compelled to attempt retribution not out of anger but out of a perceived need to show their strength and thereby avoid future victimization. This reaction to assault in a social environment that is perceived as very hostile is common and may be resistant to traditional conflict resolution approaches. In the language of these young men, the need to avoid being a "sucker" is deeply rooted in their adoption of societal notions of what it means to "be a man" but also in their ideas about the consequences of being perceived as weak or vulnerable. Some terms ("punk," "chump," and "buster") have similar meanings and represent a central notion of what it means to live in the world as a young black man in the inner city (Rich and Stone 1996). While some young men are injured due to their involvement in gangs or in the illicit economy, many more (and this fact is supported by police data) are injured as a result of interpersonal conflicts, perceived jealousy, and conflicts inflamed by the presence of drugs or alcohol.

The public health approach to violence recognizes that it is a broad issue and not isolated to the individual. In fact, more progressive approaches to violence address the whole individual, including mind, body, and spirit. Such approaches, by capitalizing on the capacity and resilience of young people, are more likely to have a lasting effect than those that focus on a single behavior.

However, despite the recent tendency to regard violence as a public health problem, amenable to a more holistic approach, recently observed decreases in violence have been accompanied by dramatic increases in the number of young black men in prison. Given what we know about the effects of trauma and violence on young men and the lack of economic opportunity in communities of color, young men who spend significant amounts of time in jail would be expected to have high rates of substance abuse, homelessness, and recidivism to jail. Jails rarely possess the resources to provide adequate drug treatment services and mental health support. Overcrowding, more and more the rule in American prisons, exposes newly incarcerated young men to even more stress and to violence played out in a more controlled environment. Many young men find these incarcerations, which are fast becoming a rite of passage in the inner city, tremendously traumatic and lacking in adequate health services.

HIV AND AIDS

Acquired immunodeficiency syndrome (AIDS) is the leading cause of death for black men between the ages of 25 and 44, and the rate of HIV infection is rising in black men at a higher rate than in any other group (Centers for Disease Control and Prevention 1998a). While 35 percent of these infections result from the use of intravenous drugs and the sharing of infected needles, a substantial proportion of them are sexually transmitted. Of these, the largest proportion (38 percent) has resulted from men having sex with men. In 7 percent of the sexually transmitted cases, the infection was attributed to heterosexual contact, and in 12 percent of the cases, no risk factor was identified. This high proportion of cases in which no risk factor can be identified is significantly higher for black men than for any other group, perhaps indicating that black men are reluctant to acknowledge risk behaviors even when diagnosed with AIDS. Blinded seroprevalence data about HIV infections also indicate that black men are at a high risk of new HIV infection.

These data point to the necessity of finding effective ways to change the behavior of young black men. National studies conducted between 1988 and 1995 among urban adolescent males have shown that while black adolescents' attitudes about premarital sex became more conservative, their behavior did not change (Leighton et al. 1998). In addition, AIDS education did not lead to any changes in sexual activity by black males, although this change did occur among nonblack males. All types of HIV risk behavior must be emphasized in educational approaches to stem the epidemic in black men. Even those behaviors that are heavily stigmatized in communities of color, such as men having sex with other men and intravenous drug use, must be openly and honestly dealt with. Young men who are struggling to understand their sexual preferences may be unable to identify with resources that characterize them as gay or bisexual. It is therefore important that resources be developed that address the unique cultural, religious, and political meanings that certain behaviors hold in the black community.

MENTAL HEALTH

Many of the mental health problems that young black men experience are related to the unique stresses they experience as a result of poverty, racism, and past trauma. In general, young black men have higher levels of stress and anxiety due to a lack of meaningful employment opportunities. The stresses of balancing multiple life pressures, often without material or social capital, may lead to feelings of hopelessness and desperation. Add to this the impact of trauma in the form of losing friends and family to violence, and we have the makings of a mental health crisis.

Over the past decade, there has been a substantial increase in suicide rates not only among black males but among young black males in particular (Centers for Disease Control and Prevention 1998b). While the suicide rate for young black men is still lower than the rate for their white counterparts, this rate is increasing more rapidly than for any other group. Insufficient data are available to help us understand the reasons for this change, but it is likely to be due to the stresses previously detailed combined with a lack of access to mental health services. Some of the suicides are by young men who are struggling with their sexual identities, since we know that a major contributor to suicides in young people is the feeling of alienation brought on by their emerging sexual preferences. Given that homosexuality is particularly stigmatized in African American communities, this alienation may be felt in an extreme manner by inner-city young black males.

Substance-abuse behaviors also provide some insight into the emotional health of young black men in the urban environment. While alcohol use rates are higher among white males than black males, young black men have a particularly high rate of marijuana use, and this rate seems to be on the increase (McCraig 1999). This is in contrast with cocaine use, which seems to be decreasing in all U.S. populations. While many use marijuana because of its much highlighted role in the pop culture, using it mainly during social interactions, a significant number of others use this drug to self-treat symptoms of anxiety. In addition, there is growing concern that marijuana use may lead to the use of more serious substances such as alcohol, cocaine, and possibly even heroin. Given that these substances are not effective in treating symptoms of anxiety and given the illicit nature of marijuana, use of this drug may lead to even more interaction with the police and the criminal justice system and increases in life stress.

While less easily quantified than specific diseases, racism and oppression stand as a constant backdrop against which these men live their lives. Harvard psychiatrist Chester

Pierce (1970) has written eloquently about the notion that microaggression, that is, small racial insults experienced on a daily basis by people of color, has an aggregate effect that is equivalent to or greater than so-called macroaggression, such as beatings or lynching. Clearly, because of the widely held stereotypes that have been applied to young black men, they are likely to experience microaggression, such as being followed by security guards in stores, arrested or harassed by the police, denied frontline employment, and treated poorly in the health care system. To the extent that the effects of these insults are additive to the other stresses of life, they may take a particular toll on the health of black men.

CANCER

Black men have a higher death rate from cancer than do other groups. Prostate cancer in particular has a disproportionate incidence among African American men. African American men have the highest incidence of prostate cancer in the world, and the rate is twice that of white men. Black men have an age-adjusted death rate from all cancers that is 50 percent higher than that for white men, despite similar or lower incidence rates for some cancers. This disproportionate death rate relates in large part to a lack of access to health care since many of these cancers can be prevented or, if detected early, limited in the harm that they cause. In addition, lifestyle factors, such as smoking, sedentary lifestyle, and diet, are linked to higher rates of cancer. To the extent that significant life stresses and lack of access to health care inhibit lifestyle changes, impoverished men of color are even less likely to adopt healthier behaviors. Community-based efforts to increase prostate screening rates for black men have met with some success; similar efforts are necessary to address other high-mortality cancers such as lung and colorectal cancers.

CARDIOVASCULAR DISEASE

Similar to cancer, black men have a higher death rate due to cardiovascular disease than any other group. Once again, the increased mortality seen here is due in part to factors that are associated with the black race, such as poverty and lack of access to health care, rather than caused by race itself. In fact, men with lower incomes are more likely to die of cardiovascular disease, regardless of race. Recently identified biases in the health care system no doubt contribute to this also. Recent studies have shown that physicians are less likely to refer black patients for certain diagnostic or therapeutic cardiac procedures, independent of their socioeconomic status (Schulman et al. 1999). Lack of access to effective primary health care, combined with lifestyle issues such as smoking, diet, and lack of exercise, renders black men at the highest risk of death due to cardiovascular disease.

ACCESS TO HEALTH CARE AND
HEALTH CARE UTILIZATION

Young men of color are less likely than others to have access to effective health care services. Young people between the ages of 18 and 24 in the United States are the least likely group to have insurance coverage. Black and Latino men are also disproportionately represented among the uninsured in some states. Fully 25 percent report having no insurance (Hoffman 1998). Young black and Latino men in particular, because of their socioeconomic position, are less likely to qualify for public sources of insurance such as Medicaid. Even though, in some states, Medicaid eligibility has been greatly expanded in the past few years, young men over the age of 18 qualify only if they are classified "long-term unemployed," defined as having been unable to find work for a period of two years or more. Otherwise, nondisabled young men cannot access Medicaid.

Most Americans, who have health insurance, obtain insurance through their workplaces. Those who occupy unskilled and nonunion jobs are less likely to be offered insurance coverage. Such insurance is prohibitively expensive for any lower-income or working-class individual to purchase on the open market. The socioeconomic position of young urban black men, with higher rates of unemployment and lower-skilled jobs, means that they have less access to health insurance. Even those who qualify for coverage may not know that they are eligible since they may lack critical information about access to health care.

Finally, even for those young men who are fortunate enough to have health insurance through their jobs or through public coverage, the current health care environment, marked by managed care competition, may limit their access to appropriate care. Fierce competition within the health care market has relegated prevention to the back burner. Decisions about the kinds of services most relevant to these men, such as community-based outreach and preventive mental health, are often made on financial grounds, and little justification is seen for outreach to the most disenfranchised groups. As a result, young black men may have insurance but still face barriers to effective preventive care.

Lack of health insurance leads to several problematic health-seeking behaviors. Young men may defer necessary care for nonemergent problems because of concern that they will be unable to pay. Consequently, they may receive care in settings such as emergency rooms or urgent care clinics that are less well equipped to deal with preventive health. Encounters in acute and emergency settings tend to be less satisfying since patients are faced with harried staff and long waiting times. Such experiences may further alienate this group from seeking care, particularly preventive health care, the mainstay of future health and wellness.

Even for those with health insurance or with the ability to obtain free care, access to culturally appropriate providers may not exist. Health care providers are not immune to general societal stereotypes of young black men. Providers who hold these unconscious preconceptions may interact with these patients based upon preconceived notions, further alienating them. Anecdotally, numerous young black men have related that providers have assumed that they were involved with gangs, sold or used drugs, or had particular attitudes, based solely upon their appearance. A young black man who was an innocent victim of random street violence related being lectured by a white provider about the need to "change [his] lifestyle" without even asking the youth about the circumstances of his injury.

Recent research supports the notion that providers unconsciously consider race when making treatment decisions in the application of expensive technologies like cardiac surgery and kidney transplantation. Schulman and colleagues (1999) found that physicians viewing videotapes of actors depicting patients with heart disease, all of whom were scripted to have the same symptoms, test results, occupation, and socioeconomic status, recommended certain high-technology cardiac diagnostic studies less often for black patients and for women. If, in the face of such highly data-driven decisions, providers consider race, then it is likely that in interfacing with young black men, racial stereotypes as well as other deeply held notions influence the interaction. This finding is of particular concern given that the vast majority of physicians are white, even in areas where the population is much more diverse.

MEDICAL EDUCATION

Medical education for African Americans began in organized fashion in 1868 with the founding of Howard Medical School, which graduated its first M.D. graduates in 1871. While, during the decade that followed, 12 more schools sprang up to educate black doctors, only two, Howard and Meharry Medical College, in Nashville, Tennessee, ultimately survived. The Flexner Report, a Carnegie Foundation–sponsored report on the state of medical education in the United States, led to the closure of inadequate medical programs, both predominantly black and white. Therefore, those two predominantly black institutions were responsible for training the vast majority of black physicians through the 1960s (Organ and Kosiba 1987; Epps, Johnson, and Vaughan 1994). Two additional predominantly black medical schools now exist, Charles R. Drew University of Medicine and Science, in Los Angeles, and Morehouse School of Medicine, in Atlanta. In addition, a number of physicians of color are trained at majority institutions.

The view of the future of African Americans in medicine is uncertain. While it is well documented that physicians of color are more likely than their majority counterparts to practice in underserved areas, fewer blacks are matriculating at U.S. medical schools. Data collected by the Association of American Medical

Colleges (AAMC) indicate that, between 1969 and 1975, the enrollment of underrepresented minorities in American medical schools increased from 3.1 to 8.1 percent. Howard and Meharry went from training 75 percent of black medical students in 1969 to only 20 percent in 1979. However, since peaking at 8.1 percent in 1975, minority enrollment in medical schools has begun to decrease. This is particularly true for black males. While organizations like the AAMC have developed innovative programs to increase the enrollment of people of color in medical school, it is clear that broader interventions designed to increase the number of black men in college and who pursue health-related careers are necessary.

CONCLUSION

By virtue of social inequality, racial bias, and lack of adequate access to health care, African American men have a worse health status than other groups. Some of these health outcomes can be traced to poverty and historical racial discrimination, while others more clearly emanate from health behaviors and risk taking. Simultaneously, African American men have, as a group, made a significant contribution to the health of black and white Americans alike.

The future health of African American men will depend upon improving their access to health care that addresses health behaviors in their social context while also providing access to primary care and appropriate technologies. Concerned African American men have the ability and power to affect the health of their communities by influencing their peers to alter unhealthy behaviors and seek regular medical care, while also teaching them to advocate for their health needs. Furthermore, increasing the representation of Africa Americans, particularly men, in medical school and other health professions will be critical to improving the health of people of color. But these outcomes will depend upon increasing the number of underrepresented groups in higher education and improving the lot of African American boys in primary and secondary education.

References

Bastian, Lisa D. and Bruce M. Taylor. 1994. *Young Black Male Victims*. Washington, DC: Bureau of Justice Statistics.

Breslau, N., G. C. Davis, P. Andreski, and E. Peterson. 1991. Traumatic Events and Posttraumatic Stress Disorder in an Urban Population of Young Adults. *Archives of General Psychiatry* 48:216-22.

Campbell, Carla. and Donald F. Schwarz. 1996. Prevalence and Impact of Exposure to Interpersonal Violence Among Suburban and Urban Middle School Students. *Pediatrics* 98(3, pt. 1):396-402.

Centers for Disease Control and Prevention. 1997. *Sexually Transmitted Disease Surveillance Report*. Atlanta, GA: U.S. Department of Health and Human Services, Centers for Disease Control and Prevention.

———. 1998a. *HIV/AIDS Surveillance Report*. Atlanta, GA: U.S. Department of Health and Human Services, Centers for Disease Control and Prevention.

———. 1998b. *Suicide Among Black Youths—United States, 1980-1995.* Atlanta, GA: U.S. Department of Health and Human Services, Centers for Disease Control and Prevention.

———. 1999a. *National Vital Statistics Report.* Vol. 47. No. 19. Atlanta, GA: U.S. Department of Health and Human Services, Centers for Disease Control and Prevention.

———. 1999b. *National Vital Statistics Reports.* Atlanta, GA: U.S. Department of Health and Human Services, Centers for Disease Control and Prevention.

Courtenay, Will H. 1998. College Men's Health: An Overview and a Call to Action. *Journal of American College Health* 46(6):279-90.

———. In press. Constructions of Masculinity and Their Influence on Men's Well-Being: A Theory of Gender and Health. *Social Science and Medicine.*

Epps, C. H., D. G. Johnson, and A. L. Vaughan. 1994. *African American Medical Pioneers.* Rockville, MD: Betz.

Fitzpatrick, K. and J. Boldizar. 1993. The Prevalence and Consequences of Exposure to Violence Among African-American Youth. *Journal of the American Academy of Child and Adolescent Psychiatry* 32:424-30.

Goins, Wendell A., Jonathan Thompson, and Cuthbert Simpkins. 1992. Recurrent Intentional Injury. *Journal of the National Medical Association* 84(5):431-35.

Hoffman, Catherine. 1998. *Uninsured in America: A Chart Book: The Kaiser Commission on Medicaid and the Uninsured.* Menlo Park, CA: Henry J. Kaiser Family Foundation.

Leighton, K., F. Sonenstein, L. D. Lindberg, C. H. Bradner, S. Boggess, and J. H. Pleck. 1998. Understanding Changes in Sexual Activity Among Young Metropolitan Men: 1979-1995. *Family Planning Perspectives* 30(6):256-62.

McCraig, Linda F. 1999. *National Hospital Ambulatory Medical Care Survey: 1997 Outpatient Department Summary.* Atlanta, GA: U.S. Department of Health and Human Services, Centers for Disease Control and Prevention.

Organ, Claude H., Jr. and Margaret M. Kosiba, eds. 1987. *A Century of Black Surgeons.* Vol. 2. Norman, OK: Transcript Press.

Pierce, Chester. 1970. Offensive Mechanisms. In *The Black Seventies,* ed. F. Barbour. Boston: Porter Sargent.

Rich, John A. and David A. Stone. 1996. The Experience of Violent Injury for Young African American Men: The Meaning of Being a "Sucker." *Journal of General Internal Medicine* 11:77-82.

Schulman, Kevin A., Jesse A. Berlin, William Harless, Jon F. Kerner, Shyrl Sistrunk, Bernard Gersh, Ross Dube, Chrisotpher Taleghani, Jennifer E. Burke, Sankey Williams, John E. Eisenberg, and José J. Escarce. 1999. The Effect of Race and Sex on Physicians' Recommendations for Cardiac Catheterization. *New England Journal of Medicine* 340(8):618-26.

Sims, Deborah W., Brack A. Bivins, Farouck N. Obeid, H. Matiloa Horst, Victor J. Sorensen, and John J. Fath. 1989. Urban Trauma: A Chronic Recurrent Disease. *Journal of Trauma* 29(7):940-47.

Williams, David R. and Chiquita Collins. 1995. U.S. Socioeconomic and Racial Differences in Health: Patterns and Explanations. *Annual Review of Sociology* 21:349-86.

Williams, David R., Risa Lavizzo-Mourey, and Reuben C. Warren. 1994. The Concept of Race and Health Status in America. *Public Health Report* 109:26-41.

ANNALS, *AAPSS*, **569**, May 2000

The Black Male
and the U.S. Economy

By SUSAN WILLIAMS McELROY and LEON T. ANDREWS, JR.

ABSTRACT: This article examines the current status of black males in the U.S. economy. It emphasizes several positive aspects of the changing status of black males over time. The authors acknowledge that the social and economic conditions of black males in the United States are troubling in many respects. However, the objective of the article is to highlight the progress and achievements of black males. Most research on black males focuses solely on the problems and rarely documents the successes and accomplishments. Black males have made significant contributions to the U.S. economy. However, little attention has been paid in the literature to their achievements in education, their professional successes, and their positive community and family involvement.

Susan Williams McElroy is assistant professor of economics and education policy at the H. John Heinz III School of Public Policy and Management at Carnegie Mellon University. Her research interests include racial and gender inequality in the U.S. labor market and the role of education in economic status.

Leon T. Andrews, Jr., received his master's degree in public policy and management from Carnegie Mellon University. He is currently working as a consultant to the Allegheny County Department of Human Services in Pittsburgh, Pennsylvania.

NOTE: The authors thank R. Landon Witcher for his contributions to this article. Toureia Williams assisted with research. Steve Haugen and Steve Hipple of the Bureau of Labor Statistics provided unpublished tabulations of employment statistics that were used in this article.

I F one had to choose a single word to describe the position of the black male in the U.S. economy, a fitting word would be "contradictory." Black males are in a precarious position in the labor market. Their unemployment rates are among the highest of any demographic group (Farley 1987; Schwartzman 1997; McElroy and Darity 1999). Their rates of participation in the paid labor force have declined during recent decades (Parsons 1980; Brown 1984; Juhn 1992). They earn less than their white male counterparts (Carnoy 1994; Schmitz, Williams, and Gabriel 1994; Durden and Gaynor 1998), even when they have completed the same amount of education (McElroy and Darity 1999). As McElroy and Darity (1999) reported, in 1998, black males aged 16 and over who were employed full-time earned an average of $468 per week, compared with white males, who earned an average of $615 per week.[1] In relative terms, then, black males employed full-time earned 76 cents for every dollar that white males earned.

By focusing solely on the difficulties facing black males in the economy, one runs the risk of overlooking the many positive advances made by black males. Some of the gains made by black males have been documented by different research efforts. For instance, economists have noted that the earnings gap between black and white males has decreased over time. They often point to black males' rising educational attainment as the central factor that explains why the earnings gap between black and white males narrowed between 1940 and 1980 (Smith and Welch 1986).

Although it is certainly important to document the changes in income disparities between black and white males over time, it is also essential to examine some of the other positive dimensions of the status of black males in the economy.

This article examines the current status of black males in the U.S. economy and emphasizes several positive aspects of their changing status over time. While we acknowledge that the social and economic conditions of black males in the United States are troubling in many respects, our objective is to highlight the achievements of black males. Much of the research on black males focuses solely on the problems and rarely highlights the successes and accomplishments. The research discusses high crime rates, high incarceration rates, high unemployment rates, and low educational attainment among black males. However, less attention has been paid to achievements in education, professional successes, and positive involvement in communities and families.

We consider black male accomplishments in three separate but related contexts. First, a significant number of black males have received a bachelor's degree or higher in recent decades. Second, black males have made inroads in professional occupations in increasing numbers. Finally, a significant number of black males are supporting themselves and their families. Although many barriers make it difficult for black males to take advantage of economic opportunities in this country, there are still a number of black males who are taking the steps necessary to achieve economic success. As authors of this article, we do not wish to diminish the efforts of other scholars and journalists who examine the problems of black males. Rather, this article focuses on the enormous progress black males have made in the economy and their outstanding achievements.

EDUCATION

While there are numerous determinants of economic success, few single factors have the impact that educational attainment does. The level of educational attainment is both a significant determinant of economic success and a major component of human capital development. (We can think of human capital as the productive capacities and abilities developed within a person.) Labor economists generally agree that high levels of educational attainment contribute to higher earnings. With higher levels of educational attainment, one has greater access to jobs with higher pay, better benefits, greater security, better working conditions, and more opportunities for advancement (Doeringer and Piore 1971).

Advancement in educational attainment

Black males have made tremendous strides in attaining higher levels of education. As a result, they have increased their potential for greater access to jobs. Let us examine the educational progress of black males over the last 30 years and their

steady improvement in earnings potential.

During the period from 1969 to the present, the average level of educational attainment for adult black males (aged 25 and over) has increased markedly from ninth grade to high school graduate. In 1969, the median number of years of schooling completed for black males aged 25 and over was 9.6, roughly a ninth-grade education (U.S. Bureau of the Census 1970). By 1991, the median years of schooling completed for black males aged 25 and over had increased to 12.4, slightly higher than a high school diploma (U.S. Bureau of the Census 1992).

Another indicator of black males' rising educational attainment is the percentage of black males who have completed high school and college. Both high school and college completion rates for black males have notably increased. We review the evidence on high school completion rates first.

High school completion

In 1964, 24 percent of black males aged 25 and over had completed high school. By 1998, the completion figure had tripled to 75 percent, as shown in Figure 1 (U.S. Bureau of the Census 1998).[2] This remarkable progress in the black male high school completion rate in those 32 years is noteworthy. First, the sheer magnitude of the increase merits mention. Second, this dramatic increase occurred over a relatively short period of time.

The amount of education black males have completed affects their earnings potential and their ability

FIGURE 1
PERCENTAGE OF BLACK MALES AGED 25 AND OVER
WHO HAD COMPLETED HIGH SCHOOL OR COLLEGE, 1964-98

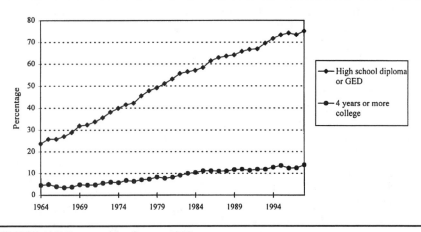

SOURCE: U.S. Bureau of the Census 1998.
NOTE: Completion of high school means having at least received a high school diploma or GED.
Completion of college means having received a bachelor's degree or higher.

to support themselves and other persons who are dependent on them financially. The steady increase over time in the percentage of black males who have completed a high school education deserves special mention because a high school diploma has become the minimum level of educational attainment required for access to jobs that pay a "living wage," that is, enough to support oneself and one's family.

The employment prospects for males of all races with less than a high school diploma have deteriorated remarkably in recent decades, in part because the demands of the labor market have changed so drastically. The U.S. economy has transformed itself from a primarily goods-producing economy to a primarily service-producing economy. One of the most profound effects of this shift has been a sizable reduction in the number of jobs in the economy for lower-skilled workers as compared with previous decades.

Furthermore, in the 1960s and, to a lesser extent, in the 1970s, there were greater opportunities for a male high school dropout (of any race) to earn enough to support himself and his family as compared with today. In today's labor market, however, high school dropouts and others at the lower end of the educational attainment spectrum face increasingly bleak prospects for earning a living wage. Clearly, the level of formal education one attains has a major effect on employment prospects and earnings potential.

In general, among workers in the U.S. labor market, there is a financial payoff in continuing one's education to high school completion and beyond. With each higher level of education, employed black males earn more on average. In 1997, black males aged 25 and over who had completed high school but no further schooling earned $22,174 per year on average.[3] They earned $6593 more (or 42 percent more) than black males who had completed ninth, tenth, or eleventh grade (U.S. Bureau of the Census 1999a).

High school graduates with no further formal schooling are the single largest educational category of black males aged 25 and over; they account for 37 percent of all black males aged 25 and over. A smaller percentage of black males (16 percent) are high school dropouts (U.S. Bureau of the Census 1999a), which means that adult black males who have completed high school outnumber black males who have not completed high school by more than 2 to 1. Clearly, more black males are completing their high school education than are not, thereby increasing their earnings potential.

Degree completion

What about college enrollment and completion of degrees at the higher educational levels by black males? Are black males making progress in this area? Yes, an increasing number of black males are enrolling in and completing college. The percentage of black males aged 25 and over who have completed college has more than tripled since the mid-1960s (U.S. Bureau of the Census 1992): in 1964, 4.5 percent of black men aged 25 and over had completed four years or more of college. By 1998, 13.9 percent of black men had attained this level of education (U.S. Bureau of the Census 1998). The

relative increase in college completion rates of black males highly parallels the relative increase in high school completion rates of black males. However, the percentage of black males who complete college (13.9 percent in 1998) is far below the percentage who complete high school (75 percent in 1998).

Impact of educational attainment on earnings

Clearly, not everyone who enrolls in college actually completes a degree. However, even if a black male enrolls in college and never graduates, he can expect to earn more after having completed some college than if he had not completed any college after receiving his high school diploma.

In 1997, black males aged 25 and over who had completed some college but no degree earned $26,635 per year on average (U.S. Bureau of the Census 1998). They earned $4461 more per year than black male high school graduates of the same age ($22,174) who had not attended college at all. In percentage terms, then, those who had attended some college earned 20 percent more than those who had not attended any college.

From 1989 to 1996, the number of black males completing higher educational degrees increased noticeably. Specifically, the number of black males receiving bachelor's, master's, professional, and doctoral degrees rose, with the largest increase occurring in the number who received their bachelor's degrees (from 22,370 in 1989 to 32,852 in 1996) (U.S. Department of Education 1998).

In 1997, black males with a bachelor's degree earned $31,631, while black males with a high school diploma earned $22,174, a differential of 43 percent (U.S. Bureau of the Census 1998). Black males who earn bachelor's degrees clearly increase their earnings potential relative to black male high school graduates. Today, many black males now have a greater probability of being in a higher income bracket, thereby enhancing their ability to provide financially for themselves and their families.

Degree completions are a clear indicator of the progress that black males have made in higher education in the United States. The number of black males completing bachelor's and graduate degrees (master's and professional degrees) has increased markedly during recent decades. More black males are graduating with professional degrees and becoming lawyers, doctors, and engineers than in the past.

PROFESSIONAL OCCUPATIONS
AND ENTREPRENEURSHIP

Black males have made notable inroads into the professional occupations. The occupational upgrading of black males in the U.S. labor market during recent decades has been nothing short of dramatic. Black males have moved out of agricultural and private household occupations into professional and managerial occupations in increasing numbers. As a result, more black males have assumed positions of leadership and authority in the last 20 years. Black males occupy high-level positions in the armed forces, the federal government, and private industry. Other black males have ventured into the entrepreneurial arena, and many have found economic success and other rewards there.

Leaders in the public sector

In the public sector, increasing numbers of black males have received appointments to some of the top positions in government. Some of these men include Rodney Slater, secretary of transportation; Colin Powell, former chairman of the Joint Chiefs of Staff; Andrew Young, former U.S. ambassador to the United Nations; and Roger W. Ferguson, Jr., vice-chairman and governor of the U.S. Federal Reserve.

Rodney Slater's appointment to the Transportation cabinet position in 1997 by President Clinton is an example of the high achievement that black males have made in the public sector. The Department of Transportation under Slater's guidance has been largely responsible for unprecedented improvements in the transportation infrastructure of America over the last two years (U.S. Department of Transportation 1999).

Colin Powell was named chairman of the Joint Chiefs of Staff in 1989 under President George Bush, making him the most powerful military officer in the United States. In 1992, he spearheaded Operation Desert Storm, commanding a successful mission of U.S. troops in the Persian Gulf. Since his retirement from the military, Powell has actively led President Clinton's national volunteer program, America's Promise.

Powell's efforts connect positively to the importance of black males in the family, a topic to which we turn in the next section.

Andrew Young had already had a long and distinguished career as a civil rights advocate before entering electoral politics during the 1970s. Young fought many civil rights battles beside Dr. Martin Luther King, Jr., before he was elected mayor of Atlanta. Mayor Young's leadership helped usher in a period of economic and political advancement of many African Americans in Atlanta. His skill and diplomacy did not go unnoticed. President Carter recognized his enormous value and appointed him ambassador to the United Nations, where he served from 1977 to 1979.

Roger W. Ferguson, Jr., received the presidential appointment to the position of governor of the U.S. Federal Reserve in 1997. In September 1999, Ferguson was confirmed by the U.S. Senate as vice-chairman of the Federal Reserve's Board of Governors. The appointment of Ferguson to this position elevates him to the second most powerful position in the world's premiere central banking system. Ferguson's accomplishments at the Federal Reserve Bank are noteworthy; they include his leadership in the bank's planning and preparations to address the year 2000 computer problem (Board of Governors of the Federal Reserve System 1999). He follows two other distinguished black men—Andrew Brimmer and Emmett Rice—who also served as governors of the U.S. Federal Reserve.

Corporate executives

In the private sector, several African American men are managing the affairs of major corporations and emerging as leaders in their fields. Reginald Lewis and Kenneth Chenault are excellent examples of accomplished African American men in the private sector.

Reginald Lewis was the founder of TLC Beatrice International Holdings, Inc. and best known throughout the financing world as one of the most successful financiers during the late 1980s. Lewis's success in the business world is attached to the leveraged buyout deal that created TLC Beatrice, one of the nation's largest black-owned companies. TLC Beatrice is one of the world's largest food and beverage holding companies.

The success attained by Lewis exemplifies the growing opportunities available to other black businesspeople (Fairclough 1999). The successful rise of Reginald Lewis is recounted in his coauthored autobiography, *Why Should White Guys Have All the Fun?* (see Hays 1999). The Lewis family maintained ownership of TLC Beatrice after Reginald Lewis's death in 1993.

Kenneth Chenault is the current president and chief operating officer of American Express. He holds the highest position of any black executive in a *Fortune* 500 company. He has been designated to become, in 2001, the company's next chairman of the board and chief executive officer. Some of Chenault's greatest abilities are his ingenuity, persuasiveness, and foresight. One of his major accomplishments at American Express involved cutting $3 billion in operating costs. Under his leadership, the company developed strategies to diversify current business operations (Whigham-Desir 1999).

Providing examples of black males who receive high accolades and recognition for their positions and responsibilities tends to overlook how other black males are making significant strides.

In the 1950s and 1960s, fewer black men had the education and skills required to qualify for professional and managerial positions than is the case today. Even for black males with a degree during that time, having a college degree did not necessarily ensure them access to these positions because of racial barriers. Some of the barriers for black men may still exist, but they are not as severe now as they were in the 1950s and 1960s.

Today, increasing numbers of black males with higher levels of educational attainment are afforded access to greater opportunities. As mentioned earlier, there are significantly more black males receiving higher education, enabling them to qualify for professional and managerial positions in existing organizations. As an alternative, other black males with similar levels of education choose the entrepreneurial path.

Entrepreneurs

Black males are experiencing increasing success in their entrepreneurial quests. There are more financially successful black male entrepreneurs than 20 years ago.

Examples of such men include Earl G. Graves, John H. Johnson, Russell Simmons, and Percy Miller (better known as Master P). Each of these men provides a better understanding of the impact black male entrepreneurs have on this economy.

A visionary entrepreneur, Earl G. Graves is publisher and chief executive officer of *Black Enterprise* magazine. *Black Enterprise* is instrumental in publicizing the successes of black male executives. Graves has received numerous awards for his accomplishments in the business world. He provides leadership to the black community. An outspoken entrepreneur, he encourages blacks to invest in and support black businesses (Graves 1997). Graves's accomplishments and ingenuity have allowed *Black Enterprise* to develop and maintain outstanding loyalty among its readership.

Another successful black male entrepreneur is John H. Johnson. He is the chief executive officer of Johnson Publishing Company, which publishes *Ebony* and *Jet* magazines. Johnson started this company in 1942 with a $500 loan on his mother's furniture. In the ensuing decades, Johnson Publishing Company grew into a multi-million-dollar business (Johnson Publishing Company 1999). Johnson has established himself as a leader in the publishing world and an eminently successful risk taker.

Russell Simmons used his ingenuity to start a small record label and develop it into a major entertainment enterprise. Although some observers questioned his judgment in developing a business around rap and hip-hop music, Simmons demonstrated that he possessed a keen business savvy. He understood the market. He has established himself as one of the premier promoters of rap and hip-hop entertainment and is credited with expanding this genre of music into popular culture (Stark 1999).

Finally, Percy Miller, better known as Master P, is the youngest black male who has achieved the greatest financial success. He developed a unique understanding of how to produce and market music that originally started in an underground market but was propelled quickly into popular culture. Miller exploited what is known as gangsta rap and used this success to explore other business ventures. As a result of his efforts and successful risks, Master P is now regarded by *Fortune* magazine as the twenty-eighth wealthiest man under 40 years old. Miller's net worth is estimated at over $360 million, exceeding that of Michael Jordan (Borden and Koudsi 1999).

The professions

Now let us note black males' success in the professional and managerial occupations. In earlier decades, such positions were less open to black males than is the case today. Overt as well as subtle forms of discrimination in the labor market ensured that the number of black males employed as professionals and managers remained small. More recently, the economic shift from goods-producing to service-producing industries affects black males in terms of the different types of jobs they hold. This

is evident when we consider the increase in the number of black males in professional occupations since 1960.

The number and percentage of black males in professional occupations has increased dramatically since 1960. In 1960, only 5 percent of the approximately 3.64 million black males in the labor force were professionals, technical workers, managers, officers, or proprietors (U.S. Bureau of the Census 1963). Counted among these men were physicians, dentists, clergyman, engineers, lawyers, and schoolteachers. By 1990, 12 percent of the approximately 4.67 million black males in the labor force were employed in managerial and professional specialty occupations (U.S. Bureau of the Census 1993a). The percentage of black males in managerial and professional occupations had more than doubled in those 30 years. This is a significant and admirable feat for black males.

Several professional specialty occupations have been particularly important for black males. Among them are physicians and lawyers. Black males are entering professional fields in greater numbers than ever before. Although there still exists a need to continue efforts that develop and sustain black males in their pursuit of professional degrees, there are many positive stories about the professional achievements of black males.

The number of black male physicians has increased significantly throughout the twentieth century. These men have contributed greatly to the advancement of medicine in numerous fields in that time. The increase in their number can be seen in the second half of the century. In 1960, there were approximately 4216 black male physicians and surgeons in the United States (U.S. Bureau of the Census 1963). By 1990, their numbers had grown to 13,707 (U.S. Bureau of the Census 1993a), an increase of over 300 percent in only three decades.

Although the increase in the number of black male physicians is partly due to an increase in the U.S. population over time, the increase in the number of black male physicians is still very positive and significant. The growing number of black male physicians reflects changes in opportunities available to black men in medicine since 1960.

The legal profession provides yet another example of black males' inroads into the professions. Over the past few decades, black males have been influential in various aspects of the legal profession, particularly in the area of civil rights. The late Thurgood Marshall played a pivotal role in the 1954 case of *Brown* v. *Board of Education of Topeka,* which mandated the end to segregation in public schools in the United States. He was later appointed to the U.S. Supreme Court, where he served until his retirement in 1991.

Today, black male lawyers have impact in the courtroom as criminal lawyers, in popular culture as entertainment lawyers, and in the boardroom as corporate lawyers. There are more opportunities available for black male lawyers in the different legal fields than ever before.

Despite the substantial increase in the number of black male lawyers and judges since 1960, black males still accounted for a small percentage of all lawyers and judges in 1990. In 1990, there were an estimated 15,542 black male lawyers and judges in the United States, nearly eight times the number in 1960 (2004). In fact, during this 30-year period, the number of black male lawyers and judges increased faster than did the total number of lawyers and judges. The total number of lawyers and judges increased threefold, one-half the rate of increase for black judges and lawyers (U.S. Bureau of the Census 1963, 1993a). Nevertheless, the percentage of all lawyers and judges who were black males did not increase substantially between 1960 and 1990. In 1960, 1 percent of all lawyers in the United States were black males (U.S. Bureau of the Census 1963). Thirty years later, in 1990, 2 percent of all lawyers in the United States were black males (U.S. Bureau of the Census 1993a).

BLACK MALES AND THEIR FAMILIES

An important, though often overlooked, aspect of the role and position of black males in the economy is the relationship to other parts of the society. There are important links between economic status and family formation, marriage, child rearing, and community development. Black males contribute to the functioning of the family at both the micro and macro levels. The contributions of black males to the family are important to the economy because their efforts build and strengthen opportunities for themselves and their families to succeed in the economy.

The micro level

The growth in the number of families headed by a female with no spouse present[4] has received enormous attention in recent decades (Ross and Sawhill with MacIntosh 1975; Garfinkel and McLanahan 1986). Family households headed by women with no spouse present account for an increasingly large share of all black families, increasing from less than one-third (28 percent) in 1970 to nearly half (47 percent) in 1998. In absolute numbers, the number of such black family households doubled during this period, from 1.36 million in 1970 to 3.93 million in 1998 (U.S. Bureau of the Census 1993b, 1999b).

A fact that is much less well known is that black family households headed by a male with no spouse present as a percentage of all black families has also doubled since 1970. The Census Bureau estimated that in 1970 there were 181,000 families headed by a black male with no spouse present, or 4 percent of all black family households. By 1998, the number had increased to 562,000, or 7 percent of all black family households (U.S. Bureau of the Census 1993b, 1999b). It would be misleading to point out the rise in the number of black family households headed by a male with no spouse present without placing this trend in perspective relative to the growth in the number of black family households headed by a female with no spouse present.

Certainly, the number of black family households headed by a male with no spouse present is much smaller than the number of black family households headed by a woman with no spouse present. Nevertheless, the growth in the number of black family households headed by a male with no spouse present has also been tremendous.

The growth in the number of black family households headed by a male with no spouse present must be taken into account when assessing the role of the black male in the family and the resulting impact on the economy. There are numerous reports suggesting that black males are not being responsible family men. The increase in the number of family households headed by a black male with no spouse present provides evidence of black males' being responsible family men.

Indeed, there is a restructuring of the nuclear, or two-parent, family, and marriage rates among blacks have been on the decline in recent decades (Tucker and Mitchell-Kernan 1995). Nevertheless, there are positive impacts for black males who decide to marry. Specifically, black males with higher education who marry increase the potential of having a family with a higher income.

The macro level

Finally, we consider the role of black males in families and communities at the macro level. Here we adopt a view of family that extends beyond one's immediate family, and even beyond the extended family. Strong and thriving family units produce strong and thriving communities. Likewise, strong communities result in more persons employed and earning a wage to better take care of themselves and their families. Many black males play vital roles in their neighborhoods and communities. Black male leadership at the macro level takes the form of involvement in professional, community, and social organizations, churches, and public service.

In 1900, black dentists, composed almost exclusively of black males, came together in Washington, D.C., to form the first professional association of black dentists, the Washington Society of Colored Dentists. The agenda of these dentists extended to the well-being of the black community. "The concern for the low economic status of their clientele produced a certain cohesiveness among the black dentists" (Kidd 1979, 68).

Because of segregation, through the 1960s and into the 1970s, black male dentists and other black male professionals primarily serviced the black community exclusively. Traditionally, black institutions of higher education (Howard University and Meharry Medical College) have educated the majority of black dentists. Historically black colleges and universities have a long history of providing the necessary education and training for many black male professionals.

One example of a community and social organization that gives support and empowerment to families and neighborhoods is 100 Black Men, Inc. This organization provides numerous activities and programs that serve over 60,000 young people. It is a constant presence in the community and has a long history of having a significant impact on the lives of young black males. Its members' efforts assist black males with rebuilding their lives and becoming a valuable asset to their neighborhood and to the economy (100 Black Men of America 1998).

Another community organization is the National African American Male Collaboration. It deserves special mention because it is an umbrella organization devoted to a single common purpose, that of improving the status of black males.

Black fraternities have existed since the turn of the century. There are five black fraternities: Omega Psi Phi, Alpha Phi Alpha, Kappa Alpha Psi, Phi Beta Sigma, and Iota Phi Theta. Each fraternity provides a strong support base for black males. Their purpose encompasses the principles of encouragement, empowerment, and service to each other and the community. With tens of thousands of black males actively involved in fraternities, there are a plethora of programs that target volunteerism in the community and activities that empower youths, families, and neighborhoods.

Churches and mosques are an integral part of the family and neighborhoods. These religious organizations have a long-standing tradition of involvement with the black family. Over the last two decades, many churches and mosques in black neighborhoods have expanded and provided services to more families. For instance, Ebenezer A.M.E. Church, pastored by the Reverend Grainger Browning, relocated to Fort Washington, Maryland, in 1983 with 13 members. Today, Ebenezer is serving over 10,000 members. Like similar black churches that serve a large membership base, it provides numerous services and programs to black families.

Black males assume many leadership roles in churches and mosques that serve black families. The involvement of black males in both churches and mosques demonstrates the efforts made by black males to be involved in families and the impact black males have in participating in activities that create sustainability and economic opportunities for families.

Another form of black male leadership can be found in public service, which ranges from positions in the president's cabinet to governor to mayor. Black males hold positions of authority and responsibility at all levels of government: federal, state, and local. Earlier we discussed the leadership roles of black males at the federal level. Also, there are black males who assume leadership roles at the state level. One of them is Douglas Wilder, the former governor of Virginia. At the local level, among the major cities in the United States that currently have black male mayors are San Francisco, California; Atlanta, Georgia; Dallas, Texas; Baltimore, Maryland; Seattle, Washington; Cleveland, Ohio; Denver, Colorado; St. Louis, Missouri;

Philadelphia, Pennsylvania; and Washington, D.C. There are also a number of black males who serve their districts in the U.S. House of Representatives.

The positions at the federal, state, and local levels where black males assume leadership and maintain high levels of responsibility are important to the family at the micro and macro levels and therefore to the economy. The black men in these positions are representing many families with their public service. Their focus involves addressing the conditions from a policy standpoint that will positively affect families and create economic opportunities.

At both the micro and macro levels, black men have played and continue to play a vital role in the family. The oft-discussed perspective that black males are not meeting their responsibilities does not completely hold true. More black males need to take responsibility for their families. However, there are a significant number and percentage of black males who are responsible and active in the family at both the micro and macro levels.

CONCLUSION

This article demonstrated how black males are making significant strides in the U.S. economy. Again, the article does not refute the reports about the conditions affecting black males. Rather, it highlights the progress and accomplishments of black males in the economy. The positive accomplishments and impact of black males are often overlooked or neglected because of the myriad problems that confront them. We demonstrated that many black males, although faced with problems, are overcoming these obstacles and carving a piece of the U.S. economy for themselves.

Notes

1. The averages reported in this section of the article are median weekly earnings and are based on data from the U.S. Bureau of Labor Statistics.

2. In 1998, the total number of black males aged 25 and over in the U.S. population was 8,578,000, and of those, 6,449,000 had received a high school diploma or a GED (general educational development) equivalency credential.

3. Throughout this article, we use the median when we report average earnings.

4. The Census Bureau distinguishes between a household and a family. "A household comprises all persons who occupy a housing unit, that is, a house, an apartment or other group of rooms, or a single room that constitutes 'separate living quarters.'" A family is defined as "a group of two or more persons related by birth, marriage, or adoption and residing together in a household. Families headed by women with no spouse present used to be called 'female-headed families.' The householder is the first adult member listed on the questionnaire. The instructions call for listing the person (or one of the persons) in whose name the home is owned or rented. If a home is owned or rented jointly by a married couple, either the husband or the wife may be listed first. Prior to 1980, the husband was always considered the household head (householder) in married-couple households" (U.S. Bureau of the Census 1998).

References

Board of Governors of the Federal Reserve System. 1999. Members of the Board of Governors. Available at http://www.bog.frb.fed.us/bios/Ferguson.htm. Accessed on 27 Oct. 1999.

Borden, Mark and Suzanne Koudsi. 1999. America's Forty Richest Under Forty. *Fortune*, 27 Sept.

Brown, Charles. 1984. Black-White Earnings Ratios Since the Civil Rights Act of 1964: The Importance of Labor Market Dropouts. *Quarterly Journal of Economics* 44(Feb.):31-44.

Carnoy, Martin. 1994. *Faded Dreams: The Politics and Economics of Race in America*. New York: Cambridge University Press.

Doeringer, P. B. and M. J. Piore. 1971. *Internal Labor Markets and Manpower Analysis*. Lexington, MA: D. C. Heath.

Durden, Garey C. and Patricia E. Gaynor. 1998. More on the Cost of Being Other Than White and Male: Measurement of Race, Ethnic, and Gender Effects on Yearly Earnings. *American Journal of Economics and Sociology* 57(1):95-103.

Fairclough, Gordon. 1999. TLC Beatrice Prepares to Sell Last of Its Holdings. *Wall Street Journal*, 27 May.

Farley, John E. 1987. Disproportionate Black and Hispanic Unemployment in U.S. Metropolitan Areas: The Roles of Racial Inequality, Segregation and Discrimination in Male Joblessness. *American Journal of Economics and Sociology* 46(2):129-50.

Garfinkel, Irwin and Sara S. McLanahan.1986. *Single Mothers and Their Children: A New American Dilemma*. Washington, DC: Urban Institute Press.

Graves, Earl G. 1997. *How To Succeed in Business Without Being White: Straight Talk on Making It in America*. New York: Harper Business.

Hays, Constance L. 1999. TLC Beatrice to Sell Remaining Divisions. *New York Times*, 28 May.

Johnson Publishing Company. 1999. About Our History. Available at http://www.ebony.com/historya.html. Accessed on 29 Oct. 1999.

Juhn, Chinhui. 1992. Decline of Male Labor Market Participation: The Role of Declining Market Opportunities. *Quarterly Journal of Economics* 107(1):79-121.

Kidd, Foster. 1979. *Profile of the Negro in American Dentistry*. Washington, DC: Howard University Press.

McElroy, Susan Williams and William Darity, Jr. 1999. Labor Market Discrimination by Race. In *Readings in Black Political Economy*, ed. John Whitehead. Dubuque, IA: Kendall/Hunt.

100 Black Men of America, Inc. 1998. Available at http://www.100blackmen.org. Accessed 27 Oct. 1999.

Parsons, Donald O. 1980. Racial Trends in Male Labor Force Participation. *American Economic Review* 70(Dec.):911-20.

Ross, Heather L. and Isabel V. Sawhill with the assistance of Ania R. MacIntosh. 1975. *Time of Transition: The Growth of Families Headed by Women*. Washington, DC: Urban Institute.

Schmitz, Susanne, Donald R. Williams, and Paul E. Gabriel. 1994. An Empirical Examination of Racial and Gender Differences in Wage Distributions. *Quarterly Review of Economics and Finance* 34(Fall): 227-39.

Schwartzman, David. 1997. Black Male Unemployment. *Review of Black Political Economy* 25(Winter): 77-93.

Smith, James P. and Finis R. Welch. 1986. *Closing the Gap: Forty Years of Economic Progress for Blacks*. Santa Monica, CA: RAND.

Stark, Jeff. 1999. Brilliant Careers. *Salon*, 6 July.

Tucker, M. Belinda and Claudia Mitchell-Kernan. 1995. Trends in African American Family Formation. In *The Decline of Marriage Among African Americans: Causes, Consequences, and Policy Implications*, ed. M. Belinda Tucker and Claudia Mitchell-Kernan. New York: Russell Sage Foundation.

U.S. Bureau of the Census. 1963. *U.S. Census of Population: 1960. Detailed Characteristics. United States Summary*. Final Report PC (1)-1D. Washington, DC: Government Printing Office.

———. 1970. *Educational Attainment: March 1969*. Current Population Reports. Series P-20. No. 194. Washington, DC: Government Printing Office.

———. 1992. *Educational Attainment in the United States: March 1991 and 1990*. Current Population Reports. Series P-20. No. 462. Washington, DC: Government Printing Office.

———. 1993a. *Census of Population and Housing, 1990: Equal Employment Opportunity (EEO) File on CD-ROM*. Machine-readable data files. Washington, DC: Bureau of the Census

———. 1993b. *Statistical Abstract of the United States 1993*. Washington, DC: Government Printing Office.

———. 1998. Percent of People 25 Years Old and Over Who Have Completed High School or College, by Race, Hispanic Origin and Sex: Selected Years 1940 to 1998 (Table A-2). Available at http://www.census.gov/population/socdemo/education/tablea-02.txt.

———. 1999a. *Educational Attainment in the United States: March 1998 (Update)*. Current Population Reports. Series P-20. No. 513. Washington, DC: Government Printing Office.

———. 1999b. *Marital Status and Living Arrangements: March 1998 (Update)*. Current Population Reports. Series P-20. No. 514. Washington, DC: Government Printing Office.

U.S. Department of Education. National Center for Education Statistics. 1998. *Digest of Education Statistics 1998*. Washington, DC: Government Printing Office.

U.S. Department of Transportation. Office of Public Affairs. 1999. Biography: Rodney E. Slater, United States Secretary of Transportation. Washington DC: U.S. Department of Transportation. Available at http://www.dot.gov/affairs/slatebio.htm. Accessed on 27 Oct. 1999.

Whigham-Desir, Marjorie. 1999. Leadership Has Its Rewards. *Black Enterprise*, Sept.

Book Department

INTERNATIONAL RELATIONS AND POLITICS

BOMBERG, ELIZABETH. 1998. *Green Parties and Politics in the European Union*. Pp. xiii, 225. New York: Routledge. $75.00. Paperbound, $25.99.

Green parties are generally rife with factions and wracked by ideological conflict. For example, members of the Green Party of New York State, in which I am active, are currently arguing over the war in Kosovo, party building and leadership, affiliations with other parties and groups, and other issues. The strife is partly due to the ordinary growing pains attendant to new parties. But there is something deeper at work here as well.

The central conflict is between the realists, who are more or less willing to compromise Green values in the name of effectiveness, efficiency, and coalition politics, and the fundamentalists, who are opposed to (nearly) any dilution of the Green program. This dualism, of course, suffers from the weakness of all such dyads: it does not capture the complexity or nuances of actual conflicts. But almost every political issue confronted by Greens brings some version of this conflict to the fore, and so it is with Green parties in the European Union (EU), the subject of Elizabeth Bomberg's excellent new book.

Bomberg begins with an overview of Green politics and actors in Western Europe, deftly and concisely covering an enormous territory. She introduces the "green strategic conundrum," the dilemma over doctrinal purity versus participation in real, existing polities. In chapter 2, she makes a compelling case for the increased importance of the EU as the premier regional site for environmental policymaking. The Greens, she makes clear, have had no alternative but to press their issues at the European level. But they have not been content to accept the institutions of European integration as designed by others; chapter 3 puts forward the Greens' alternative theoretical conceptions of a "Europe of the regions" based on the principles of decentralism and subsidiarity. In practice, however, as Bomberg shows in chapter 4, the pressures of four European Parliament (EP) elections, with Green candidates running increasingly professional campaigns, have pushed the Green dream of a fundamentally different Europe to the background.

When she turns to the Greens' organization and performance within the EP, we see a steadily more coherent Green caucus beset not just by the inescapable strategic conundrum but also by cultural and structural divisions between national Green parties. Bomberg scrutinizes the Greens' impact on EU policymaking in chapters 6 and 7. She finds in chapter 6 that the Greens have had a limited impact on the EU's environmental policymaking process, with some notable exceptions. She examines three cases in greater detail in chapter 7: vehicle emissions, biotechnology, and packaging waste. Bomberg claims that varied Green success (greatest for vehicle emissions) is due primarily to the heroic efforts of individual Green members of the EP. She shows that the Greens are hindered by paltry resources (staff, money, and so on) in comparison to coalitions of corporate behemoths, like those in the packaging industry. Her discussion of Green lobbying against biotechnology has been overcome by events. Public opposition to Monsanto's soybeans, among other genetically engineered Frankensteins, has grown explosively.

Green Parties and Politics in the European Union closes with an assessment of the insoluble conundrum: what makes the Greens attractive to voters (strong, unwavering principles) conflicts with the daily realities of EU politics (compromise and deal making). Bomberg makes clear that this is an existential dilemma for Greens. Green parties have no choice, short of splintering, but to confront and negotiate the dilemma.

This is a book that deserves a wide readership, from scholars to practitioners to undergraduates to the educated public interested in European and Green politics. Rare is the book that is of use to both researchers and beginning students. It is clearly written, coherently organized, cogently argued: a model of comparative public policy scholarship.

STEVE BREYMAN

Rensselaer Polytechnic Institute
Troy
New York

HERBST, SUSAN. 1998. *Reading Public Opinion: How Political Actors View the Democratic Process*. Pp. x, 256. Chicago: University of Chicago Press. Paperbound, $16.00.

This work firmly establishes Susan Herbst as one of the leading theorists of public opinion. Her previous books have illuminated the historical and social contexts in which opinion emerges and through which it is defined. In *Numbered Voices*, we were reminded convincingly that publics in previous eras were organized in communities and that they expressed their voices in ways that both affirmed their identities within those communities and made creative political use of their public voices. She concluded that the emergence of mass opinion polls in the present era not only distracts attention from arguably more important forms of opinion but drowns out distinctive social voices that lose their identities through the constructed homogeneity of polling. Her next work, *Politics at the Margin*, is among the best historical analyses of the origins of publics in modern democracy, looking at the means through which marginal political groups such as women have gained their share of the public sphere.

Reading Public Opinion, the latest work in Herbst's impressive oeuvre, is in many ways the most ambitious. The focus is on contemporary politics. Instead of looking at possible opinion formations emanating from citizens, Herbst turns the tables and asks the provocative question of what the public looks like from the vantage of political elites. This way of problematizing opinion engages directly with democratic theory. In particular, looking at publics and public interests through the eyes of elites enables Herbst to question the appropriateness of the often disconnected and abstracted ways in which academics conceptualize and measure opinion.

Her interviews with journalists, party activists, legislative staffers, communication directors, and press secretaries in the Illinois state capital provide a richly textured look at how actors who operate in the same environment do so with vastly different conceptions of publics and their opinions. Yet these elites all share one startling perspective: none regards publics as broad aggregations of citizen viewpoints that should be counted routinely in their political or journalistic navigation through political situations. The formal consideration of polled opinion for purposes other than spin is the exception rather than the rule of political insider thinking. For staffers (and, one presumes, their elected bosses) the front line of meaningful public opinion is the lobbyist corps, whose interests are perceived to be those of the public. More generalized publics figure mainly into political positioning and election strategies as politicians respond to popular reactions to legislation. For journalists, the public is a vague, sleepy lot. The real opinions that matter are those carried on the insider buzz. This conception may explain a lot about why general publics perceive journalists as out-of-touch insiders: apparently, they are. For their part, party activists see party leaders and representatives as the sources of true opinions that represent the best interests of all, even when their opinions are removed from those expressed in polls. We see in this a primary reason why party activists may preserve party ideological divisions against the warnings of strategists that such divisions may prove fatal at election time. These foundations on which opinion is incorporated into the legislative and representative processes, and in journalistic renderings of these processes, make a great deal of sense in a political context, but they are at odds with much of the contemporary theory and the empirical work underlying mainstream analyses of politics.

Herbst concludes that her findings are reminiscent of Lippmann's phantom public, as captured in the idea that general publics are creatures of political rhetoric and are creations of public relations and the engineering of consent. Thus a compelling point of the work is that the ways in which academics and pollsters generally regard opinion offer little insight into how opinion is actually incorporated into the daily interactions and calculations of the elites most responsible for making government work and for publicizing the results. As with all of Herbst's work, this trenchant idea is stated with subtlety. Unlike many critics, Herbst is less interested in toppling conventional wisdom than in understanding how opinion processes actually affect the communication and expression of preferences and the operation of government. This is an important book that adds another dimension to Herbst's rigorous effort to understand opinion processes in different social and historical settings.

LANCE BENNETT

University of Washington
Seattle

HILL, KEVIN A. and JOHN E. HUGHES. 1998. *Cyberpolitics: Citizen Activism in the Age of the Internet.* Pp. ix, 207. Lanham, MD: Rowman & Littlefield. $49.00. Paperbound, $18.95.

As we sit in front of our computer terminals, we have all wondered how the Internet and related technologies are changing our world, especially the political aspects of these technologies. *Cyberpolitics* attempts to answer this question by analyzing the political content of the Internet in its various forms.

This book maps out the political implications of the World Wide Web in three areas. First, have these new technologies expanded access to political information and opened new participation opportunities? Second, are there apparent political biases in the users of these new technologies? Third, and most important, what are the implications of these new technologies for the quality and operation of the democratic process?

A tremendous amount has already been written about the Internet, chat rooms, and the Web, but this literature is largely impressionistic and based on anecdotal evidence. This leads some authors to claim that the Internet will create a democratic utopia, while others see these technologies as potentially weakening the democratic process.

Hill and Hughes rise above this speculation by providing a rich and diverse empirical study of these technologies. They use national survey data to examine the social and political characteristics of Internet users. They sample newsgroups and analyze their content, as well as the political content of chat rooms or Internet Relay Chats. There is also a brief exploratory content analysis of several political Web sites. All the pieces are here to provide a baseline study of the political implications of this brave new world.

The "cybercitizens" who utilize the Internet tend to be younger, better-educated males—the generation that came to age wielding a joystick (or a mouse). These users are also more likely to be Democrats, although their beliefs reflect a mix of liberalism and skepticism toward big government. Furthermore, rather than rejecting conventional political action, Internet users are more interested in politics, more likely to vote, and more likely to use conventional information sources such as newspapers.

A different pattern emerges for the political content of Usenet and chat room conversations. Political discourse on the Web tends to be politically neutral, but when ideological biases exist, they are distinctly conservative and antigovernment. This is surprising since Hill and Hughes had just demonstrated that most Internet users are liberal. They offer a provocative explanation (which deserves more study): a small group of conservative activists are actively attempting to shape Internet discourse.

The chapter on international newsgroups suggests a link between the Internet and global democratization. Hill and Hughes find that the level of government criticism existing in newsgroups about specific nations is related to the level of democracy in a nation. Critical comments decrease as democracy increases; this holds globally and within most regions of the globe. Such Internet criticisms of repressive government may represent a type of virtual protest against these regimes. This is unlikely to alter the course of politics in a nation such as Cuba or China—but providing a forum for such discussion is still a positive benefit of the World Wide Web.

Cyberpolitics charts a course between the rhetoric of Internet utopians and dystopians. This is not high theory, but it does offer important practical evidence on the political implications of these new technologies. In the end, Hill and Hughes conclude, "The Internet is a supplement to political discourse, not a gigantic paradigm shift." The Internet does represent a new channel of information, and it does provide access to nonmainstream groups. But the evidence of this book suggests that the ability of these technologies to wield a true transformative impact appears limited.

RUSSELL DALTON

University of California
Irvine

NINO, CARLOS SANTIAGO. 1996. *The Constitution of Deliberative Democracy*. Pp. ix, 246. New Haven, CT: Yale University Press. $40.00. Paperbound, $17.00

At the beginning of a new century, the modern human rights revolution stands at a crossroads. Numerous countries, from Latin America to Eastern Europe to Africa and the Caribbean, are attempting to make the precarious transition from dictatorship to democracy—from repressive regimes to ones committed to the rule of law. At the same time, however, thousands of innocent people have been murdered, tortured, and brutalized in these very same nations.

It remains unclear which of the paths will predominate in the coming years. Unfortunately, what is clear is that we understand little about the causes of human rights abuses, the content of human rights norms, and the prescriptions for addressing massive violations of these rights. There remain huge gaps in our understanding of the philosophical and moral justifications of human rights, democracy, and constitutionalism, and we remain uncertain about the methods for dealing with these complex issues on a practical level. This gap is reflected in the paucity of first-rate literature.

One noted exception is the work of Carlos Santiago Nino, a unique Argentine professor, lawyer, and political actor, who has bridged the gap between democracy, human rights theory, and practice. As an adviser to President Raul Alfonsín directly after the "dirty war" of 1976-83 that led to the deaths of at least 9000 Argentines by a brutal military junta, Nino also became one of the chief architects of the government's decision to place members of the junta on trial for the atrocities perpetrated under their rule.

In *The Constitution of Deliberative Democracy*, published posthumously, Nino brought his lifelong work to bear on the relationship between democracy, constitutionalism, and human rights. The main question, according to Nino, is how to justify democracy. He attempts to answer this complicated question by examining various interpretative and justificatory theories of democracy, and he argues that democracy is a normative concept, not simply an end in itself but a means for the creation of a more just society. Nino then concludes that democracy is best justified by its epistemic value. This theory assigns a value to democratic politics because it enlarges the range of interests that will be taken into account in the formulation of public policy. For Nino, democracy is a surrogate for the informal practice of moral discussion, and, in an imperfect world, democracy is the best means available for discovering moral truth.

Putting the greatest emphasis on the practice of rational deliberation, Nino assigns value to democracy based on a processing of preferences. His view relies on the virtue of democracy to transform people's self-interested preferences into more altruistic and impartial ones. His view further assumes that the method of achieving this goal is that of collective deliberation—dialogue. Further, Nino argues that collective deliberation has value in itself because it provides reasons for believing that the solution endorsed by the consensus agrees with what is prescribed by valid moral principles, which, in turn, provide us with autonomous reasons to act. Moreover, he contends that majority decision making preceded by a process of deliberation constitutes a more effective method of ascertaining the moral good than any person's individual reflection. Thus Nino's theory assumes an intrinsic relationship between democratic politics, the law resulting from it, and morality.

According to Nino, deliberative democracy supports constitutionalism. It also bears on the way power is organized under a constitution. In his theory, what he refers to as the three dimensions of constitutionalism—a historical constitution, an ideal constitution of rights, and an ideal constitution of power—need not conflict but, rather, can reinforce one another.

Another goal of Nino's work is to provide a horizon and blueprint for the design and adjustment of political institutions. His theory of deliberative democracy suggests how these changes can be made. For example, he argues for a more important role for ideologically committed political parties, and he critiques the presidential system.

The Constitution of Deliberative Democracy is an extraordinary book written by an extraordinary man about the burning issues of our time. It is extremely thought provoking and intellectually challenging. Even more important, it invites further development and argument, a goal Nino himself constantly strove to achieve.

IRWIN P. STOTZKY

University of Miami
Coral Gables
Florida

OBER, JOSIAH. 1998. *Political Dissent in Democratic Athens: Intellectual Critics of Popular Rule.* Pp. xv, 417. Princeton, NJ: Princeton University Press. $35.00.

This book is first rate: intelligent, judicious, original, a seamless performance, and on a fundamental topic, Athens's elite literary critics of its democracy. Seven chapters each discuss a single writer (or at most two): Ps.-Xenophon ("The Old Oligarch"); Thucydides; Aristophanes (*Ecclesiazusae*); Plato (with Sokrates); Isokrates (*Antidosis* and *Areopagitikos*); Aristotle (*Politics*); and Ps.-Aristotle (*Political Regime of the Athenians*) with Theophrastos. Each chapter cogently, brilliantly explicates these critics' views on democracy's problems and what (if anything) might be done about them. Beyond this, for Ober, these critics constituted a community of dissident intellectuals. Each chapter suggests links and reactions between

their works, from Ps.-Xenophon's "dead end" in the face of democracy's success, through Aristotle's final, workable solution to democracy's problems a century later, and the moderating of antidemocratic criticism.

Discussion of the many strengths of this volume would greatly exceed the space allotted. On virtually every page I find I have scrawled enthusiastic comments or "use in class!" Beginners as well as experts will profit from each synthetic chapter. Ober's text is consistently accessible to the nonspecialist. One signal rhetorical quality lies in Ober's almost total lack of polemic or even discussion of competing positions. This absence of controversy gives the impression that everything inside is translucent truth that all accept. The style is a marvelous *captatio benevolentiae*.

Page by page, I have remarkably few criticisms. For future reflection, I make four general remarks. First, one great strength of the volume is that it makes a century of antidemocratic criticism coherent. However, Ober's community of dissidents may be too restricted and not so much a community. If, for example, Aristotle echoes themes found in Isokrates (such as "the ancestral democracy"), many such themes were older than Isokrates and more widely disseminated. We may therefore question whether "Aristotle follow[ed] Isocrates' lead." Athens's democracy had many more elite literary critics than seven, beginning (for me) with Sophocles' *Ajax* and *Antigone* and culminating in the wider and now public discontent after 350, for example, in Demosthenes and Aeschines, which led to significant modifications of Athens's democratic constitution. Ober alludes to the latter only at the end of his volume. Although less consistently antidemocratic and much harder to disentangle, these critics might profitably be added to the mix.

Within the study of each critic also, the search for coherence means that important problems are sometimes smoothed over. As with his contemporary Euripides, often Thucydides' complexities make him especially worth pondering: for example, toward Perikles (whose first speech is indeed answered by the Corinthians, and the funeral oration by the plague), or toward Athens's brutalities on Melos, paralleled by Sparta's earlier treatment of the Plataians (and Sparta was not a democracy). Over his long life, Isokrates' views were all over the map (at the end of the book, Ober recognizes this). None of these texts is so transparent as in Ober's illuminating explication. The compelling seamless coherence of this book masks a more disjointed, contradictory reality.

Third, Ober sometimes (knowingly) pushes the envelope, for example, in the two provocative hypotheses that start and end the volume. First, he claims, after 404 one had to criticize democracy to be considered a serious intellectual. True, most intellectuals whose work is preserved do criticize democracy. However, barring Aristophanes, these texts were written in part because their antidemocratic authors could not speak in public. Pro-democratic thinkers could speak publicly, without the need for writing. It is hard to imagine that no intellectuals (including, for example, dramatists) in fourth-century Athens took the side of democracy. (Both Ober and I argue from silence.) Second, toward the end of the volume, Ober's major hypothesis that Aristotle thought the Macedonians could enact his ideal regime in an Asian colony must remain speculative.

My fourth and last criticism is that chapter 1 ends with an extended discussion of speech act theory, rather awkwardly located. This perhaps does not accomplish much and is rarely exploited later.

Future work notwithstanding, Ober's book is a great achievement. It is a volume I shall read again.

ROBERT W. WALLACE
Northwestern University
Evanston
Illinois

WEART, SPENCER R. 1998. *Never at War: Why Democracies Will Not Fight One Another*. Pp. xii, 424. New Haven, CT: Yale University Press. $35.00.

The 93 pages of endnotes in this book devoted almost entirely to the listing of sources (many in French, Germany, Italian, and Spanish) are one indication of the scope of this work. Another is a comment by Weart about his research regarding medieval Italy: "It cost me a year of research into the detailed history of each Italian city to recognize this crucial transition."

The thesis inspiring this prodigious feat of historical distillation is that republics have not and will not fight wars against each other. Most of the political scientists who have evaluated this idea in the last decade or so have focused on the era since World War II. Skeptics wonder whether peace between democracies in that era might be accounted for by the opposition from Communist states, for example. But Weart examines relationships between republics in ancient Greece, medieval and Renaissance Italy, the Swiss Forest States, the Hanseatic League, and, in fact, wherever and whenever he has been able to find them in the history of the entire world up to the contemporary era.

His historical investigation is guided by a few simple, intuitively plausible concepts and propositions. He defines "republics" as states in which political decisions are made in competitive processes by a body of citizens who hold equal rights. If the body of citizens in question represents less than one-third of the male population, the republic is categorized as oligarchic. If more than two-thirds of the adult males have political rights, that political community is categorized as democratic. A republic is considered well established if its government tolerates peaceful opposition from all important domestic political rivals. Republics in existence for three years can be assumed to have developed a republican political culture. Political culture is defined as involving the beliefs that people have about how they ought to deal with each other when groups are in conflict. A war is defined as organized violence by political units across boundaries that involves at least 200 deaths resulting from combat.

The keystone of Weart's theory is the idea that political leaders will generalize from domestic political experiences when they deal with foreign counterparts. Political leaders in well-established republics will expect, when they deal with other republics, that political conflicts can and should be dealt with in a peaceful manner. This tendency is so strong that Weart finds in his study of republics from the Peloponnesian War to the present that similar republics have virtually never fought wars against each other. There has been only one war between well-established oligarchic republics, in 1656. There have been no wars between well-established democratic republics.

There is historical interpretation involved in coming to these conclusions, and opponents to Weart's thesis might come to different conclusions. But Weart does seem inclined to be fair. He writes clearly. He is certainly thorough. He has provided virtually a mountain of documentation available to anyone who cares to question his conclusions.

I wonder if Weart has paid enough attention to imperialist colonization by democratic France, Britain, and the United States. At one point, he seems inclined to define Communist countries as oligarchic republics, which brings to mind questions about just how broad that category is. But basically this volume seems to me to present a powerful argument in favor of the idea that one simply cannot understand conflict between states (or other independent political communities) without taking into account the pervasive impact of fundamental differences between autocratic and democratic (or republican) political regimes.

JAMES LEE RAY

Vanderbilt University
Nashville
Tennessee

AFRICA, ASIA, AND LATIN AMERICA

CAMP, RODERIC AI. 1997. *Crossing Swords: Politics and Religion in Mexico*. Pp. ix, 341. New York: Oxford University Press. $65.00.

Roderic Camp, professor of government at Claremont McKenna College, has published extensively on the modern Mexican scene. In his latest work, he takes the same approach that he used earlier in analyzing Mexican intellectuals, politicians, entrepreneurs, and military personnel and applies it to the Mexican clergy and the Catholic Church.

Camp begins by establishing the analytical framework he will employ. The work involves an examination of both the relationship between church and state and the interrelationship between religion and politics. These relationships involve 14 "premises," which Camp explores. Camp devotes a chapter to a historical overview of church-state relations, with the emphasis on the post-1910 period, especially the constitutional reforms of the presidential administration of Carlos Salinas in 1991-92.

Camp then devotes two chapters to a discussion of current issues confronting the Catholic Church that he categorizes as politics, partisanship, development, moral challenges, and spiritual challenges. The church considers it unacceptable to favor a particular political party but believes it proper to play a political role. There is a discussion of the church's connection—or lack of it—to the various political parties and its involvement in promoting the integrity of the electoral system and pursuing social justice issues. Camp also examines the religiosity and the religious intensity of the Mexican people and their social and political consequences.

The next three chapters deal with the social origins, recruitment, education, and attitudes of the clergy, with the emphasis on those priests who become bishops. A number of elements influence the decision to become a priest, especially the family environment and being closely related to someone in the religious life. An examination of the career tracks of those bishops who held office from the 1960s through the 1990s indicates the importance of serving at the diocesan seminary in becoming a bishop. Unlike political leaders, bishops are more likely to come from a working-class background and have strong regional and rural connections.

Camp also examines the informal and structural linkages between church and state. In the absence of strong institutional connections, personal linkages are the most important; as one goes down the political administrative structure, personal linkages between church and state become stronger and more important.

Camp also covers the Mexican church's international linkages, including the key role played by the papal nuncio and the impact of foreign finances and personnel.

There is an entire chapter devoted to the structure of the diocese as the basic unit of the church and to the decision-making power of the bishop in his diocese. Mexican bishops tend to have lengthy tenures and enjoy considerable autonomy. Their power and influence are major factors in the decentralized nature of the church, which is often viewed—especially by Mexican politicians—as a monolithic organization.

Camp concludes his work by comparing and contrasting the views of the church held by politicians, bishops, and priests. All three groups find it difficult to distinguish between social activism and political activism. Camp concludes that mediation and negotiation will serve as the cornerstones of the church's approach to the state in the future.

As in many of his earlier works, Camp often relies on the collective-biography approach, with much of the information derived from his personal interviews with participants on both sides and all levels of church-state relations. These interviews are the most extensive ever conducted by Camp and took place between 1985 and 1995, spanning the periods immediately before and after the constitutional reforms of 1991-92. The work does not presuppose any knowledge about the structures and functions of the Catholic Church that Camp details. *Crossing Swords* provides valuable data and conclusions about one of the most important institutions in Mexico. It makes an excellent companion piece to Camp's earlier works, such as his recent study of the Mexican military, *Generals in the Palacio* (1992).

DON M. COERVER

Texas Christian University
Fort Worth

HUGHES, LINDSEY. 1998. *Russia in the Age of Peter the Great*. Pp. xxix, 602. New Haven, CT: Yale University Press. $35.00.

Lindsey Hughes's book joins the classic works of S. M. Solov'ëv, V. O. Kliuchevskii, and P. N. Miliukov on the reign of Peter the Great and will be one of the volumes that everyone interested in Russia in the 1682-1725 period will need to read.

Hughes masterfully presents most of the major historiographic disputes (What evolved from the past, and what was new? What was the role of Peter's personality? What was native, and what was imported from the West? What proved to be ephemeral, and what endured?) as she discusses the major relevant topics of the era: war and military change, the constantly reforming government, economic development, social change, the building of St. Petersburg and the arts, education and religion, Peter's court, his personality, his family, and major assistants. The reader may be assured that much of the recent scholarship on these topics is accurately presented as well as that Hughes herself has read and creatively used most of the published primary sources and also some unpublished archival materials in Russia. Especially creative is Hughes's use of the large number of contemporary non-Russian commentaries on the period.

The major element that is surprising to me in this book is the presentation of the Petrine use of Greek and Roman motifs, which adumbrated the post-1730 neoclassical period decades before it became the dominant mode. The appeal of the neoclassical was to make the isolated Russian a man of the world, but Peter obviously had prepared the ground for such thoughts.

Historiography buffs wanting to know where Hughes comes down on the major issues of continuity, innovation, impact, and Peter's personality may be disappointed by a lack of decisiveness on these issues, which typically is the result of a sophisticated approach recognizing that black-and-white presentations are too simplistic. Yet on some issues, a more specific authorial verdict might be welcome, for it is hard to comprehend how Peter both brought Russia out of Asiatic barbarism and backwardness to Western modernity and also held Russia back two centuries by reinforcing the caste system and crushing all glimmerings of a civil society. In the case of the reform of the church (the abolition of the Patriarchate and its replacement by the Holy Synod, a government department), the reader is likely to believe that the reform was more radical than it really was because the effective secularization of church administration by the creation of the Monastery Chancellery in the Ulozhenie of 1969 is not mentioned.

My major problem with the book is Hughes's presentation of society, which I find confusing. She uses the words "nobility" and "nobles" very loosely to refer to everyone from the handful of boyars down through the tens of thousands of rural landholders and landowners and even some people who had no land or serfs at all. (At least she is to be congratulated for eschewing the word "gentry," which is equally inapplicable. I prefer the term "service class.") At the other end of society, the presentation of slaves (sometimes "servants") is not as accurate as it might be. I also am not impressed very much by the utility of a semiotic approach indicating that some of Peter's problems stemmed from his inability to communicate with his subjects. I would prefer to argue that most of society was right-brained and that Peter's nauseatingly continuous use of violence was the only way to communicate with Russian society. Preliterates (nonreaders) could not be appealed to by left-brained rationality.

RICHARD HELLIE

University of Chicago
Illinois

MILLER, MARTIN A. 1998. *Freud and the Bolsheviks: Psychoanalysis in Imperial Russia and the Soviet Union.* Pp. xvii. 237. New Haven, CT: Yale University Press. $30.00.

Following the lifting of Soviet-era ideological restrictions and the opening of previously inaccessible archives, Western and Russian scholars alike have begun to reassess numerous controversial aspects of Soviet history. Martin Miller's analysis of the complex fate of Freudian theory and practice in the USSR is one example of this valuable new scholarship. While Miller is not the only researcher to have tackled this subject in the past decade, both his approach and the scope of his analysis distinguish this work from others that have preceded it.

The chronological boundaries of his study are the first appearance of Freudian concepts and psychoanalytic practitioners in Russia in the late nineteenth century and the demise of the Soviet system in 1991. For most of the twentieth century, the conventional wisdom has been that Freudian theory never really took hold in Russia and that the Bolsheviks, under Stalin, eliminated whatever traces of a psychoanalytic community continued to exist there at the end of the 1920s. The official Soviet stance on the subject was consistently, even stridently, critical, giving most observers every reason to assume that Stalin had indeed succeeded in "killing Freud."

As Miller convincingly demonstrates, however, the reality was much more complex. Officially, Freud may have met an untimely end at the hands of the ideological purists, but, as was characteristic of so many other aspects of the Soviet system, the unofficial reality was something else altogether. Miller carefully, yet concisely, traces the history of formal policies toward Freudian ideas, practitioners, and institutions. Some of this story has already been told. More significant, however, he reveals the manner in which and the extent to which Soviet scholars and practitioners managed (particularly after the death of Stalin) to facilitate discussions of Freudian ideas by participating in the ongoing critique of it. A prime example is the case of V. N. Dobren'kov, a Moscow sociologist who in the mid-1970s "achieved a very Soviet distinction—in a very public manner, he became the country's leading expert on a Western intellectual whose work was officially not yet available to read." Through his examining of the writings of scholars such as Dobren'kov and others, Miller also makes it clear that the Soviet critique of Freud was based upon more than single-minded "ideological commitments." Rather, many of the criticisms leveled against Freudian theory by Soviet analysts were not only similar to those of their Western peers but sometimes even anticipated them.

Official Soviet treatment of things Freudian has varied radically over the course of the twentieth century. Freudian theory had very powerful supporters among the early Bolsheviks, and, perhaps partly as a result of that, its opponents later attacked it with particular vengeance. The somewhat ironic upshot of this, as Miller points out, is that the Bolshevik government has the distinction of being the only one either to sponsor "a state-supported and government-funded psychoanalytic institute" or to set about "literally closing down the entire structure of psychoanalytic work."

These dramatic shifts in the status of Freudian thought serve as a good indicator of changes occurring within the larger Soviet polity and society. Miller utilizes this theme not only to shed new light upon an incompletely understood chapter in the history of psychoanalytic theory but to open a window onto the whole of Soviet history as well. Among the strengths of this book are its readability and its accessibility. Both of these qualities, in combination with its relative brevity, should attract a wide readership that includes not only scholars of Russia and of psychoanalytic history but also a much broader audience of nonspecialists.

JULIE V. BROWN

University of North Carolina
Greensboro

EUROPE

KERTZER, DAVID I. 1998. *Politics and Symbols: The Italian Communist Party and the Fall of Communism*. Pp. xi, 211. New Haven, CT: Yale University Press. $32.50. Paperbound, $15.00.

On 11 November 1989, only two days after the fall of the Berlin Wall, Achille Occhetto, the secretary of the Italian Communist Party (PCI), made a speech to a group of Resistance veterans in Bologna calling for the radical transformation of the party he led. What followed in little more than a year was the dramatic change of a party, the largest of its kind outside the Communist-bloc states, into a post-Communist Democratic Party of the Left (PDS) and a neo-Communist Refounded Communist Party (RC).

The change Occhetto and his supporters promoted was not achieved without considerable emotional turmoil and organizational strain. During 1990, the PCI leadership held an extraordinary Central Committee meeting, a special

National Congress in Bologna (the PCI's nineteenth) and, finally, at the end of January 1991, a twentieth and last national gathering in Rimini.

David Kertzer provides a fascinating account of the PCI's transformation in these months from a particular perspective. Too often, he writes, political scientists neglect the symbolic aspects of party politics—the roles of naming, myths, and rituals—in seeking to understand the attachments that people develop to nations and political organizations of all kinds. *Politics and Symbols* is a case study that emphasizes the importance of such symbolism.

For Americans raised in the anti-Communist atmosphere of the Cold War era, it is difficult to believe but true nonetheless that millions of Italians willingly came to think of the PCI as a church that expressed a secular religion, one replete with saints (for example, Antonio Gramsci), devils (namely, capitalism and the United States), and near-holy experiences (that is, the Resistance to Fascist-Nazi rule during World War II). For those who came to think of the PCI in these highly emotive terms, particularly if they were party members for any length of time, the bonds between personal and collective identity became exceptionally close. As Kertzer points out repeatedly and with great effect, many people's identities—how they thought of themselves and how they wished to be understood by others—were based on their ties to the party. As one long-time militant put it, the effect on those whose lives were so closely tied to the PCI of Occhetto's decision to give up the Communist label and transform their beloved party into another formation was the equivalent of the pope's indicating he no longer believed in Jesus.

The abandonment of the Communist name and the symbol of the hammer and sickle along with such rituals of party life as the singing of "Bandiera Rossa" and the "Internationale" was too much for some. The RC continues to keep the old faith alive. But the majority of party members, after going through considerable public distress, were willing to follow Occhetto into the new PDS.

Much of Kertzer's excellent and instructive case study is devoted to analyzing the symbolic meanings of the transformation. Despite the author's highly persuasive argument about the importance of understanding the symbolic component at work in the PCI's death and rebirth, the change is also explicable as a rational choice as well. After all, the PCI's name had kept it out of power for decades. At the time that Occhetto announced his *svolta*, the party had been losing members and voters for years. Both the former and latter were aging rapidly. The Communist movement was collapsing on a worldwide basis. Occhetto's appeal for a new post-Communist party therefore seems like the perfectly rational calculation of a sensible party politician. Should we forget that the decision has paid off? Less than a decade later, the PDS is far and away the largest party in Italy's ruling coalition, and its leader, Massimo D'Alema, is the country's prime minister. Wouldn't these developments make Anthony Downs smile?

LEONARD WEINBERG

University of Nevada
Reno

SHAPIRO, GILBERT and JOHN MARKOFF. 1998. *Revolutionary Demands: A Content Analysis of the Cahiers de Doléances of 1789.* Pp. xxxi, 684. Stanford, CA: Stanford University Press. $75.00.

Revolutionay Demands is both an innovative study of the famous *cahiers de doléances*, the lists of popular grievances

compiled all across France on the eve of the Revolution of 1789, and an effort to reawaken interest in computer-assisted content analysis. Together with Markoff's recent study of peasant movements during the Revolution, *The Abolition of Feudalism* (1996), based largely on the same data, this volume effectively challenges many long-standing assumptions about the *cahiers* and about French public opinion at the time of the summoning of the Estates-General. Whether it will inspire other researchers to commit the time and resources required to emulate Shapiro and Markoff's efforts is less clear.

The over 40,000 *cahiers* are a unique body of documentation: a massive survey of public opinion in a society about to explode into one of history's most significant upheavals. Shapiro and Markoff made separate analyses of the general *cahiers* submitted by the assemblies of nobles and the Third Estate in each of the nearly 200 *bailliages*, or electoral districts (the clergy's *cahiers* are omitted, since they have never been systematically catalogued), and of a statistically representative sample of the parish *cahiers* produced in each French village. They argue convincingly that these three sets of documents represent three distinct groups, each of which played a vital role in the unfolding of the revolutionary process: the doomed aristocrats; the country's prosperous, educated urban elites; and the peasants, who made up some 85 percent of the population.

Historians have drawn on the *cahiers* in explaining the causes of the Revolution for over a century, but Shapiro and Markoff contend that previous studies have been too unsystematic or too narrowly focused to provide reliable results. They have attempted to code and analyze all the grievances in the entire body of surviving general *cahiers* and in their sample of the parish *cahiers*. They have furthermore sought to classify both the subjects mentioned in the grievances and the actions sought with respect to them. Rather than simply feeding the *cahiers* into a computer, they developed an elaborately described and carefully justified process combining coding by human readers and computerized analysis of the resulting data. In their view, this procedure overcomes the handicaps, such as confusion due to linguistic ambiguity, that bedevil purely machine-based analyses while still providing a scientific rigor unattainable with the informal procedures of conventional historical analysis.

Shapiro and Markoff's description of their methodology—the most original part of the book—and their critique of the sources occupies the first half of their volume. The second half contains eight previously published essays based on their data, seven by one or both coauthors and one by historian Timothy Tackett. These serve to demonstrate the variety of subjects that their database can address, ranging from the degree of conflict and consensus among and between nobles, bourgeois elites, and peasants on the eve of 1789 to the population's image of the king. Their work has unquestionably thrown considerable new light on the origins of the French Revolution and especially on the attitudes of the peasantry, exploding clichés about the rural population's lack of political interests or acumen, although these findings are laid out more clearly in Markoff's *Abolition of Feudalism*. They have also provided a working model of a successful approach to large-scale content analysis, one that should be of interest to social science researchers in many fields. The labor-intensive nature of their approach, however, leaves open the question of how many historical subjects warrant a comparable investment of time and effort.

JEREMY D. POPKIN

University of Kentucky
Lexington

UNITED STATES

MAY, CHRISTOPHER N. 1998. *Presidential Defiance of "Unconstitutional" Laws: Reviving the Royal Prerogative.* Pp. xiv, 215. Westport, CT: Greenwood Press. $59.95.

This is a book about a very special type of executive discretion. While most constitutional scholars would agree that the president should have some flexibility in enforcing the law, especially when the law is not appropriate to the exigencies of the moment, the type of discretion discussed in this book is a special case. On occasion, presidents have taken it upon themselves to disregard duly constituted laws for no other reason than their personal belief that the law they are required to enforce is unconstitutional. Christopher May makes a clear and convincing case that the responsibility for deciding the constitutionality of a law lies not with the president but with the courts. With this argument I fully agree.

Nevertheless, I would hardly go so far as to suggest that these incidents represent an attempt by the president to return to the royal prerogative. Rather, I see a system of the separation of powers at work in all its subtleties. It seems to me that in almost all the instances in which the president has refused for constitutional reasons to enforce a law, he is justified in doing so not because he seeks to return to the status of king but because Congress has made a clear attempt to encroach on the executive power. Specifically, I am referring to instances in which Congress has imposed a legislative veto (of the kind outlawed in *Chadha*) or encroached on the power of presidential appointments.

In theory, the president should veto acts of Congress he sees as unconstitutional. However, in the real world, Congress often bundles in legislation that the president does not want with what the president desperately needs (annual appropriations, for instance). Thus the president is forced to sign the legislation, disregard those provisions he sees as unconstitutional, and hope that the courts make a determination.

It is at this point that May and I sometimes disagree. May makes a rather tortured argument that a president's attempt to disregard what he sees as an unconstitutional law sometimes goes unchallenged because no one has standing to sue. I am not a lawyer, but to me this means that if no one has standing, harm against someone cannot be demonstrated. Thus the action constitutes a nullity. If someone is harmed, he or she will be able to object, and, because, as the author points out, picking and choosing laws to enforce is so clearly beyond the president's constitutional authority, the courts will agree with the president or order him to comply. Furthermore, it seems to me that members of Congress always have standing to sue in instances when the president chooses to ignore duly constituted laws (see, for instance, *Crockett* v. *Reagan*, 558 F. Supp. 893, 1982).

Thus I am not nearly as alarmed as May in what I see in these actions. I would be alarmed if the president chose to ignore a court order to comply with the law, but that is not the problem here. I would also be alarmed if the president were required to comply with some of the more egregious encroachments imposed by Congress on his authority. This book makes an excellent case for the slam-dunk proposition that the president has little or no authority to ignore laws he thinks are unconstitutional. But that is not in the main what is going on here. I see these actions as an attempt on the part of the president to protect his office from the unconstitutional encroachments of others, not as an attempt to supplant the authority of the courts.

DANIEL P. FRANKLIN

Georgia State University
Atlanta

McELROY, JOHN HARMON. 1999. *American Beliefs: What Keeps a Big Country and a Diverse People United.* Pp. xii, 259. Chicago: Ivan R. Dee. $25.00.

John McElroy's *American Beliefs* could have been a Fourth of July speech to a veterans' group in the 1940s. He writes as if the outpouring of scholarship by historians during the past half century had not occurred. However, a good number of his sweeping generalizations are not especially controversial. Belief in social mobility and support for the written Constitution, for example, have been part of the creed that most Americans accept. As he notes, most immigrants came to America to seek freedom or a better economic life. They often found these, or certainly better conditions than at home. If they did not improve their lot much, their children and grandchildren usually did. He stresses the nation's reverence for the Constitution, but it is important to remember that many saw its faults and demanded amendments to bring more Americans into the political process. McElroy scarcely considers the Civil War and Reconstruction amendments and the addition giving women the right to vote. He often assumes that the nation's beliefs developed early and did not change significantly over time.

McElroy frequently reminds his readers that Americans encountered a wilderness and civilized it in a relatively short period of time. One is barely aware that Indians lived in this wilderness, and the term "civilized" is not clearly defined. Does it mean cities and economic growth, or does it mean something else? Surely, one of the beliefs of white Americans about the frontier was that it belonged to them to develop and not to the Indians, whom they despised.

McElroy also praises America not only on its own terms but by comparison to other nations. At times, this can be annoying, and, of course, he picks his comparisons with care. America is progressive and Brazil is backward, as indeed are most European nations. He might have compared the United States to Scandinavian countries during the past 50 years, but such a comparison would have not been so strongly in America's favor. He insists that social mobility is more common for Americans than it is in Europe, but in recent years scholars have noted that the mobility rates of Europe and America are very similar. There is no mention that in spite of the impressive achievements of the American economy, the poverty rates in the United States are higher than they are in Europe. In one of the more amusing comparisons in discussing voting, he says that England did not become a full democracy until 1928. McElroy, of course, is referring only to property qualifications; women, who got the vote only in 1919 in America, do not count. Nor do southern African Americans, who did not get the vote until the civil rights era of the 1960s.

The fact that he omits women, Indians, and blacks as well as Asians and Latinos in discussing democracy and the frontier is perhaps the major flaw in this ambitious work. For the most part, they do not appear in his story. Thus we hear that, around the time of the American Revolution, the "people" through their elected representatives created their government. Surely, it is not debunking to point out who had the right to vote and hold political power at different times in American political history.

Unfortunately, one of the beliefs that tied white Americans together until recent decades is the belief that Indians, blacks, Hispanics, and Asians were inferior. The problem for many American historians is to explain why beliefs in republicanism and democracy developed in a racist society that until 1865 sanctioned slavery. By the way, England abolished slavery before the United States did.

In the last few pages, McElroy makes his politics clear. He is disturbed by the trends of the past 30 years. With alarm, he points to failing schools, drugs, AIDS, and broken homes, and few persons would disagree with him. But he also attacks multiculturalism (whatever that means), high taxes, dependency upon the government, *Roe* v. *Wade*, flag burning, and the absence of prayer in the public schools. He also sees much moral decay (shorthand for gay rights perhaps?). It is well to remember that the last few decades have also seen unprecedented gains for women, blacks, and other minorities, who, after all, make up the majority of the United States. History is often complex.

I do not know how well this book will sell. It might do better if the publisher replaced the redwood trees on the jacket, for readers might think it a book about the environment. It would be better for the book to have a red, white, and blue cover, which would also be more appropriate.

DAVID M. REIMERS

New York University
New York City

SOCIOLOGY

COHEN, MARK NATHAN. 1998. *Culture of Intolerance: Chauvinism, Class, and Racism in the United States*. Pp. ix, 315. New Haven, CT: Yale University Press. $27.50.

Anthropology is a discipline that has a lot to say about the world, but one that has had great difficulty getting its message across. Since Margaret Mead, no anthropologist has captured the attention of the American public by convincingly demonstrating, as did Mead, why the study of human cultural and biological diversity should matter to them. Lay and even not-so-lay people continue to associate anthropology with the study of bones and the exotically irrelevant. Why this is so is a complex question and one that is well beyond the scope of this review. Nevertheless, it is a question that lies at the heart of Mark Nathan Cohen's new book, *Culture of Intolerance*.

Cohen's book is an impassioned and far-reaching critique of cultural assumptions that underpin how many Americans understand issues ranging from human biological variation to the meaning of such slippery principles as freedom, justice, and social equality. Like the members of any society, Cohen observes, Americans hold taken-for-granted assumptions about the world that shape how they think and behave. Since these deeply held assumptions (such as the existence of human races) typically enjoy considerable cultural as well as political authority, they are often experienced as unquestionable truths. "Americans," Cohen writes,

for all our protestation of freedom of speech, of thought, and of action, are no exception. Our culture trains us to be ignorant of alternative sets of assumptions, other options, and other lifestyles. . . . If we can't expose our assumptions to careful examination and modification or discard them as needed, we are no freer, no more progressive, and no less tradition-bound than any other people. (7-8)

Cohen captures the historical mission and promise of anthropology: that the disciplined study of human cultural and biological diversity would yield evidence that could be used to challenge the view that modern Western societies (or, more accurately, modern white people) were superior to those found in the rest of the world. Read in this light, *Culture of Intolerance* is at once a powerful demonstration of anthropology's critical promise and a symptom of its failed mission.

Nowhere is anthropology's failure to get through more apparent and, perhaps,

more tragic than in the case of the race question in America. Cohen begins his critique with a rigorous exegesis of contemporary anthropological understandings of human biological variation that demonstrates that distinct races of people do not exist. Yes, human populations differ biologically, but those manifold differences (in, for example, blood type, skin color, and hair texture) cannot be clumped together to form discreet racial groups. Genetically speaking, we are all far too mixed up.

Cohen then moves on to challenge ethnocentrism and other forms of intolerance that often find support in tradition-bound assumptions about what is natural. In each case, whether it be American attitudes concerning taxes and private property or the growing intolerance toward affirmative action programs, Cohen masterfully brings a wealth of anthropological knowledge and insight to bear on pressing political and economic issues and debates within American society. The message is that, if we are to do away with the culture of intolerance, then we must educate the public in ways that promote a more critical awareness of our own cultural biases and a broader and more complex vision of the possibilities for human freedom and equality.

Few readers would take issue with Cohen's assessment of the myriad forms of cultural intolerance and their devastating social consequences. However, some (myself included) would find Cohen's proposals for transforming this culture wanting. What is surprisingly absent from Cohen's critique is a textured analysis of the political interests and power relations that undergird the beliefs and attitudes addressed in the book. Indeed, the very notion of a *culture* of intolerance, rooted in a set of wrongheaded assumptions, tends to obscure the political and historical specificity of what are a very diverse set of interest-laden doctrines, ideologies that are constructed and exercised within particular social and, above all, institutional locations. To be sure, the concept of race is based on erroneous assumptions concerning the nature of human differences. What gives this fiction its extraordinary social force and durability, however, is an institutional arrangement of power in American society that, by practicing racial inequality, produces and reaffirms racialized ways of understanding social differences and antagonisms.

Cohen's neglect of this politics of intolerance leads him to propose an ambitious but rather sketchy program of educational reform and development that disengages the question of cultural beliefs and attitudes from far messier problems of political power. For example, addressing the issue of economic justice in America, Cohen argues, "We have to teach the rich and powerful to recognize that luck, affirmative action, and enormous contributions from the society that nurtured them (often, but not always, accompanied by hard work and ability) got them where they are." If the exodus of American corporations to offshore sources of cheap labor teaches us anything, it is that America's rich and powerful know very well whence their wealth and power derive. It is doubtful that education alone will lead them to the path of social responsibility and economic justice.

Culture of Intolerance offers a compelling critique of racism, class prejudice, and other forms of intolerance that find their roots in taken-for-granted assumptions about the nature of human differences. Cohen demonstrates, as have anthropologists before him, that the way that we do things as a society is not written in stone, let alone in so-called human nature. But herein lies the historical weakness of anthropology's critical reflection on American society: if our purpose is to abolish intolerance and its underlying structures of inequality, then we must do more than reveal alter-

natives; rather, we must take on the much more daunting task of understanding and communicating just how those alternatives might be realized in a politically and economically stratified society. In this regard, *Culture of Intolerance* poses a formidable challenge to us all.

STEVEN GREGORY

New York University
New York City

HANNIGAN, JOHN. 1998. *Fantasy City: Pleasure and Profit in the Postmodern Metropolis*. Pp. xvi, 239. New York: Routledge. Paperbound, $22.95.

Fantasy City is a fascinating study of what the author calls "urban entertainment destinations" (in an almost simultaneously published book, *Enchanting the Disenchanting World*, I have alternately called the same set of phenomena "the new means of consumption" and "cathedrals of consumption"). These include shopping malls, mega-malls, superstores, fast-food restaurants and other chains, theme parks, casino-hotels, "eatertainment," "retailtainment," and the like. What is distinctive about this book is that it employs an urban optic in analyzing these phenomena. This perspective helps in understanding a number of issues, but it is simultaneously unhelpful with others. The latter is due to the fact that many of these means of consumption, as Hannigan acknowledges at many points in the book, are not urban in origin, are not necessarily or even primarily located in the cities, and have an impact that is certainly not limited to the cities. Nevertheless, to the degree that they are urban or affect the city, Hannigan's analysis tells us much about them and how they are shaping the postmodern city for both good and ill.

The analysis of urban entertainment centers is embedded in a discussion of the long-standing need of middle-class city dwellers for safe entertainment. While these centers do, in the main, serve this function, they do so at the cost of having private space replace public space, reinforcing the gap between rich and poor, destroying the local, and transforming the city itself "into a hyperreal consumer commodity."

Hannigan begins with the "golden age" of urban entertainment (1895-1930) as exemplified by the heyday of New York's Coney Island. However, by the 1950s, the cities had declined dramatically as entertainment centers (race and crime are central factors) with the development of suburbia and suburban fun centers like drive-in movies and Disneyland. Yet, by the 1980s, the cities began to make a comeback with urban developments such as Baltimore's Harborplace, Boston's Faneuil Hall, and South Street Seaport in New York City and, in the 1990s, with the coming of Disney to the cities, most obviously in the resuscitation of New York's Times Square.

Hannigan attributes the success of urban entertainment centers to several factors. First, consumers seem drawn to their technological wizardry. Second, people, especially those with money, acquire cultural capital as they visit and become knowledgeable about more of these locales. Third, they offer consumers sanitized environments, or what Hannigan calls "riskless risk." Fourth, they provide a comfortable environment in which to meet and interact with others. Hannigan also links the growth of these centers to three major social trends: the "McDonaldization" of society, which makes it possible to replicate these centers all over the world; the proliferation of themed environments; and the building of synergies between a range of enterprises associated with urban entertainment centers. In this context, Hannigan also discusses what I have called the "implosion" of the new means of consumption,

or, more specifically, the convergence of "shopping, dining, entertainment and education" in "shopertainment" (for example, Niketown), "eatertainment" (Hard Rock Cafe, for example), and "edutainment" (for example, museums where the line between education and entertainment has been blurred).

What I found most informative in this book was the discussion of some of the nuts and bolts of developing a fantasy city. For example, there are the strategies of the major players in the development of such a city: corporate investors, real estate developers, entertainment companies, and retail operators. Then there is the relationship between public and private interests. The public sector makes various contributions, such as land, improvements in infrastructure, help in financing, and regulatory relief. Hannigan provides an interesting discussion of the public pursuit of sports franchises, concluding that these are hard to justify on the grounds of economic gain to the community. Similarly interesting are discussions of gambling in Las Vegas and the efforts to extend casinos elsewhere in the country as well as a useful discussion (but now dated in light of the economic crisis in that part of the world) of the development of cathedrals of consumption in the Far East.

In the concluding chapter, Hannigan wonders whether the city can be saved by Mickey Mouse and, more generally, urban entertainment centers. His response is generally negative since the cathedrals of consumption do not create wealth within the community, do not foster "casual, serendipitous encounters" between urban residents, and threaten the distinctiveness of the local community.

This is a well-researched, interesting book that is another important step in correcting the productivist bias in sociology and other social sciences. However, the entities of concern to Hannigan are not limited to the city; in fact, they are far more likely to be suburban and even small-town phenomena. They are of great importance and worthy of study in their own right and not just because of their impact on the city.

GEORGE RITZER

University of Maryland
College Park

HOWELL, MARTHA C. 1998. *The Marriage Exchange: Property, Social Place, and Gender in Cities of the Low Countries, 1300-1550.* Pp. xv, 278. Chicago: University of Chicago Press. $52.00. Paperbound, $19.00.

Martha Howell's new book extends her earlier work on the interrelationships of gender and economic change at the boundary between the medieval and early modern periods. In *Women, Production, and Patriarchy in Late Medieval Cities* (1986), Howell laid out a sophisticated and nuanced approach to the historical economics of gender, based on a comparative analysis of urban economies. Her new work adopts a narrower archival focus—on the city of Douai—but, at the same time, broadens in theoretical scope to consider not only women's changing labor status but also conceptual shifts in the meaning of property, marriage, kinship, and gendered identity.

Based on a meticulous study of marriage contracts, wills, and other archival material, Howell finds gradual but decisive shifts taking place in Douai across the late medieval centuries: from customary to contractual law in marital arrangements and from a focus on the conjugal couple to a preference for linear descent in property and inheritance law. These changes brought a decrease in widows' inheritance rights and a shift away from conceiving of women as potential producers of wealth. Parts of this story

are well known as broad historical trends. But in Douai, according to Howell, the changes were not imposed from above; instead, she sees them evolving in the individual choices made by people weighing their economic options. Further, Howell finds such transformative decisions being made not only at the top of the social scale but also among ordinary residents. Given this broad base, Howell argues persuasively that analysis of legal change must be linked with exploration of its social and cultural reference points.

Howell's most stimulating commentary focuses on this issue of intersections between legal texts, socioeconomic practice, and cultural conceptions (or what Howell calls, in her sometimes jargon-prone style, the "social imaginary"). Working from an analysis of marriage contracts and property transfer, Howell sees Douai's inhabitants as shifting toward a conceptualization of property as fixed inheritance rather than as tools for production. In the new scenario, women were increasingly situated as conduits for property rather than as active managers or producers of wealth. She analyzes women's use of testamentary practices, arguing that women's greater tendency to connect concrete objects with particular people and social relationships can be seen as both a product of women's socioeconomic limitations and a means of creating their own social meanings. Connecting her findings with broader historical discussions of the changing nature of marriage and family life, Howell points to the paradox that it was only as marriage lost some of its economic cohesion that its emotional qualities were emphasized.

Some aspects of the analysis raise questions that could be further explored—in particular, the question of how we should understand the case of Douai in relation to broader European changes. As the center of a declining cloth industry, Douai experienced changes that read almost like decapitalization— less centralization, greater artisan independence, and slower circulation of goods, but also social changes (such as a declining role for women as producers of wealth) that many historians, especially after reading Howell's first book, associate with the clichéd but inescapable rise of capitalism. This seeming puzzle needs more comment. Also, Howell's case for fundamental change in Douai's overall social structure is sometimes hampered by scanty evidence about the situation preceding the change.

The great achievement of this intensive case study lies in its forging of new links between the sometimes hazy realm of cultural discourse and the nuts and bolts of archival detail. It makes an important contribution to historical thinking about the interconnections of gender, law, and society.

JOY WILTENBURG

Rowan University
Glassboro
New Jersey

LANDRINE, HOPE and ELIZABETH A. KLONOFF. 1996. *African American Acculturation: Deconstructing Race and Reviving Culture.* Pp. ix, 182. Thousand Oaks, CA: Sage. Paperbound, $18.95.

African American Acculturation is an engaging, scholarly, and stimulating monograph. The subtitle of the book aptly identifies Landrine and Klonoff's two main aims: to argue, first, that African Americans and European Americans are ethnic groups and not races and, then, to illustrate that "the best approach to understanding an ethnic group is to analyze the extent to which members participate in their own culture versus the culture of the dominant society."

Landrine and Klonoff present these points forcefully and typically persuasively.

The first chapter of the book is dedicated to the goal of deconstructing race. Landrine and Klonoff draw on evidence from a range of fields (anthropology, history, sociology) to make a strong case that race is a social construction and that racialization develops to facilitate the exploitation of certain groups. The authors are passionate and firm in their arguments. They chastise psychology for its support of race as a biological concept: "Why would African Americans want to major, let alone pursue graduate education, in a discipline that persists in trying to prove them inferior?" Their conclusion is unequivocal: "Race is not a biological or genetic category."

How successful are the authors in achieving their objective of deconstructing race? On one hand, the arguments are careful and logical. Even for people like me who were already sympathetic to this point, chapter 1 is very informative and useful. On the other hand, the type of evidence brought to bear on the social construction of race will probably not be sufficient to change the minds of people who search out and believe in biological and genetic markers of race. Nevertheless, it is not necessary to debunk race as a biological concept entirely in order to make a compelling case for understanding African Americans as an ethnic group. That case is made in a persuasive way in the remainder of the book.

Acculturation is hypothesized not to be a slow, steady, evolutionary transformation of the group as a whole but, rather, to proceed through the "rapid fracturalization" of individuals and isolated, smaller groups. Beginning in the second chapter, Landrine and Klonoff address questions about why some people become acculturated and others do not, about what variables predict acculturation, and about whether acculturation is a unidirectional or reversible process. They consider, but perhaps a little too briefly, the relationship between their scale and other measures of group identity and esteem. Chapters 3 through 5 present empirical evidence about the development and validation of the African American Acculturation Scale (chapter 3), and the relation between acculturation and indices of physical health (chapter 4) and mental health (chapter 5). Some of this information was previously published, but much of it is new. Readers should find these studies to be carefully conducted and informative. The last chapter represents a synopsis of the authors' goals, arguments, and supportive evidence, and it offers concrete, promising suggestions for future research.

In summary, *African American Acculturation* is a thoughtful text that represents a refreshing balance of disciplinary perspective and criticism, of passion and science, and of looking backward and thinking ahead. It succeeds in some objectives better than others, and it will appeal to some readers more than others. The important point is that, overall, the book is clearly both successful and appealing. It should be of interest and value to psychologists, sociologists, counselors, and educators for its theoretical, empirical, and practical implications and applications, and it should contribute substantially and constructively, as the authors hoped, to "a genuine appreciation of cultural diversity."

JOHN F. DOVIDIO

Colgate University
Hamilton
New York

OTHER BOOKS

ABALOS, DAVID T. 1996. *Strategies of Transformation Toward a Multicultural Society: Fulfilling the Story of Democracy.* Pp. xix, 189. Westport, CT: Praeger. $55.00.

ABSHIRE, DAVID and BROCK BROWER. 1996. *Putting America's House in Order: The Nation as a Family.* Pp. xiv, 189. Westport, CT: Praeger. $19.95.

BABKINA, A. M. 1998. *Terrorism: An Annotated Bibliography.* Pp. 327. Commack, NY: Nova Science. No price.

BAILEY, F. G. 1996. *The Civility of Indifference: On Domesticating Ethnicity.* Pp. xvi, 184. Ithaca, NY: Cornell University Press. $37.50. Paperbound, $15.95.

BASU, AMRITA and ATUL KOHLI, eds. 1998. *Community Conflicts and the State in India.* Pp. viii, 287. New York: Oxford University Press. $29.95.

BAYOR, RONALD H. 1996. *Race and the Shaping of Twentieth-Century Atlanta.* Pp. xvi, 334. Chapel Hill: University of North Carolina Press. $29.95.

BEAUCHAMP, DAN E. 1996. *Health Care Reform and the Battle for the Body Politic.* Pp. xiv, 173. Philadelphia: Temple University Press. $49.95. Paperbound, $16.95.

BECNEL, THOMAS A. 1996. *Senator Allen Ellender of Louisiana: A Biography.* Pp. xv, 300. Baton Rouge: Louisiana State University Press. $30.00.

BEDERMAN, GAIL. 1995. *Manliness and Civilization: A Cultural History of Gender and Race in the United States, 1880-1917.* Pp. xiii, 307. Chicago: University of Chicago Press. $27.50.

BLICKLE, PETER. 1997. *Obedient Germans? A Rebuttal: A New View of German History.* Pp. xviii, 126. Charlottesville: University Press of Virginia. Paperbound, no price.

BONIFACE, PASCAL. 1999. *The Will to Powerlessness: Reflections on Our Global Age.* Pp. 153. Kingston, Canada: Queen's Quarterly. Paperbound, no price.

BREEN, T. H. 1989. *Imagining the Past: East Hampton Histories.* Pp. xii, 306. Athens: University of Georgia Press. Paperbound, $19.95.

CASPER, GRETCHEN and MICHELLE M. TAYLOR. 1996. *Negotiating Democracy: Transitions from Authoritarian Rule.* Pp. viii, 287. Pittsburgh, PA: University of Pittsburgh Press. $44.95. Paperbound, $19.95.

CHATTERJEE, PARTHA, ed. 1998. *Wages of Freedom: Fifty Years of the Indian Nation-State.* Pp. x, 327. New York: Oxford University Press. $32.00.

COLLINS, ELIZABETH FULLER. 1997. *Pierced by Murugan's Lance: Ritual, Power, and Moral Redemption Among Malaysian Hindus.* Pp. viii, 246. DeKalb: Northern Illinois University Press. Paperbound, no price.

COLUMBUS, FRANK, ed. 1998. *Asian Eccnomic and Political Issues.* Vol. 1. Pp. vi, 226. Commack, NY: Nova Science. No price.

COMBS, JAMES E. and DAN NIMMO. 1996. *The Comedy of Democracy.* Pp. viii, 203. Westport, CT: Praeger. $55.00.

COPPER, JOHN F. 1998. *Taiwan's Mid-1990s Elections: Taking the Final Steps to Democracy.* Pp. x, 243. Westport, CT: Praeger. $59.95.

CUNNINGHAM, NOBLE E., JR. 1996. *The Presidency of James Monroe.* Pp. xvi, 246. Lawrence: University Press of Kansas. $29.95.

DE LA GARZA, RODOLFO O. and LOUIS DESIPIO. 1999. *Awash in the Mainstream: Latino Politics in the 1996 Election.* Pp. xiii, 283. Boulder, CO: Westview Press. $60.00.

DIGGINS, JOHN PATRICK. 1996. *Max Weber: Politics and the Spirit of Trag-*

edy. Pp. xvi, 334. New York: Basic. $35.00.

DIRKS, NICHOLAS B., ed. 1998. *In Near Ruins: Cultural Theory and the End of the Century.* Pp. xvi, 308. Minneapolis: University of Minnesota Press. $49.95. Paperbound, $19.95.

ECCLES, STEPHEN and CATHERINE GWIN. 1999. *Supporting Effective Aid: A Framework for Future Concessional Funding of Multilateral Development Banks.* Pp. xvi, 97. Washington, DC: Overseas Development Council. Paperbound, $13.95.

ELLIOTT, GREGORY. 1998. *The Merciless Laboratory of History.* Pp. xxi, 340. Minneapolis: University of Minnesota Press. $39.95.

EPSTEIN, T. SCARLETT, A. P. SURYANARAYANA, and T. THIMMEGOWDA. 1998. *Village Voices: Forty Years of Rural Transformation in South India.* Pp. 240. Walnut Creek, CA: AltaMira Press. Paperbound, $24.95.

FERMAN, BARBARA. 1996. *Challenging the Growth Machine: Neighborhood Politics in Chicago and Pittsburgh.* Pp. xv, 192. Lawrence: University Press of Kansas. $35.00. Paperbound, $14.95.

FINNEGAN, MARGARET. 1999. *Selling Suffrage: Consumer Culture and Votes for Women.* Pp. xii, 222. New York: Columbia University Press. $49.50. Paperbound, $17.50.

FREEDMAN, ESTELLE B. 1996. *Maternal Justice: Miriam Van Waters and the Female Reform Tradition.* Pp. xvii, 458. Chicago: University of Chicago Press. $34.95.

FROHNEN, BRUCE. 1996. *The New Communitarians and the Crisis of Modern Liberalism.* Pp. viii, 271. Lawrence: University Press of Kansas. $29.95.

GALLHOFER, IRMTRAUD N. and WILLEM E. SARIS. 1996. *Foreign Policy Decision-Making: A Qualitative and Quantitative Analysis of Political Argumentation.* Pp. xv, 276. Westport, CT: Praeger. $65.00.

GAUS, GERALD F. 1996. *Justificatory Liberalism: An Essay on Epistemology and Political Theory.* Pp. xiv, 374. New York: Oxford University Press. $55.00. Paperbound, $29.95.

GREENBERG, KENNETH S. 1996. *Honor and Slavery: Lies, Duels, Noses, Masks, Dressing as a Woman, Gifts, Strangers, Humanitarianism, Death, Slave Rebellions, the Proslavery Argument, Baseball, Hunting, and Gambling in the Old South.* Pp. xvi, 176. Princeton, NJ: Princeton University Press. $24.95.

GUARDINI, ROMANO. 1998. *The End of the Modern World.* Pp. xxvi, 220. Wilmington, DE: Intercollegiate Studies Institute. $24.95.

HAAS, MICHAEL, ed. 1999. *The Singapore Puzzle.* Pp. ix, 208. Westport, CT: Praeger. $57.95.

HALE, DENNIS and MARC LANDY, eds. 1999. *Bertrand de Jouvenel, Economics and the Good Life: Essays on Political Economy.* Pp. ix, 308. New Brunswick, NJ: Transaction. Paperbound, no price.

HALL, RICHARD L. 1996. *Participation in Congress.* Pp. xiv, 293. New Haven, CT: Yale University Press. $35.50.

HAUPTMANN, EMILY. 1996. *Putting Choice Before Democracy: A Critique of Rational Choice Theory.* Pp. ix, 138. Albany: State University of New York Press. Paperbound, $14.95.

HERRMANN, PETER. 1999. *European Integration Between Institution Building and Social Process: Contributions to a Theory of Modernisation and NGOs in the Context of the Development of the EU.* Pp. vii, 159. Commack, NY: Nova Science. $59.00.

HERRMANN, WILFRED A. 1998. *Asia's Security Challenges.* Pp. x, 345. Commack, NY: Nova Science. No price.

HILL, SAMUEL S. 1996. *One Name but Several Faces: Variety in Popular Christian Denominations in Southern History*. Pp. xiv, 128. Athens: University of Georgia Press. $20.00.

HINDESS, BARRY. 1995. *Discourses of Power: From Hobbes to Foucault*. Pp. viii, 183. Cambridge, MA: Blackwell. $49.95. Paperbound, $19.95.

HOROWITZ, LEONARD. 1996. *Emerging Viruses: AIDS and Ebola, Nature, Accident or Genocide?* Pp. xxv, 544. Rockport, MA: Tetrahedron. $49.95.

JOHNSON, CHARLES S. 1996. *Shadow of the Plantation*. Pp. xxxii, 215. New Brunswick, NJ: Transaction. Paperbound, no price.

KAASE, MAX and KENNETH NEWTON. 1996. *Beliefs in Government*. Pp. xvii, 217. New York: Oxford University Press. $45.00.

KAKAR, SUDHIR. 1996. *The Colors of Violence: Cultural Identities, Religion, and Conflict*. Pp. xiii, 217. Chicago: University of Chicago Press. Paperbound, $14.95.

KAMMEN, CAROL, ed. 1996. *The Pursuit of Local History: Readings on Theory and Practice*. Pp. 240. Walnut Creek, CA: AltaMira Press. Paperbound, $24.95.

KLEINMAN, SHERRYL. 1996. *Opposing Ambitions: Gender and Identity in an Alternative Organization*. Pp. viii, 152. Chicago: University of Chicago Press. Paperbound, no price.

KRYZANEK, MICHAEL J. 1999. *Angry, Bored, Confused: A Citizen Handbook of American Politics*. Pp. xviii, 292. Boulder, CO: Westview Press. $59.00. Paperbound, $17.00.

KUGLER, RICHARD L. 1998. *Changes Ahead: Future Directions for the United States Overseas Military Presence*. Pp. xxvii, 174. Santa Monica, CA: Rand. Paperbound, $20.00.

KUPPENHEIMER, L. B. 1996. *Albert Gallatin's Vision of Democratic Stability: An Interpretive Profile*. Pp. xii, 152. Westport, CT: Praeger. $55.00.

LEVINE, ROBERT A. 1998. *Western Europe, 1979-2009: A View from the United States*. Pp. xvii, 61. Santa Monica: Rand. Paperbound, $15.00.

LEVY, FRANK. 1998. *The New Dollars and Dreams: American Incomes and Economic Change*. Pp. xiii, 248. New York: Russell Sage Foundation. $39.95. Paperbound, $16.95.

LORENTE, J. PEDRO. 1998. *Cathedrals of Urban Modernity: The First Museums of Contemporary Art, 1800-1930*. Pp. xiii, 322. Brookfield, VT: Ashgate. $83.95.

LOW, D. A. and HOWARD BRASTED, eds. 1998. *Freedom, Trauma, Continuities: Northern India and Independence*. Pp. 237. Walnut Creek, CA: AltaMira Press. $45.00.

MACLEOD, EMMA VINCENT. 1998. *A War of Ideas: British Attitudes to the Wars Against Revolutionary France, 1792-1802*. Pp. viii, 240. Brookfield, VT: Ashgate. $78.95.

MAEHR, MARTIN L. and CAROL MIDGLEY. 1996. *Transforming School Cultures*. Pp. xiv, 252. Boulder, CO: Westview Press. $60.00. Paperbound, $18.00.

MARGULIES, HERBERT F. 1996. *Reconciliation and Revival: James R. Mann and the House Republicans in the Wilson Era*. Pp. xv, 242. Westport, CT: Greenwood Press. $57.95.

MARSH, DAVID, JIM BULLER, COLIN HAY, JIM JOHNSTON, PETER KERR, STUART McANULLA, and MATTHEW WATSON. 1999. *Postwar British Politics in Perspective*. Pp. x, 251. Malden, MA: Polity Press. Paperbound, $29.95.

McADAM, DOUG, JOHN D. McCARTHY, and MAYER N. ZALD. 1996. *Comparative Perspectives on Social Movements*. Pp. xiv, 426. New York: Cambridge University Press. $54.95. Paperbound, $18.95.

McELRATH, JOSEPH R., JR., ROBERT C. LEITZ III, and JESSE S. CRISLER, eds. 1999. *Charles W. Chesnutt: Essays and Speeches.* Pp. xxxvii, 596. Stanford, CA: Stanford University Press. $60.00.

MICHAEL, MIKE. 1996. *Constructing Identities.* Pp. viii, 179. Thousand Oaks, CA: Sage. $65.00. Paperbound, $21.95.

MIRZA, HAFIZ, ed. 1998. *Global Competitive Strategies in the New World Economy: Multilateralism, Regionalization and the Transnational Firm.* Pp. xv, 338. Northampton, MA: Edward Elgar. $95.00.

MORLEY, JAMES W., ed. 1998. *Driven by Growth: Political Change in the Asia-Pacific Region.* Rev. ed. Pp. xiv. 391. Armonk, NY: M. E. Sharpe. $65.00. Paperbound, $24.95.

NAIR, JANAKI. 1998. *Miners and Millhands: Work, Culture and Politics in Princely Mysore.* Pp. 324. Walnut Creek, CA: AltaMira Press. $44.95.

NIE, NORMAN H., JANE JUNN, and KENNETH STEHLIK-BARRY. 1996. *Education and Democratic Citizenship in America.* Pp. xxi, 268. Chicago: University of Chicago Press. $48.00. Paperbound, $16.95.

PACKHAM, ERIC S. 1998. *Success or Failure? The United Nations Intervention in the Congo After Independence.* Pp. 326. Commack, NY: Nova Science. Paperbound, no price.

PAILLARD, BERNARD. 1998. *Notes on the Plague Years: AIDS in Marseilles.* Pp. xx, 293. New York: Aldine de Gruyter. $49.95. Paperbound, $23.95.

PERSONS, GEORGIA A., ed. 1999. *Race and Ethnicity in Comparative Perspective.* Vol. 7. Pp. ix, 313. New Brunswick, NJ: Transaction. Paperbound, $24.95.

PLOTKIN, ZALMAN. 1998. *Even in America.* Pp. xv, 87. Pittsburgh, PA: Dorrance. Paperbound, $10.00.

RADIN, BERYL A., ROBERT AGRANOFF, ANN O'M. BOWMAN, C. GREGORY BUNTZ, J. STEVEN OTT, BARBARA S. ROMZEK, and ROBERT H. WILSON. 1996. *New Governance for Rural America: Creating Intergovernmental Partnerships.* Pp. xiii, 242. Lawrence: University Press of Kansas. $29.95. Paperbound, $17.95.

RAO, SRINIVASA. 1998. *Perceptual Error: The Indian Theories.* Pp. xii, 150. Honolulu: University of Hawaii Press. Paperbound, $20.00.

REARDON, DAVID C. 1996. *Making Abortion Rare: A Healing Strategy for a Divided Nation.* Pp. xv, 204. Springfield, IL: Acorn. $24.95. Paperbound, $14.95.

REED, ADOLPH, JR. 1999. *Without Justice for All: The New Liberalism and Our Retreat from Racial Equality.* Pp. ix, 460. Boulder, CO: Westview Press. $25.00.

ROCHLITZ, RAINER. 1996. *The Disenchantment of Art: The Philosophy of Walter Benjamin.* Pp. vi, 298. New York: Guilford. $26.95.

RONEY, JOHN B. 1996. *The Inside of History: Jean Henri Merle d'Aubigne and Romantic Historiography.* Pp. vi, 214. Westport, CT: Greenwood Press. $59.95.

RONFELDT, DAVID, JOHN ARQUILLA, GRAHAM E. FULLER, and MELISSA FULLER. 1999. *The Zapatista Social Netwar in Mexico.* Pp. xiii, 168. Santa Monica, CA: Rand. Paperbound, $15.00.

ROWLAND, C. K. and ROBERT A. CARP. 1996. *Politics and Judgment in Federal District Courts.* Pp. xi, 211. Lawrence: University Press of Kansas. $29.95.

RYDEN, DAVID K. 1996. *Representation in Crisis: The Constitution, Interest Groups, and Political Parties.* Pp. x, 309. Albany: State University of New York Press. Paperbound, $21.95.

SACHS, CAROLYN. 1996. *Gendered Fields: Rural Women, Agriculture, and Environment.* Pp. xiv, 205. Boulder, CO: Westview Press. $54.95. Paperbound, $19.95.

SCHULTZ, DAVID A. and CHRISTOPHER E. SMITH. 1996. *The Jurisprudential Vision of Justice Antonin Scalia.* Pp. xxv, 245. Lanham, MD: Rowman & Littlefield. $62.50. Paperbound, $23.95.

SIFF, EZRA Y. 1999. *Why the Senate Slept: The Gulf of Tonkin Resolution and the Beginning of America's Vietnam War.* Pp. xix, 172. Westport, CT: Praeger. $49.95.

SINGH, HIRA. 1998. *Colonial Hegemony and Popular Resistance: Princes, Peasants, and Paramount Power.* Pp. 274. New Delhi: Sage. $44.95.

SKEEN, C. EDWARD. 1999. *Citizen Soldiers in the War of 1812.* Pp. ix, 229. Lexington: University Press of Kentucky. $27.50.

STOCKHOLM INTERNATIONAL PEACE RESEARCH INSTITUTE. 1998. *SIPRI Yearbook 1998: Armaments, Disarmament and International Security.* Pp. xxxiv, 638. New York: Oxford University Press. $115.00.

STOKES, GALE, ed. 1996. *From Stalinism to Pluralism: A Documentary History of Eastern Europe Since 1945.* 2d ed. Pp. 294. New York: Oxford University Press. $39.95. Paperbound, $16.95.

STREZHNEVA, MARINA. 1999. *Social Culture and Regional Governance: Comparison of the European Union and Post-Soviet Experiences.* Pp. xiv, 269. Commack, NY: Nova Science. $59.00.

STUDDERT-KENNEDY, GERALD. 1998. *Providence and the Raj: Imperial Mission and Missionary Imperialism.* Pp. 273. Walnut Creek, CA: AltaMira Press. $36.00.

THOMAS, RICHARD W. 1996. *Understanding Interracial Unity: A Study of United States Race Relations.* Pp. ix, 230. Thousand Oaks, CA: Sage. Paperbound, no price.

THORNTON, RUSSELL, ed. 1999. *Studying Native America: Problems and Prospects.* Pp. xvii, 443. Madison: University of Wisconsin Press. $65.00. Paperbound, $27.95.

TINE, WARREN VAN, C. J. SLANICKA, SANDRA JORDAN, and MICHAEL PIERCE. 1998. *In the Workers' Interest: A History of the Ohio AFL-CIO, 1958-1998.* Pp. viii, 219. Columbus: Ohio State University Press. $27.95. Paperbound, $16.95.

TOLIVER, SUSAN D. 1998. *Black Families in Corporate America.* Pp. xiii, 193. Thousand Oaks, CA: Sage. $47.50.

TOMBLIN, BARBARA BROOKS. 1996. *G. I. Nightingales: The Army Nurse Corps in World War II.* Pp. ix, 254. Lexington: University Press of Kentucky. $29.95.

TREFOUSSE, HANS L. 1999. *Impeachment of a President: Andrew Johnson, the Blacks and Reconstruction.* Pp. xvi, 252. Bronx, NY: Fordham University Press. $29.95. Paperbound, $18.95.

VON FURSTENBERG, GEORGE M. and MICHAEL K. ULAN. 1998. *Learning from the World's Best Central Bankers.* Pp. xxiii, 248. Norwell, MA: Kluwer. $110.00.

WALT, STEPHEN M. 1996. *Revolution and War.* Pp. x, 365. Ithaca, NY: Cornell University Press. $35.00.

WEED, CLYDE P. 1995. *The Nemesis of Reform: The Republican Party During the New Deal.* Pp. xiv, 293. New York: Columbia University Press. $37.50.

WESTAD, ODD ARNE, ed. 1999. *Brothers in Arms: The Rise and Fall of the Sino-Soviet Alliance, 1945-1963.* Pp. xxii, 404. Stanford, CA: Stanford University Press. $45.00.

WESTERFIELD, DONALD L. 1996. *War Powers: The President, the Congress, and the Question of War.* Pp. xix, 245. Westport, CT: Praeger. $55.00.

WILLARD, CHARLES ARTHUR. 1996. *Liberalism and the Problem of Knowledge: A New Rhetoric for Modern De-* *mocracy.* Pp. x, 384. Chicago: University of Chicago Press. $55.00. Paperbound, $17.95.

WILSON, FRANK L., ed. 1998. *The European Center-Right at the End of the Twentieth Century.* Pp. xv, 279. New York: St. Martin's Press. $49.95.

INDEX

Health of African American men
  access to health care, 155-58
  cancer, 155
  cardiovascular disease, 155
  health insurance, 156
  human immunodeficiency virus (HIV) and
    acquired immunodeficiency syndrome
    (AIDS), 153-54
  mental health, 154, 156
  racism in administration of health care,
    151, 155, 157
  violence, 151-53
HEALTH OF AFRICAN AMERICAN MEN,
  THE, John A. Rich, 149-59
Homosexuality, in African American communities, 153, 154

INCARCERATED AFRICAN AMERICAN
  MEN AND THEIR CHILDREN: A
  CASE STUDY, Garry A. Mendez, Jr.,
  86-101
Incarceration of African American males, 25
  prisoners' attitudes toward parenting, 86-
  101

Jackson, Jesse, 13, 33, 35
Johnson, John H., 167
Journalists, black, 126

Karenga, Mawana Ron, 115-16
King, Martin Luther, Jr., 47-50, 54

Lewis, Reginald, 166

Master P, 168
MCELROY, SUSAN WILLIAMS and LEON T.
  ANDREWS, JR., The Black Male and
  the U.S. Economy, 160-75
Media
  broadcast media, and black men, 129-32
  portrayal of black males, 25, 121-24, 126,
    129, 132, 151
  print media, and black men, 109-10, 125-29
  see also Publishers, African American
MEDIA AND THE BLACK RESPONSE,
  THE, Lewis Diuguid and Adrienne Rivers, 120-34
Medical education, and African Americans,
  157-58
  see also Occupations, professional and
  managerial, of black males
MENDEZ, GARRY A., JR., Incarcerated African American Men and Their Children:
  A Case Study, 86-101
Mfume, Kweisi, 20-21, 45

MILLER, JAKE C., African American Males
  in Foreign Affairs, 29-41
Million Man March, 52
Minstrel shows, 72-73, 129
Montgomery Bus Boycott, 48
Music, and African American males, 75-78,
  111, 114

Nation of Islam, 50, 51-52
National Association for the Advancement of
  Colored People (NAACP), 13, 19, 21, 44,
  45, 47, 65, 83,127
  and racial discrimination in the armed
  forces, 36
National Trust for the Development of
  African-American Men, 86-101
New York State prisons, attitudes of impris-
  oned fathers toward parenting, 86-101
North American Free Trade Agreement, effect
  on U.S. employment, 35

OBI, SUNDAY O., see OBIAKOR, FESTUS E.,
  coauthor
OBIAKOR, FESTUS E., SUNDAY O. OBI, and
  PATRICK GRANT, Foreign-Born African American Males: Turning Barriers
  into Opportunities, 135-48
Occupations, professional and managerial, of
  black males, 109, 110, 165-66, 168-69,
  171
  racism, 167, 168, 171
Organization of Afro-American Unity
  (OAAU), 50, 51

Powell, Adam Clayton, Jr., 18-20
Powell, Colin, 14, 24-25, 32, 33, 37, 39, 165-66
Publishers, African American, 128-29, 167
Racism, 16-19, 21, 24, 25, 78, 103-6, 112-16,
  135-48, 151, 155, 157, 167, 168, 171
  in the armed forces, 33-34, 36-38
  and the health of African American men,
  154-55, 158
  and U.S.-African relations, 34-35
  and urban school reform, 63, 64-66, 68
Randolph, A. Philip, 13, 45-47
REFORM FOR TROUBLED TIMES: TAKE-
  OVERS OF URBAN SCHOOLS, A,
  Robert L. Green and Bradley R. Carl,
  56-70
Religious organizations, and black males,
  171-72
RICH, JOHN A., The Health of African American Men, 149-59
RIVERS, ADRIENNE, see DIUGUID, LEWIS,
  coauthor
Robinson, Randall, 33